DYNAMIC VISION
From Images to Face Recognition

DYNAMIC VISION
From Images to Face Recognition

Shaogang Gong

Queen Mary and Westfield College

Stephen J McKenna

University of Dundee

Alexandra Psarrou

University of Westminster

Imperial College Press

ICP

Published by

Imperial College Press
57 Shelton Street
Covent Garden
London WC2H 9HE

Distributed by

World Scientific Publishing Co. Pte. Ltd.
P O Box 128, Farrer Road, Singapore 912805
USA office: Suite 1B, 1060 Main Street, River Edge, NJ 07661
UK office: 57 Shelton Street, Covent Garden, London WC2H 9HE

British Library Cataloguing-in-Publication Data
A catalogue record for this book is available from the British Library.

DYNAMIC VISION
From Images to Face Recognition

ISBN 1-86094-181-8

This book is printed on acid and chlorine free paper.

Printed in Singapore by Fulsland Offset Printing

To my Parents and Aunt Mae

Shaogang Gong

To Collette

Stephen McKenna

To my Parents

Alexandra Psarrou

Contents

As you set out for Ithaka
hope your road is a long one,
full of adventure, full of discovery.

— C.P. Cavafy, Ithaka

Preface

Face recognition is a task that the human vision system seems to perform almost effortlessly, yet the goal of building computer-based systems with comparable capabilities has proven to be difficult. The task implicitly requires the ability to locate and track faces in scenes that are often complex and dynamic. Recognition is difficult because of variations in factors such as lighting conditions, viewpoint, body movement and facial expression. Although evidence from psychophysical and neurobiological experiments provides intriguing insights into how we might code and recognise faces, its bearings on computational and engineering solutions are far from clear. In this book, we describe models and algorithms that are capable of performing face recognition in a dynamic setting. The key question is how to design computer vision and machine learning algorithms that can operate robustly and quickly under poorly controlled and changing conditions.

The study of face recognition has had an almost unique impact on computer vision and machine learning research at large. It raises many challenging issues and provides a good vehicle for examining some difficult problems in vision and learning. Many of the issues raised are relevant to object recognition in general. In particular, face recognition is not merely a problem of pattern recognition of static pictures; it implicitly but crucially invokes many more general computational tasks concerning the perception of moving objects in dynamic and noisy scenes. Consideration of face recognition as a problem in dynamic vision is perhaps both novel and important. The algorithms described in this book have numerous potential applications in areas such as visual surveillance, multimedia and visually mediated interaction.

There have been several books and edited collections about face recognition written over the years, primarily for studies in cognitive psychology or related topics [38, 39, 41, 42, 43, 46, 378]. In more recent years, there has been an explosion of computer vision conferences and special workshops dedicated to the recognition of human faces and gestures [162, 163, 164, 165, 166, 167, 168, 365]. Surprisingly, however, there has been no book that provides a coherent and unified treatment of the issue from a computational and systems perspective. We hope that this book succeeds in providing such a treatment of the subject useful for both academic and industrial research communities.

This book has been written with an emphasis on computationally viable approaches that can be readily adopted for the design and development of real-time, integrated machine vision systems for dynamic object recognition. We present what is fundamentally an algorithmic approach, although this is founded upon recent theories of visual perception and learning and has also drawn from psychophysical and neurobiological data.

We address the range of visual tasks needed to perform recognition in dynamic scenes. In particular, visual attention is focused using motion and colour cues. Face recognition is attempted by a set of co-operating processes that perform face detection, tracking and identification using view-based, 2D face models with spatio-temporal context. The models are obtained by learning and are computationally efficient for recognition. We address recognition in realistic and therefore poorly constrained conditions. Computations are essentially based on a statistical decision making framework realised by the implementation of various statistical learning models and neural networks. The systems described are robust to factors such as changing illumination, poor resolution and large head rotations in depth. We also describe how the visual processes can co-operate in an integrated learning system.

Overall, the book explores the use of visual motion detection and estimation, adaptable colour models, active and animate vision principles, statistical learning in high-dimensional feature spaces, vector space dimensionality reduction, temporal prediction models (e.g. Kalman filters, hidden Markov models and the Condensation algorithm), spatio-temporal context, image filtering, linear modelling techniques (e.g. principal components analysis (PCA) and linear discriminants), non-linear models (e.g. mixture models, support vector machines, nonlinear PCA, hybrid neural networks), spatio-temporal models (e.g. recurrent neural networks), perceptual integration, Bayesian inference, on-line learning, view-based representation and databases for learning.

We anticipate that this book will be of special interest to researchers and academics interested in computer vision, visual recognition and machine learning. It should also be of interest to industrial research scientists and managers keen to exploit this emerging technology and develop automated face and human recognition systems for a host of commercial applications including visual surveillance, verification, access control and video-conferencing. Finally, this book should be of use to post-graduate students of computer science, electronic and systems engineering and perhaps also of cognitive psychology.

The topics in this book cover a wide range of multi-disciplinary issues and draw on several fields of study without requiring too deep an understanding of any one area in particular. Nevertheless, some basic knowledge of applied mathematics would be useful for the reader. In particular, it would be convenient if one were familiar with vectors and matrices, eigenvectors and eigenvalues, some linear algebra, multivariate analysis, probability, statistics and elementary calculus at the level of 1st or 2nd year undergraduate mathematics. However, the non-mathematically inclined reader should be able to skip over many of the equations and still understand much of the content.

Shaogang Gong
Stephen McKenna
Alexandra Psarrou

October 1999, London and Dundee

Nomenclature

Vectors are column vectors, i.e. $\mathbf{x}^{\mathrm{T}} \equiv [x_1\, x_2\, \ldots\, x_N]$. A list is written as $(x_1, x_2, \ldots x_N)$ while a set or sequence is denoted by $\{x_1, x_2, \ldots x_N\}$. Furthermore, $\{(x_1, y_1), (x_2, y_2), \ldots (x_N, y_N)\}$ denotes a set or sequence of lists. Other commonly used symbols in the book are:

N, n	Input space dimensionality, index
M, m	Number of examples, index
C, c	Number of classes, index
K, k	Number of basis functions or discrete states, index
T, t	Number of time-steps (frames), time variable or index
i, j	Indices
x, y	Coordinates in the image plane
s, r, a	Scale, orientation and aspect ratio in the image plane
θ, ϕ	Tilt and yaw (rotation out of the image plane)
κ, ξ	A constant, an error variable
λ	Eigenvalue, wavelength or a hidden Markov model
$\sigma, \boldsymbol{\mu}, \boldsymbol{\Sigma}$	Standard deviation, mean vector and covariance matrix
$\mathbf{u}, \boldsymbol{\alpha}$	Eigenvector, a representation vector
$\mathbf{a}$	Parameter vector
$\mathbf{x}, \mathbf{q}, \mathbf{y}$	Observation, state and interpretation label vectors
$\tilde{\mathbf{x}}, \mathbf{x}^*$	An approximation to $\mathbf{x}$, a prediction of $\mathbf{x}$
$\boldsymbol{\gamma}, \boldsymbol{\xi}$	Rotation in depth (both yaw and tilt)
$\mathcal{X}, \mathcal{Q}, \mathcal{Y}$	Sets or sequences of observations, states, interpretations
$\mathcal{O}, \mathcal{S}$	Object, scene background
$|\boldsymbol{A}|,\ \boldsymbol{A}^{\mathrm{T}},\ \boldsymbol{I}$	Determinant and transpose of matrix $\boldsymbol{A}$, identity matrix
$\Re^N$	N-dimensional space of reals
$f(\cdot), d(\cdot), h(\cdot)$	A function, a distance function and a similarity function
$P(\cdot), E(\cdot), L(\cdot)$	Probability, expectation and likelihood
$p(\cdot)$	Probability density function (PDF)
$G(\cdot),\ \phi(\cdot)$	Gaussian function (normal distribution), kernel function
$I(\cdot)$	Intensity function (monochrome image)
$\mathcal{E}(\cdot), \mathcal{L}(\cdot), \mathcal{R}(\cdot)$	Error function, loss function and risk functional
$\|\mathbf{x}\|$	L_2 norm of $\mathbf{x}$ (Euclidean length)
$\ln$	Logarithm to base e
$\otimes$	Convolution

Acknowledgements

We should like to express our considerable gratitude to the many fine people who have helped us in the process of writing this book. The experiments described herein would not have been possible without the work of PhD students, research assistants and post-docs at QMW and the University of Westminster. In particular, we want to thank J.J. Collins, Yongmin Li, Peter Loft, Jeffrey Ng, Eng-Jon Ong, Yogesh Raja, Sami Romdhani, Jamie Sherrah, Jonathan Tanner, Fernando de la Torre, Paul Verity and Michael Walter for their contributions to this work. We are indebted to Hilary Buxton, Robert Koger and Dennis Parkinson, all of whom read a draft carefully and gave us many insightful comments and suggestions.

We should also like to thank the anonymous reviewers for their constructive feedback as well as John Navas at Imperial College Press and R. Sankaran at World Scientific Publishing for the kind help we have received in the final stages of preparing this book. The book was typeset using LATEX.

Our thanks are also due to Wolfgang Konen and Elke Sassmannshausen at ZN GmbH in Bochum, Johannes Steffens at Eyematic Interfaces Inc., James Kottas at Miros Inc. and Martin Levine at VisionSphere Technologies Inc. for kindly responding to our enquiries concerning their companies' products which are summarised in Appendix B.

We gratefully acknowledge the financial support that we have received over the years from UK EPSRC, EU ESPRIT and HCM networks, the BBC, BT and Safehouse Technologies Inc. Finally, we should like to thank our families and friends for all their support.

Perchance the best chance of reproducing the ancient Greek temperament would be to cross the Scots with the Chinese.

— Murray Christopher Grieve (Hugh McDiarmid), Lucky Poet

PART I

BACKGROUND

1   About Face

O why was I born with a different face?
Why was I not born like the rest of my race?

— *William Blake, Letter to Thomas Butts*

1.1   The Visual Face

Faces play a vital role in our daily lives with their varied repertoire of intricate and often subtle functions. Our faces contain sense organs of which our eyes are the most useful in allowing us to sense the dynamic world around us. But what information do our faces convey to others? One way in which we use our faces to communicate is through the production of audible speech. However, the *visual* face alone conveys a plethora of useful information. Indeed, speech is accompanied by facial motion as a result of which lip-reading is possible. Facial expressions produced by visible deformation of the face provide us with a guide to judging mood, character and intent. We are constantly 'reading' one another's faces and such processes clearly play an important part in social interaction and communication. All these changes in facial appearance due to expression and speech occur on a rather short time-scale. There are of course more enduring visual cues provided by a person's face and these allow us to estimate such factors as age, gender, ethnic origin and *identity*. It is this last use, *as a visual cue for identification*, that will form the main thread of this book. We have begun by pointing out the other functions of faces because identification is inevitably performed in the presence of all the variations in facial appearance to which these give rise. Whilst your appearance changes all the time, your identity is one thing with which you are stuck!

Faces form a unique class of objects. They share a common structure: *the facial features are always configured in a similar way.* Given their similarity, it is remarkable that we can discriminate between so many different people based upon facial appearance alone. This seems even more remarkable when we consider that we perform recognition in the presence of widely varying viewing conditions.

The perception of faces is highly dynamic, both in space and time and with respect to a given context. In human perception and behaviour it is certainly the case that we use more than just static facial appearances in discriminating between different faces. Visual context constrains our expectation: the object sitting behind a desk is more likely to be human than the object on top of the bookcase! Other sources of information such as body gestures and gait also provide useful cues. It is important to realise that above all, the perception of faces is a spatio-temporal, *dynamic vision* task. Whilst it is true that we can often identify someone from a static photograph, in the real world we usually observe and identify faces in a dynamic setting. Facial appearance alters due to relative motion of the face and the observer. Changes in lighting and the environment also affect appearance. Therefore, face perception involves rather more than the perception of static pictures of faces. In particular, it would seem to require the ability to detect and track faces as they move through cluttered scenes which are themselves often complex and dynamic.

1.2   The Changing Face

The process of identifying a person from facial appearance has to be performed in the presence of many often conflicting factors which alter facial appearance and make the task difficult. It is therefore important to examine the sources of variation in facial appearance more closely. One can consider that there are two types of variation. A face can change its appearance due to either *intrinsic* or *extrinsic* factors. Intrinsic variation takes place independently of any observer and is due purely to the physical nature of the face. Extrinsic variation, on the other hand, arises when the face is *observed* via the interaction of light with the face and the observer. It is the intrinsic variations that one must learn to understand and interpret. This is largely what we mean by the *perception of faces*. Perceptual tasks have to be performed consistently and robustly under all sorts of changes in external conditions characterised by the extrinsic sources of variation. In general, faces exhibit many degrees of intrinsic variability which are difficult to characterise analytically. Table 1.1. lists some rather obvious perceptual tasks and the corresponding intrinsic sources of variation. These are not independent and the list is by no means exhaustive. If these perceptual tasks are to be performed effectively, intrinsic variability must be analysed and modelled. The visual appearance of a face also varies due to a host of extrinsic factors such as those highlighted in Table 1.2.

Table 1.1   Intrinsic sources of variation in facial appearance.

Source	Possible Tasks
Identity	Classification, known-unknown, verification, full identification
Facial expression	Inference of emotion or intention
Speech	Lip-reading
Sex	Deciding whether male or female
Age	Estimating age

Table 1.2   Extrinsic sources of variation in facial appearance.

Source	Effects
Viewing geometry	Pose
Illumination	Shading, colour, self-shadowing, specular highlights
Imaging process	Resolution, focus, imaging noise, sampling of irradiant energy distribution, perspective effects
Other objects	Occlusion, shadowing, indirect illumination

Typically, the appearance of a face alters considerably depending on the illumination conditions and in particular due to self-shadowing. The characteristics of the camera (or eye) used to observe the face also affect the resulting image quality. Other objects present in the scene can cause occlusion and cast shadows as well as altering the nature of the incident

light. However, one of the most significant sources of variation is pose
change. It is worth emphasising that the pose of a face is determined by the
relative three-dimensional (3D) position and orientation of the observer. It
is, therefore, an extrinsic rather than an intrinsic source of variation because
viewing geometry requires the presence of an observer. The main cause of
pose change is relative *rigid motion* between the observer and the subject.
A face undergoes rigid motion when it changes its position and orientation
in 3D space relative to the observer. However, a face can also undergo
non-rigid motion when its 3D shape changes due for example to speech or
facial expression. This results in intrinsic variation of appearance. Whilst
these two types of motion usually occur together, it is more convenient to
treat them separately. If perceiving faces implies interpreting the intrinsic
variations in a manner which is invariant to other changes, such invariances
are often best achieved if the extrinsic variations are modelled so that their
effects can be negated. For instance, the perception of identity should
ideally be pose invariant and as such, the ability to determine the pose of a
face can play an important role in perceiving identity. In this context, rigid
motion provides strong visual cues for understanding pose. Whilst non-
rigid facial motion is also likely to provide useful cues for identification, it
clearly plays an even more important role in communication and perception
of expressions.

1.3   Computing Faces

Over the last quarter of a century, scientists and engineers have endeav-
oured to build machines capable of automatic face perception. This effort has been multi-disciplinary and has benefited from areas as varied
as computer science, cognitive science, mathematics, physics, psychology
and neurobiology. Computer-based face perception is becoming increasingly desirable for many applications including human-machine interfaces,
multimedia, surveillance, security, teleconferencing, communication, ani-
mation, visually mediated interaction and anthropomorphic environments.
Consequently, there has been a strong research effort during recent years
in the study and development of computational models, algorithms and
computer vision systems for automatic face perception [162, 163, 164, 165,
166].

Broadly speaking, in order to recognise faces or indeed any visual objects, one needs to resolve a *stimulus equivalence* problem. Visual stimuli in the form of images of a particular object or class of objects should have something in common that differentiates them from images of other objects. Such commonalities should exist regardless of most reasonable extrinsic and intrinsic changes. Computationally then, how can we represent and measure characteristics that remain unique to faces under different conditions? In fact, it is rather difficult and computationally unrealistic to consider a single, general solution to the problem of modelling faces undergoing all the intrinsic and extrinsic variations. In this book, we mainly focus on the perception of faces for identification under extrinsic variations such as pose change caused by movement. In other words, we assume that the computations are either approximately invariant to most intrinsic variations such as age and expression, or that intrinsic variation is constrained so as to have little effect on facial appearance. Although there is evidence that the perception of faces involves dedicated neural hardware, face perception has many aspects in common with our perception of moving objects in general. In order to understand the nature of *visual perception*, let us briefly introduce some of the processes involved.

In order to perceive objects, artificial and biological vision systems must solve two general problems: that of *segmentation* (also known as *parsing*), and that of *recognition*. The problem of segmentation involves computation to divide images into regions that correspond to bodies of physical objects in the scene. The problem of recognition is to label such bodies as instances of known objects. The segmentation problem is further addressed by two sub-problems known as the problem of *spatial grouping* (also known as *unit formation*) and the *correspondence problem* [326]. Whilst the process of grouping determines which image elements (pixels) belong to a single physical body, correspondence tries to establish associations over time between image elements that are representations of the same scene entity. Both these tasks are non-trivial to accomplish. This is especially true if the perceived objects are constantly in motion and can be partially occluded due to a change of viewpoint: the problem of the *curse of projection* due to the 3D world being under-constrained in its 2D images. Given highly incomplete information, for example, how does the perceptual process decide if a face seen now is the same face seen in the past?

Dynamic perception of faces is necessarily complex. One can readily expect that visual perception of moving objects such as human faces relies upon a range of computational processes including for instance, the measurement of visual cues such as motion and colour, selective attention, face detection, pose estimation, view alignment, face tracking, modelling of identity and identification. Such *perceptual processes* are closely coupled since the information extracted and the computation involved in each process are intrinsically dependent upon those of the others. However, in order to understand the computations required when perceiving faces, it is convenient and even necessary to decompose such a process into a number of clearly definable tasks. Let us now examine such a decomposition in more detail.

Perceptual Grouping and Focus of Attention

In any visual scene there is always a large amount of information to process. A necessary computational task is *perceptual grouping* which *focuses attention* on areas in the field of view where faces are likely to be present. This task is essentially one of determining small attentional windows within the visual field where further computation should be directed. Pre-attentive visual cues such as motion and colour are useful for focusing attention. Notice that focus of attention need not involve determining whether faces are present or where exactly faces are located in the scene.

Detection

The function of determining the presence of a face and locating it within the scene is *face detection*. This task requires a model to discriminate faces from all other visual objects or patterns. It does not require any of a face's intrinsic variability to be interpreted. In particular, it does not involve identification. Face detection is also known as *basic-level* or *entry-level* recognition. It can also be considered to involve the tasks of face image segmentation and face alignment.

Tracking

In a dynamic and cluttered visual scene, the location and appearance of a face can change continually. The task of following a face through a visual scene requires *tracking* which in essence involves establishing *temporal correspondence*. Attentional windows and detected face image regions need to be constantly updated, maintaining an appropriate degree of correspondence over time so that points of reference within these windows and regions are consistent.

Identification

Beyond entry-level recognition, the task of *identification* requires a function to discriminate between different faces. In the study of object recognition in general, such a task is often regarded as being *sub-ordinate level* or *within-category* recognition where all faces together constitute a category. It might seem that the problem of identification has just been defined. In fact, the exact nature of the identification task can vary quite significantly. Consider, for instance, a database consisting of a set, $\mathcal{Y}$, of M known faces. Several different identification tasks can be envisaged. In fact, at least four tasks can be defined as follows.

(1) **Classification**: The task is to identify a face under the assumption that it is a member of $\mathcal{Y}$.
(2) **Known-Unknown**: The task is to decide whether or not a face is a member of $\mathcal{Y}$.
(3) **Verification**: The identity of a face is supplied by some other non-visual means and must be confirmed using face images. This is equivalent to the known-unknown task with $M = 1$.
(4) **Full identification**: The task is to determine whether a face is a member of $\mathcal{Y}$ and if so to determine its identity.

It seems clear that any computational treatment of the *dynamic perception of faces* will involve functions that must at least perform the above tasks well. As a result of decomposing face perception in this way we must address another issue in perceptual processing: that of integration.

Perceptual Integration

Despite that the perception of faces, in common with that of other dynamic visual objects, can be conveniently modelled as an assembly of sub-tasks performed independently by a set of functions, such functions can only be effective and even computationally viable if they are closely coupled. This requires the task of *perceptual integration* or *perceptual control*. Closely coupled information processing implies that the performance of any individual process is highly correlated to and dependent upon the effectiveness of the others. In contrast, conventional approaches to vision have often modelled the computations as independent sequential processes. This has been motivated by the need for simplicity and tractability. However, overwhelming neurobiological evidence suggests that perception is only effective if it is performed by closely coupled, co-operative processes with feedbacks [143, 144].

Visual Learning and Adaptation

Humans are born with a certain innate knowledge of faces and subsequently learn to distinguish between different faces. How much knowledge of faces must be *hard-wired* into the process of face perception and how can this process then *bootstrap* using this knowledge so as to learn to recognise many different faces? Since visual information is always subject to noise and occlusion due to the generally ill-posed nature of inverse projection, model learning is often more difficult than expected. In fact, learned models need to be updated and tuned to specific recognition and tracking tasks. The ability to adapt previously learned models reflects another aspect of perceptual integration in which learned or hard-wired models are improved during the process of performing a perceptual task. The perception of moving objects and faces can also benefit greatly if recognition not only tracks and matches visual appearance with known models, but also interprets patterns of behaviour. This has been shown to be important in the perception of moving objects in general [244, 246].

Other functions are also deemed necessary although they may not be so intuitively apparent. For example, an effective system should exhibit the following functionality:

Learning from examples

A face must be known before it can subsequently be identified. It will therefore be necessary for a system to acquire identity models from observations. Such a *learning from examples* approach may be necessary not only for identification, but also for the other functions described above.

Understanding Pose

Among all the extrinsic and intrinsic sources of variation in facial appearance, pose changes are particularly problematic for the tasks of face detection, tracking and identification. One way of coping with pose change is to make pose explicit by estimating it. Although it may seem unnecessary to estimate pose explicitly in order to perform recognition in a manner that is invariant to pose, it will be useful computationally to consider *pose understanding* as a required task.

Real-time Computation

We must also consider performance issues related to computational complexity and accuracy. Many aspects of dynamic perception require computation to be performed on-line under certain time constraints and even in real-time. Real-time performance is often not a luxury but rather a necessity for visual interpretation of moving faces in dynamic scenes because correct perception needs to be performed within the spatio-temporal context. It is worth noting here that real-time does not imply that processing must be performed at full video frame-rate as long as computation proceeds correctly. In addition to constraints on computational speed, there will also be constraints of accuracy imposed on a system. Systems should be robust with graceful degradation of performance rather than complete failure.

Computer vision systems for automatic face recognition are now beginning to be deployed outside the laboratory in applications such as access control [190]. These systems typically assume a single face imaged at high resolution in frontal or near-frontal view. The environments in which they operate are highly constrained compared to the scenarios in which humans perform recognition. In fact, face recognition is a task which the human vision system seems to perform almost effortlessly in our everyday lives where the conditions are far more varied and challenging than those often artificially imposed for automated systems. Beyond the practical applications, another reason for building artificial face recognition systems is the belief that many of the computational and cognitive issues raised may provide insights into how object recognition in general is performed by the brain.

1.4 Biological Perspectives

This book is largely concerned with a computational approach to building artificial systems capable of perceiving and recognising dynamic faces. It is important to point out that the approach taken is not necessarily biologically plausible and we make no claims about furthering understanding of face recognition and perception in any biological visual systems. However, it will be interesting and possibly even enlightening to draw some parallels with biological systems. We will therefore pause towards the end of each chapter to reflect upon evidence from psychophysical and neurobiological studies. The reader should note that such studies are often somewhat inconclusive by their very nature.

In general, psychophysical and behavioural studies investigate our ability to recognise faces under various experimentally controlled conditions. The conclusions which can be drawn are often rather limited. In particular, most studies have focused on examining static *picture recognition* rather than real *face recognition* [38]. Equally intriguing and interesting is evidence from neurobiological studies that there exist cells in the cortex dedicated to the interpretation and recognition of faces. Visual neurons in the superior temporal sulcus (STS) area of the temporal cortex of monkeys (and sheep) have been found which respond with good specificity to different aspects of facial information [263]. Some face-selective cells respond differently to different people's faces, although not usually only to one person's face [16]. Others are sensitive to eye gaze and pose. The responses of such cells could provide information upon which behavioural responses to different people's faces are based.

1.5   The Approach

Provided that perceptual integration can be properly addressed, dynamic perception of faces can be decomposed into a set of visual tasks which in turn are performed by appropriate computational functions. The aim of this book is to examine how this decomposition can be achieved effectively and to suggest appropriate functions. In recognition of the fact that such a decomposition is perhaps rather artificial, we also examine the means for perceptual integration and control. Furthermore, since computation is mediated by representation, it is necessary to address the role of representation and to determine how best to model faces so as to facilitate perception and recognition. It should be realised that the adoption of a particular representational scheme will constrain the choice of approach taken in determining the computational framework for building a system for face recognition. Representation schemes are discussed in Chapter 2.

A further aim of this book is to illustrate the means for engineering an effective artificial system capable of *learning to model* and subsequently recognising dynamic faces from example images. Chapter 3 introduces the reader to statistical machine learning and to a number of learning techniques used later in the book.

Part II describes methods for performing the tasks of perceptual grouping, focusing of attention, face detection and face tracking. These are performed in the presence of large pose changes and Chapter 6 is devoted to coping with this particular form of extrinsic variation.

In Part III, the task of identification is explored. Initially, this task is eased by constraining the pose to be approximately frontal and upright. Chapter 8 deals with identification under large pose changes and Chapter 9 considers the role of temporal information in identification.

Part IV addresses the problem of perceptual integration and explores potential roles for computing faces within the context of dynamic vision in broader terms. It describes ways in which tasks can be closely coupled for the perception of faces. The appendices include a treatment of databases for development, evaluation and application as well as a look at the current state of commercial applications. Finally, we give detailed descriptions of many of the algorithms used.

2   Perception and Representation

A theory has only the alternative of being right or wrong. A model has a third possibility: it may be right, but irrelevant.

— *Manfred Eigen*

Visual perception is carried out through information processing and the computations involved are mediated by representation. Indeed at an algorithmic level the purpose of all computation can be regarded as the transformation of one representation into another. The complexity of a computation is determined as much by the choice of a representation as that of the algorithm. It is essential to ask what forms of representation are suitable for mediating effective computation for the perception of dynamic visual objects such as human faces. In other words, what information is most relevant to the perception of faces and what form of representation enables such information to be extracted from moving faces and utilised under the demands of temporal and computational constraints? Interpretation of moving objects in a changing scene is perhaps only meaningful in the appropriate context, especially the temporal context. This is somewhat different from the interpretation of static pictures where temporal constraints do not heavily influence the outcome of a perceptual task. Later we will need to consider the representation of temporal information but for now let us focus on representation of spatial information.

Meaningful perception requires knowledge. The computational mechanisms involved in the perception of human faces must at some stage appeal to stored knowledge of faces. Such knowledge needs to be represented in a form that can be used for efficient and effective matching with the visual input (after an appropriate transformation). In a biological system, this knowledge will have been learned either from direct experience or through a process of evolution. Correspondingly, in artificial systems, knowledge can be either *hard-wired* (innate) or learned by the system. In either case, representation should support learning from experience. Representation is dependent on previous experience and models learned from previous proximal data should be used to drive the form of representation used.

We need to ask how knowledge of complex, deformable, 3D objects like faces might be represented. More specifically,

(1) How can a representation capture the diversity of different people's faces?

(2) Should stored face representations aim to capture only the relevant intrinsic sources of variability and rely on other more general perceptual mechanisms to achieve invariance to extrinsic sources of variability?

(3) Alternatively, can domain specific knowledge be used to obtain some invariance to extrinsic variability?

2.1   A Distal Object

We will now try to begin to answer these questions. A classical pattern recognition approach may suggest that a representation of a face for the purpose of recognition should be based on the extraction of a relatively small set of features from an image in a predetermined manner. This *feature set* would be chosen to be sufficiently descriptive to enable recognition to be performed whilst exhibiting a degree of invariance to the expected variations in appearance due, for example, to pose, illumination and expression. An intuitive approach of this kind would be to measure geometric relationships between salient, localised facial features such as eyes, nose, mouth, eyebrows and chin outline. This was indeed the approach taken by one of the early attempts at building artificial models of faces [182]. Alternatively, the features can be based on more diffuse characteristics such as texture and colour. Such *feature-based* approaches have been proposed for face detection [317] and identification [182]. However, they rely on fixed feature sets which discard information in a rather *ad hoc* manner based upon their designers' prior knowledge. It is not at all clear how to define and extract an optimal feature set. Indeed it has been shown computationally that geometrical feature-based approaches are inferior in some ways to simple template matching [48]. Although intuitively attractive, such a local feature-based approach is flawed. Recent studies increasingly suggest a more holistic approach to representation [49, 209]. Bearing this in mind, let us now consider the problem of representation from first principles.

A person's face forms part of the surface of a *distal* object. We wish to form a *proximal* representation of this distal face from observations of it. The distal face can be characterised for this purpose by its shape and surface properties in as much as these affect the patterns of light energy reflected from it:

$$\mathcal{O}_{distal} \equiv (\mathcal{O}_{shape}, \mathcal{O}_{surface}) \tag{2.1}$$

Once these intrinsic shape and surface reflectance properties have been fixed, the visual appearance of the face then depends on the extrinsic sources of variation mentioned earlier. If these shape and surface properties could be faithfully represented in some form, images of the face could then be generated using computer graphics techniques to control the extrinsic sources of variation and render the images. Such a representation could thus be used as a *generative* model, albeit a rather restrictive one which could only generate one particular face with a particular facial expression. Pursuing this chain of thought further, we would next ask how to obtain a generative model capable of generating any face with any facial expression and incapable of generating anything else. Such a model would provide a general purpose model of faces. One approach to such representation is to assume that all faces admit an unknown, common parameterisation, $\boldsymbol{\alpha}$, and that these parameters are sufficient to determine both the 3D shape of the face and its surface reflectance properties:

$$(\mathcal{O}_{shape}, \mathcal{O}_{surface}) = f(\boldsymbol{\alpha}) \tag{2.2}$$

If such a model can be established, an instantiation of $\boldsymbol{\alpha}$ yields a particular face exhibiting a particular facial expression. This all suggests that one approach to representation of faces is to attempt to recover their 3D shape and to characterise their surface reflectance properties. Their 3D structure could be represented explicitly in a 3D co-ordinate system or implicitly using combinations of 2D views set in correspondence. Let us now examine these two possibilities.

2.2   Representation by 3D Reconstruction

One approach to obtaining a proximal representation of the distal face object is to attempt to recover its three-dimensional (3D) structure explicitly from the visual input [217]. If this *representation-by-reconstruction* can be achieved to provide a proximal representation of a face, visual tasks such as recognition might then be performed by utilising certain aspects of information captured by such a representation. For instance, a scheme can be envisaged in which a 2D image pattern is compared with projections of stored 3D models. Such a matching process is based on the assumption that the projected image of the potential candidate 3D model can be brought into *alignment* with the image pattern of interest through transformation. In theory, this alignment can be achieved, at least for rigid objects, by establishing correspondences between a few feature points on the image and the 3D model [345]. In practice, robust alignment is both nontrivial and computationally expensive.

Accurate 3D reconstruction, even of a 3D shape alone, has proven to be notoriously difficult to achieve and has never been fully implemented in computer vision. Many so-called *shape-from-X* methods have been proposed for reconstruction and some can be found in most textbooks on computer vision. However, these general purpose algorithms give disappointing results when applied to faces. Instead, researchers have used active sensing devices [6, 279, 353] or carefully calibrated stereo vision [348] in order to acquire 3D head models. These methods constitute engineering solutions to head model acquisition rather than methods for visual learning and perception of faces. Once a database of such 3D head models is available, a parametric representation of faces might be learned [6] (Equation (2.2)). Furthermore, once such a parameterisation was available, it could be used to constrain the reconstruction problem so that recovery of a 3D shape from a 2D face image becomes more accurate [6]. However, even if this is possible, many difficulties with the 3D reconstruction approach remain.

It can be stated that so far we have been concerned with obtaining a representation which is in some sense isomorphic with the distal object. Such models are useful in graphics as they provide generative models for synthesising and rendering any image of any face. In visual perception, however, the problem is one of analysis rather than synthesis and the aim of representation is not to enable recovery of a parameterisation analogous to α. Rather, the goal of representation is to obtain from the visual input an instantiation of a *proximal face* parameterisation which describes the distal object in some way that is relevant for visual interpretation. In fact, different models and different representation schemes are appropriate to different perceptual tasks. For example, a representation for face detection need not contain sufficient information for the interpretation of facial expressions. Bearing this in mind, one neither needs nor should seek a representation which is isomorphic with the distal object [101]. It is also clear that such attempts are unlikely to be computationally viable. In fact it is neither necessary nor desirable to assume that 'representation is reconstruction' without consideration of the perceptual tasks which the representation is required to mediate [101]. In particular, full 3D reconstruction is neither appropriate nor computationally viable for recognition tasks. However, it may be more relevant for certain visuomotor tasks.

An alternative approach which avoids explicit 3D reconstruction is to represent the shape and surface properties of faces *implicitly* using 2D views. Let us now explore such an approach.

2.3   Two-dimensional View-based Representation

A more attractive approach to representation avoids the need to construct explicit 3D models altogether. It can be shown that under certain restrictive assumptions, it is possible to faithfully represent the 3D structure of objects such as faces *implicitly* without resorting to explicit 3D models at all [23, 310, 311, 346, 347]. Such a representation essentially consists of multiple two-dimensional (2D) views together with dense correspondence maps between these views. Let us examine how this might be achieved.

The 2D image coordinates of a point on a face at an arbitrary pose can be represented as a linear combination of the coordinates of the corresponding point in a set of 2D images of the face at different poses provided that its shape remains rigid. These different views span the space of all possible views of the shape and form a *vector space*. The shape of the face can then be represented by selecting sufficient feature points on the face. Assuming that there is no self-occlusion, two perspective views are sufficient to model the shape of a face [311]. Three views are needed for orthographic projection [347]. In reality, however, self-occlusions are rather common when faces rotate in depth and more views of a face are required for effective representation. In fact, enough views are needed to cover the various *aspects* of a face. However, given sufficient 2D views, the 3D shape can be faithfully represented in terms of these views provided that correspondences can be established between the selected feature points in the different views. In general however, faces undergo non-rigid deformation and these results unfortunately no longer hold.

If shape ($\mathcal{O}_{shape}$) can be represented by combinations of 2D views, it is logical to ask if the surface reflectance properties of the face ($\mathcal{O}_{surface}$) can also be recovered. Given correspondence between views, the local photometric characteristics or *texture* associated with each point can be used to predict the texture of other views of the face. However, this texture varies as viewing conditions alter. As with shape, a linear combination of a few 2D views is sufficient to recover the desired information as long as certain restrictive conditions hold. In particular, if we ignore self-shadowing, assume that the face is a Lambertian surface and assume a single collimated light source, then three otherwise identical views taken under three linearly independent light source directions are sufficient to reconstruct the face under any light source direction [310]. In practice however, these assumptions are unlikely to be realistic.

We have explored the notion that a 2D view-based representation of both shape and surface reflectance properties may be achieved from which faithful reconstruction of the geometry and texture of a face is possible. Such representation requires dense correspondences to be established between different 2D views. Correspondence needs to be performed in a manner which is insensitive to the expected variations in the texture whilst the texture is principally determined by the surface characteristics of the object and the illumination conditions. Unfortunately, the computation of dense correspondences is both expensive and unstable by its very nature; it is intrinsically an ill-posed problem. However, this difficulty should not lead us to reject view-based representation but to ask whether dense correspondence is really necessary. As in the case of 3D reconstruction, we should ask whether a view-based scheme needs to faithfully represent 3D structure, albeit implicitly. Since visual recognition is the primary concern, accurate reconstruction unnecessarily places a heavy computational burden on the perceptual process. Reconstruction is, in fact, a more difficult and general requirement. We should therefore consider view-based representation without dense correspondence.

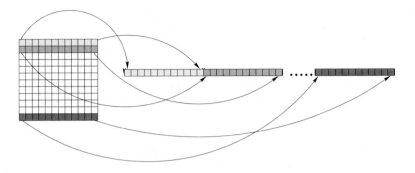

Figure 2.1   A vector space representation of a raster image array.

2.4   Image Template-based Representation

View-based representation which avoids the need for dense correspondence
can be achieved by aligning views using linear transformations involving
translation, rotation and uniform scaling in the image plane. This results
in a simple representation in terms of the pixel intensity values of the aligned
view images. We will refer to such a representation as *template-based*. Each
view is considered to form a high-dimensional vector in which each element
codes the intensity of a single pixel in the transformed image [63]. For
example, a typical monochrome image of 128×128 pixels is represented
as a vector of $128^2 = 16384$ elements. The ordering of the pixels in the
vector must be consistent, e.g. a raster scan as shown in Figure 2.1. This
simple, template-based representation retains essentially all the information
in the image although it does not attempt to separate shape and texture
information.

Any representation of visual objects based on intensity images is subject
to sensory noise and other extrinsic sources of variation such as lighting and
background clutter. This is especially true of template-based representations with images encoded directly as vectors in a multi-dimensional space.
Image preprocessing is necessary in order to ensure that a representation
is less sensitive to extrinsic variations. Image preprocessing is usually performed by spatial filtering that aims to extract salient local and holistic
features as well as to reduce image noise. In fact, the same preprocessing
methods facilitate computations aimed at establishing correspondence and
are therefore evident in most view-based representation schemes. Commonly used filters include symmetric filters such as Difference of Gaussian

(DoG) and Laplacian of Gaussian (LoG), and directional filters such as Gaussian derivatives and Gabor wavelets. Different filters may be appropriate for different visual tasks and computations. For example, let us briefly consider the use of Gabor wavelets (details are given in Appendix C). A Gabor wavelet transform yields images which are locally normalised in intensity and decomposed in terms of spatial frequency and direction in the image plane. It thus provides a mechanism for obtaining:

(1) some degree of invariance to intensity due to global illumination, skin tone and hair colour changes,

(2) selectivity in scale by providing a pyramid representation, and

(3) selectivity in orientation. This permits investigation into the role of locally oriented features with variations such as pose change.

We shall introduce and describe different filtering methods throughout the course of this book when they are deployed for specific purposes.

2.5   The Correspondence Problem and Alignment

A face modelled by multiple 2D views can be compared with an image by comparing appropriate model views after a suitable transformation. This is the notion of *multiple-views-plus-transformation* [333, 346]. Such an approach makes it possible to learn models directly from example images. However, there remains the difficult problem of establishing correspondence between a candidate image and the stored views of a face. In between the two extremes of template-based representation and separate representations of shape and texture by dense correspondence, one can consider a range of possible 2D representation schemes differing in the degree of correspondence used. The method used to establish correspondence will depend upon the degree of correspondence required by the representation scheme.

Affine transformation: Affine transformations can be applied to a face image to bring it into correspondence with another face image. Such transformations apply translations, rotations, scaling and shearing to an image. We refer to this form of correspondence as *alignment*. Alignment treats the images as holistic templates and does not in general bring all points on the face images into accurate correspondence. The template-based representation scheme discussed earlier requires a restricted form of alignment without shearing transformations, i.e. translation, rotation and uniform scaling of images only.

Sparse correspondence: Alternatively, a feature-based approach can be used to establish correspondences only between a small set of salient feature points. Correspondences between other image points can then be approximated by interpolating between these salient feature points. Typically, semantically meaningful features are selected. These can be the corners of the eyes, nose and mouth for example.

Dense correspondence: Finally, an attempt to establish dense correspondence can be made. This was the form of correspondence required by the view-based representation schemes in our earlier theoretical discussion. Dense correspondence is based on local image structure and is established either at points on a regular grid or at locations of sufficient intensity gradient. Dense correspondence maps are commonly established by computing *optical flow*, a dense apparent motion field consisting of displacement vectors between pairs of corresponding image points in two different views [157]. In general, a dense correspondence map is difficult to compute and necessarily expensive. Besides, an optical flow field can only be established if the neighbouring views are sufficiently similar [23].

Figure 2.2 shows (a) two face images taken at similar viewing angles and (b) their mean image. Also shown are the mean of the two images after the faces have been brought into correspondence by (c) affine transformation (translation, rotation and uniform scaling) and (d) feature-based warping.

It may seem that denser correspondences would always provide more accurate view transformations. However, one cannot ignore computational viability. This is especially true in visual scenes of moving objects. In dynamic perception of moving faces, establishing correspondences within a given time constraint is not only desirable but necessary. In fact, it is important to ask:

(1) What degree of correspondence is needed for each visual task?
(2) What degree of correspondence is computationally feasible within the spatio-temporal context of a dynamic scene?

(a)

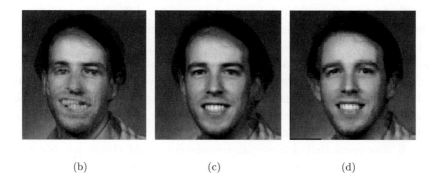

(b)   (c)   (d)

Figure 2.2 Faces brought into correspondence under different transformations. (a) Images of two different faces. (b) Averaging the two images. (c) Averaging after affine alignment (without shearing). (d) Averaging after warping using 18 facial feature points.

Table 2.1 Establishing appearance-based representation.

Correspondence	Computation	2D Texture	2D Shape
affine	alignment	image template	
sparse	feature-based	approx. shape-free	approx. warped
dense	optical flow	shape-free	warped

Higher-order correspondence separates shape and texture information more effectively. Facial attributes such as gender, age, identity and expression should be more separable in the feature space resulting from higher-order correspondence. At the extreme of full optical flow, shape and texture can be modelled as separate vector spaces. This is what underlies *morphing* in computer graphics. As we have emphasised, however, the objectives of visual perception are analysis rather than detailed synthesis. Lower-order alignment places more emphasis on the subsequent interpretation methods. Different representation schemes and thus different degrees of correspondence are desirable for different perceptual tasks. Table 2.1 summarises a range of strategies for achieving correspondence.

Extrinsic variations, such as pose and illumination change, can alone make correspondence difficult to establish. However, intrinsic variations and changes of identity make matters even more problematic. A notable difficulty is that a point on the surface of a face can be made invisible by a change of facial expression. In fact there are many reasons why correspondence between two face images of the same person cannot always be defined because of intrinsic variation:

(1) Closing of the mouth resulting in occlusion of the inner mouth.
(2) Closing of the eyelids resulting in occlusion of the eyes.
(3) Change of hairstyle (either facial or head hair) or simply partial occlusion due to hair movement or growth.
(4) Occlusion due to spectacles.
(5) The application of make-up.
(6) The appearance and disappearance of facial features and lines due to expression changes.
(7) Skin wrinkling due to aging.
(8) Changes in skin marks and blemishes.

Detailed correspondence maps between images of *different* people's faces
are clearly even more problematic to define. A point on one person's face
may not have a clearly corresponding point on another person's face. As
a result of such difficulties, consistent, dense correspondence is simply not
viable. Therefore, intrinsic variation cannot in general be modelled in an
entirely structural or geometric manner. Rather, intrinsic variation must
be handled to some extent using statistical models of appearance variation,
through learning.

We have not yet mentioned the dynamic nature of representation. So far
it all seems rather static, or *atemporal*. However, the correspondence problem is as much about temporal correlation between views over time as it is
about alignment and transformation between views. This is especially true
if the change of view is caused by relative motion between the subject and
the observer. The fact that the correspondence problem can be resolved
through computing optical flow, an apparent visual motion field, reflects
its temporal nature. It may appear that temporal change just provides
another source of useful cues for the estimation of atemporal, proximal representations. In fact, the spatio-temporal constraint is essential for solving
the correspondence problem and should be at the core of representation.
It is the temporal change and its associated causal context that are often
used as the most important visual cues in human vision. For example,
idiosyncrasies of an individual's facial expression changes can be modelled
and subsequently used as cues for identification. The role of temporal information in representation and visual interpretation will be discussed at
greater length in Chapter 10.

2.6   Biological Perspectives

There is now converging evidence from both psychophysical and neurobiological studies to suggest that face recognition in the human vision system
employs viewer-centred, 2D view-based representation rather than explicitly 3D representation [49, 209]. For instance, the existence of cells in visual
cortex that are sensitive to eye gaze and head pose can be taken to suggest
viewer-centred representation [264].

Feature-based representation: Several psychophysical studies have investigated whether faces are encoded and represented in terms of in-

dividual facial features or in terms of a more holistic, configurational representation scheme. Initial evidence for feature-based face representation comes from observations in which very young children seem to show differential fixation to eyes. In particular, infants seem to learn to attend to people's eyes before they attend to their mouths [58, 112, 124]. Psychology has by and large shown that what is learned or developed first is used most (or best) in later adulthood. Therefore one should also expect that adults fixate eyes more than other parts of the face. This is indeed what has been observed [374]. If fixation frequency or duration can be considered as an indication of selective processing and if eyes and mouth are the features most looked at, then perhaps it is reasonable to suggest that the eyes and the mouth are also salient features which play an important role in the perception of faces. Series of experiments have since attempted to verify such a hypothesis for feature-based representation and have tried to identify facial features that best aid the recognition of faces [32, 84, 147]. However, it has been pointed out that such experiments can be misleading because the subjects involved respond to the demands of a particular task with specific strategies which may be rather unlike their usual modes of processing [261]. In particular, Friedman *et al.* [119] have shown that the saliency ranking of facial features does not completely predict face recognition performance. Changing one feature rated low (e.g. forehead) did not produce greater decrement in recognition performance than changing a feature rated high (e.g. nose). The study has also shown that although observers were quite good at differentiating between two different faces, they could rarely specify which specific facial features were different. This suggests that the perception of a face may in fact use a holistic (i.e. configural) representation rather than local features.

Holistic representation: Support for the use of a holistic face representation can be drawn from experiments which show that subjects can provide only vague and limited details when asked to describe even well known faces [83]. Bachmann [9] carried out experiments on the effects of image resolution on face recognition. In fact, it is rather surprising to discover that images of resolution varying between 18 and 74 pixels per face were almost equally effective in providing information on facial identity. This is despite the fact that the outlines of the original faces were similar and that 'easy cues' for discrimination, such as clothing, were absent. This further suggests a more global, configuration sensitive scheme of representation.

One study attempted to develop a unified representational framework, based on holistic encoding of facial information, to account for the effects of inversion (rotation through 180° in the image plane), race and distinctiveness in face recognition [350]. Experiments showed that (subjective) similarity between faces could account for the effects of all three factors. It was suggested that faces may be coded as points in a multidimensional space, defined by dimensions that serve to discriminate faces. Such a representation suggests that the location in a Euclidean multidimensional space provides an appropriate metaphor for the mental representation of a face. Two specific models within this framework were identified: a *norm-based coding model* and a purely *exemplar-based model.* In a norm-based coding model it is assumed that faces are encoded in terms of their deviation from a single general face norm or prototype located at the origin of the space. Faces can be seen as an example of a perceptual category that includes in its representation information about the central tendencies. The origin of the multidimensional space is defined as the central tendency of the dimensions. It is assumed that the values of the feature dimensions of the population of faces experienced will vary normally around the central tendency (at least for faces from the observer's own "race"). Therefore, typical faces (close to the central tendency) will be seen more often than distinctive faces (distant from the central tendency). This framework also accounts for our discriminating ability in face recognition and explains the results of experiments which show that previously unfamiliar faces that are rated as distinct or unusual are more accurately recognised in a recognition memory paradigm. Conversely, typical faces are more likely to be incorrectly identified as having been seen before.

Additional support for the holistic representation of faces can be drawn from the study of caricatures. A *face caricature* is obtained through a process of exaggerating the distinctive features that individuate a particular face. Artists vary in the amount of distortion they impose on distinctive features but they agree closely in terms of which ratios they should distort the most and which they should distort the least. This provides evidence for the role of the overall configuration rather the individual features in recognition [261].

Despite the tendency towards a more holistic representation, it is conceivable that both feature-based and holistic representations are present in human vision and used for the perception of faces according to age and the data available. Experiments have shown that the ability to recognise faces improves with age and is related to the increase in the efficiency of a schemata for processing facial information [57, 115]. There are indications that the development of face recognition is from feature-based representation, which dominates during early childhood, to holistic representation which prevails in adulthood [62, 176].

2.7 Discussion

An effective representation scheme for object recognition in general and face recognition in particular is clearly important since representation underpins all computation and has strong implications for effectiveness and efficiency [101]. In this chapter, several alternative representation schemes were introduced. Explicitly three-dimensional schemes were considered and rejected in favour of two-dimensional, appearance-based representation on computational, neurobiological and psychophysical grounds. Appearance-based schemes vary in the extent to which they separate 2D shape and texture information. At the simplest level, template-based representation relies on images being brought into coarse correspondence using affine transformations in the image-plane. Representation is then essentially in terms of pixel values. The other extreme of appearance-based representation attempts to separate 2D shape from 2D texture by establishing dense correspondence using optical flow algorithms. This is both computationally difficult and inappropriate for the visual tasks considered in this book because dense correspondence cannot in general be defined for faces. Certain visual tasks will, however, benefit from analysing structural information. Therefore, a finer degree of correspondence than used in the template-based approach is needed. In such cases, sparse correspondence established at the level of common structure between faces is computationally more attractive and feasible. This allows deformation of 2D shape to be modelled and makes explicit an approximation to a face's 2D shape-free texture.

Now that we have considered face representation, we need to examine how such representations are to be acquired, adapted and used to mediate the visual tasks needed for dynamic face perception. In particular, a successful vision system will need to learn and adapt its representations if it is to function robustly in a changing environment. In order to address this problem, let us lay some foundations by introducing methods for machine learning before considering how specific vision tasks can be performed.

3   Learning under Uncertainty

I am an adaptive system, whose survival and success, whatever my goals, depend on maintaining a reasonably veridical picture of my environment of things and people. Since my world picture approximates reality only crudely, I cannot aspire to optimize anything; at most, I can aim at satisficing.

— *Herbert Simon*

The information processing involved in visual perception is in general both subject to noise and inherently ill-posed. A number of factors contribute to the incomplete and uncertain nature of perception, including sensory noise, unknown object surface properties, changing lighting conditions and ambiguities arising from perspective projection of the 3D scene to its 2D images. *Nothing is certain.* As emphasised earlier, faces are usually observed undergoing variations due to a range of extrinsic factors including unknown illumination and noisy sensing. A powerful and perhaps the only effective way to extract relevant information about faces from noisy images is through *learning.* Indeed, we consider learning to be an important part of any robust artificial system for the perception of faces. Whilst most intrinsic facial variations are difficult to model analytically, they can be modelled probabilistically through statistical learning. Viewer-centred representations in particular lend themselves to learning from example images. Inevitably, learning is to some extent context-dependent and data used for learning are usually selected to reflect typical as well as boundary conditions of the spatio-temporal context. It is not hard to see that context-dependence can be advantageous provided that the context does not change significantly over time. This raises the issue of adaptability. A system should ideally adapt to new conditions through a process of *learning and forgetting.*

We will adopt statistical learning as part of the underlying framework for modelling visual perception of faces. Particular learning algorithms will be described throughout the book within the context of the various visual tasks. However, let us first introduce some basic concepts of statistical learning in a more abstract fashion. Here, we distinguish between different types of learning problems and outline some general learning algorithms to be applied later in the book. More details of some of these algorithms are given in Appendix C. More extensive treatments of statistical machine learning can be found elsewhere [27, 92, 96, 120, 351].

3.1   Statistical Learning

We consider images of objects and faces, and similarly features extracted from these images, to form probabilistic observation feature vectors. Their semantic interpretations are also subject to uncertainty. We will sometimes refer to these interpretations as *labels*. The relationship between the observations and their labels can be modelled probabilistically. Such models can be estimated through statistical learning given sufficient observations.

The goal of *statistical learning* is to estimate an unknown *inference function* from a finite, often sparse, set of observations. Let $\mathbf{x} \in \mathcal{X}$ be a random *observation feature vector* drawn from a finite set of observations $\mathcal{X}$. Let $y \in \mathcal{Y}$ be the interpretation of $\mathbf{x}$ from a probable set $\mathcal{Y}$ given by a random variable with probability $P(y)$. For example, $\mathcal{X}$ might be a set of face images and $\mathcal{Y}$ a set of corresponding names or identity labels associated with those face images. The probability of observing the pair $(\mathbf{x}, y)$ is given by the *joint probability*

$$P(\mathbf{x}, y) = P(\mathbf{x})P(y|\mathbf{x}) \qquad (3.1)$$

where $P(\mathbf{x})$ is the probability of observing $\mathbf{x}$ and $P(y|\mathbf{x})$ is the *conditional probability* of y given $\mathbf{x}$. This conditional probability describes the probabilistic relationship between the observation $\mathbf{x}$ and its interpretation y.

If $P(y|\mathbf{x})$ is known, an interpretation y can be inferred for any given observation $\mathbf{x}$. In practice, this inference function will not be known. However, given a set of observations and their labels, it is possible to estimate the inference function from these data through *inductive learning*. Once learning has been performed, interpretations can be *predicted* for novel, previously unseen observations. This prediction is known as *inference*.

Although digital images consist of discrete values, it will often be useful to treat observations as *continuous* random variables. A set of observations is then characterised by the distribution of these variables. Such a distribution is described by a *probability density function, $p(\mathbf{x})$*. In particular, a univariate density function is defined as:

$$p(x = a) = \lim_{\epsilon \to 0} \frac{P(a < x \le a + \epsilon)}{\epsilon} \qquad (3.2)$$

The probability of $\mathbf{x}$ lying in some interval is obtained by integrating the probability density function over that interval. In particular, all density functions integrate to unity:

$$\int p(\mathbf{x})d\mathbf{x} = 1 \qquad (3.3)$$

Given a large enough set of observations, $\mathcal{X} = \{\mathbf{x}_1, \mathbf{x}_2, \ldots, \mathbf{x}_M\}$, it is possible to estimate the probability density function, $p(\mathbf{x})$. This density estimation task can be performed using *inductive learning* without the use of labels $\mathcal{Y} = \{y_1, y_2, \ldots, y_M\}$.

3.2   Learning as Function Approximation

Inductive learning can be defined as a problem of *functional approximation by risk minimisation* [351]. A *learning machine* is an algorithmic implementation of some family of functions $f(\mathbf{x}, \mathbf{a})$, where $\mathbf{a}$ is a parameter vector. Within this framework, we regard learning to be the same problem as *model estimation* or *function approximation*. Given a finite set of observations and their corresponding interpretations, $\{(\mathbf{x}_1, y_1), (\mathbf{x}_2, y_2), \ldots, (\mathbf{x}_M, y_M)\}$, the learning problem is to find a function from the available family of functions that can approximate the observations with minimal *risk* defined as:

$$\mathcal{R}(\mathbf{a}) = \int \mathcal{L}(y, f(\mathbf{x}, \mathbf{a})) \, dP(\mathbf{x}, y) \qquad (3.4)$$

where $\mathcal{L}(y, f(\mathbf{x}, \mathbf{a}))$ is a *Loss* function measuring the discrepancy between y and the learning machine's approximation of y given by $f(\mathbf{x}, \mathbf{a})$. Risk is the loss integrated over the joint probability distribution $P(\mathbf{x}, y)$. Learning aims to find a function $f(\mathbf{x}, \mathbf{a}_0)$ that minimises the risk functional. The expected risk cannot be minimised directly because $P(\mathbf{x}, y)$ is unknown.

Such a minimisation can be used to estimate the *regression*, $E[y|\mathbf{x}]$, of y on $\mathbf{x}$. The regression is the function of $\mathbf{x}$ that gives the mean value of y conditioned on $\mathbf{x}$. This function provides an optimal predictor of y given $\mathbf{x}$ when the loss is measured as:

$$\mathcal{L}(y, f(\mathbf{x}, \mathbf{a})) = [y - f(\mathbf{x}, \mathbf{a})]^2 \qquad (3.5)$$

If the probability distribution only allows y to take one value given any particular $\mathbf{x}$, then the regression is not really an average but simply the allowed value. A *classification* task in which each observation is assigned to a particular class or discrete set can be formulated as a special case in which y takes discrete values e.g. $y \in \{-1, 1\}$.

In order to estimate a regression or a classification function, a set of observations with known labels must be available. Estimation of such functions is often called *supervised* learning. If the labels are unknown or if all the observations have the same label, then only *unsupervised* learning is possible. In this case, the function to be approximated is the *probability density function*, $p(\mathbf{x})$, that describes the distribution of $\mathbf{x}$. The loss function is then typically defined as the negative log of the density. In other words, learning a density function entails finding a function $p(\mathbf{x}, \mathbf{a}_0)$ that minimises the risk functional of Equation (3.4) given the loss function:

$$\mathcal{L}(p(\mathbf{x}, \mathbf{a})) = -\log p(\mathbf{x}, \mathbf{a}) \qquad (3.6)$$

In the learning framework outlined so far, we must consider the following in order to construct a learning machine:

(1) **Type of function**: This is usually a regression, classification, or probability density function.

(2) **Implementation of functions**: There are many ways to define and implement suitable families of functions. These include networks based on multi-layer perceptrons, radial basis functions, linear discriminant functions, polynomial functions, Gaussian density functions and mixture density models.

(3) **Learning algorithm**: A method for model estimation is usually based on optimisation to minimise some approximation to the expected risk. This usually takes the form of either empirical risk minimisation or structural risk minimisation as will be explained shortly.

The choice of the family of functions to implement should depend upon:

(1) The true nature of the underlying probability distribution.
(2) The amount of training data available.

In broad terms, simple parametric functions with only a few parameters introduce a strong bias, while functions with many parameters are capable of modelling a greater range of functions but introduce high variance. The selection of a model must address this trade-off. This has been called the *bias-variance dilemma* [123]. In fact, results from statistical learning theory show that it is not the *number* of parameters that should be controlled but the *capacity* of the functions. It is important to restrict the family of functions to one with a capacity that is appropriate given the amount of training data available [351].

A learning algorithm cannot minimise the expected risk directly because $P(\mathbf{x}, y)$ is unknown. However, one approach to learning is to approximate the risk, $\mathcal{R}$, by the *empirical* risk $\mathcal{R}_{emp}$:

$$\mathcal{R}_{emp}(\mathbf{a}) = \frac{1}{M} \sum_{m=1}^{M} \mathcal{L}(y_m, f(\mathbf{x}_m, \mathbf{a})) \tag{3.7}$$

An algorithm which sets the parameters so as to minimise $\mathcal{R}_{emp}$ performs learning using the principle of *empirical risk minimisation*. For example, the classical maximum-likelihood method* for density estimation sets the parameters by minimising empirical risk with the loss function given in Equation (3.6):

$$\mathcal{R}_{emp}(\mathbf{a}) = -\frac{1}{M} \sum_{m=1}^{M} \log p(\mathbf{x}_m, \mathbf{a}) \tag{3.8}$$

Similarly, the classical least-squares method minimises empirical risk with the loss function given in Equation (3.5):

$$\mathcal{R}_{emp}(\mathbf{a}) = \frac{1}{M} \sum_{m=1}^{M} [y_m - f(\mathbf{x}_m, \mathbf{a})]^2 \tag{3.9}$$

However, this conventional minimisation of empirical risk does not guarantee good generalisation. In order to guarantee an upper bound on generalisation error, statistical learning theory tells us that the *capacity* must

---

*See Vapnik [351] for a discussion of the limitations of maximum likelihood.

be controlled. In order to achieve this, functions whose capacity can be computed are needed. This is the idea behind *support vector machines*. Instead of simply minimising empirical risk, functions of appropriate capacity are chosen using *structural risk minimisation* (SRM). SRM provides a well defined quantitative measure for the *capacity* of a learned function to generalise over unknown test data. Due to its relative simplicity, Vapnik-Chervonenkis (VC) dimension [351] in particular has been adopted as one of the more popular measures for such a capacity. By choosing a function with a low VC dimension and minimising its empirical error to a training data set, SRM can offer a guaranteed upper bound (in probability) on the generalisation error.

3.3   Bayesian Inference and MAP Classification

The joint probability of an observation and its interpretation variables can be rewritten in terms of conditional probabilities:

$$P(\mathbf{x}, y) = P(\mathbf{x}|y)\,P(y) = P(y|\mathbf{x})\,P(\mathbf{x}) \qquad (3.10)$$

This is captured by *Bayes' theorem*:

$$P(y|\mathbf{x}) = \frac{P(\mathbf{x}|y)\,P(y)}{P(\mathbf{x})} \qquad (3.11)$$

where the conditional probability $P(\mathbf{x}|y)$ is known as the *likelihood*, and $P(\mathbf{x})$ is known as the *prior* probability of observing $\mathbf{x}$. If the *posterior* probability, $P(y|\mathbf{x})$, can be computed then inference can be performed. Bayes' theorem is useful because it expresses the posterior probabilities in terms of quantities which are sometimes easier to estimate. It shows how to combine prior knowledge in the form of the prior probabilities $P(\mathbf{x})$ and $P(y)$ with the likelihood estimate for an observation.

If an observation feature vector $\mathbf{x}$ takes continuous values, its probability measures are given by a density function and Bayes' theorem is then given by

$$P(y|\mathbf{x}) = \frac{p(\mathbf{x}|y)\,P(y)}{p(\mathbf{x})} \qquad (3.12)$$

Once inference has been performed, an interpretation is often made based upon the outcome. For example, a face classification task requires the observed face image $\mathbf{x}$ to be associated with one of C possible class labels $y_c \in \{y_1, \ldots, y_C\}$. A straightforward approach to the interpretation of the observed face image, which minimises the probability of misclassification, is to assign the image the class label y_c with the largest posterior probability:

$$P(y_c|\mathbf{x}) \geq P(y_i|\mathbf{x}) \text{ for all } i, i \neq c \qquad (3.13)$$

The label y_c is the best interpretation for the novel input observation. Classification based on such a rule is known as *maximum a posteriori* (MAP) classification. In order to apply the MAP rule using Equations (3.12) and (3.13), the likelihood density functions $p(\mathbf{x}|y_c)$ with respect to each possible label are required. In other words, C class-conditional density functions need to be known or computed. They can be regarded as the learned knowledge and are usually estimated from a selected training data set of *labelled observations*: observations with known interpretations.

3.4 Learning as Density Estimation

Let us remind ourselves that the task of learning can be defined as function approximation. Furthermore, inference based on Bayes' theorem implies that such approximations can be performed using likelihood density functions. In other words, this is the problem of estimating probability density functions that aim to approximate the underlying distribution of images or features. Density estimation is the most general and difficult type of learning problem. It is often the case that visual observations are very limited and possibly insufficient for constructing a viable training set for density estimation.

There are a host of methods which essentially all aim to perform learning through density estimation [296]. In broad terms, there are three types of model for density estimation: non-parametric, semi-parametric and parametric. The choice of which to adopt depends upon the nature of the available training set and knowledge of the nature of the problem domain.

3.4.1 Parametric Models

Density estimation can be constrained by assuming that the density function has a particular explicit, parametric form. This is especially appropriate if knowledge about the problem domain suggests a specific functional form. Density estimation then consists of finding values for the parameters in order to minimise expected risk. This is usually performed using the *maximum likelihood* approach for minimising empirical risk as defined by Equation (3.8). Only parameters of relatively simple parametric models can be estimated using closed analytic solutions. A commonly used parametric form for density estimation is the Gaussian (or normal) distribution. Here we describe the process of Gaussian density estimation by way of an example. In the case of a one-dimensional input variable (the univariate case), a Gaussian density function is given by:

$$p(x) = \frac{1}{(2\pi\sigma^2)^{1/2}} \exp\left(-\frac{(x-\mu)^2}{2\sigma^2}\right) \tag{3.14}$$

where μ is the mean value, σ^2 the variance and σ the standard deviation of x. In general, an N-dimensional Gaussian model is given by:

$$p(\mathbf{x}) = \frac{1}{(2\pi)^{N/2}|\mathbf{\Sigma}|^{1/2}} \exp\left(-\frac{1}{2}[\mathbf{x}-\boldsymbol{\mu}]^{\mathrm{T}}\mathbf{\Sigma}^{-1}[\mathbf{x}-\boldsymbol{\mu}]\right) \tag{3.15}$$

where $\boldsymbol{\mu}$ and $\mathbf{\Sigma}$ are the mean vector and covariance matrix of the random vector $\mathbf{x}$. A 2D Gaussian density function is illustrated in Figure 3.1. The expression $[\mathbf{x}-\boldsymbol{\mu}]^{\mathrm{T}}\mathbf{\Sigma}^{-1}[\mathbf{x}-\boldsymbol{\mu}]$ defines a distance measure between $\mathbf{x}$ and the mean, $\boldsymbol{\mu}$, known as the *Mahalanobis* distance. The mean and the covariance matrix are the expectations of $\mathbf{x}$ and $[\mathbf{x}-\boldsymbol{\mu}][\mathbf{x}-\boldsymbol{\mu}]^{\mathrm{T}}$ given by:

$$\boldsymbol{\mu} = E[\mathbf{x}] = \int \mathbf{x}p(\mathbf{x})d\mathbf{x} \tag{3.16}$$

$$\mathbf{\Sigma} = E[(\mathbf{x}-\boldsymbol{\mu})(\mathbf{x}-\boldsymbol{\mu})^{\mathrm{T}}] = \int (\mathbf{x}-\boldsymbol{\mu})(\mathbf{x}-\boldsymbol{\mu})^{\mathrm{T}}p(\mathbf{x})d\mathbf{x} \tag{3.17}$$

The problem of density estimation with an assumed Gaussian model entails the estimation of the mean vector and the covariance matrix from a limited data set, $\mathcal{X}$. Determining the mean vector and covariance matrix requires $(N^2 + 3N)/2$ parameters to be estimated since the covariance matrix is symmetric. It can be shown that minimising the empirical risk as defined in Equation (3.8) gives the *maximum likelihood estimation* of $\boldsymbol{\mu}$ and $\mathbf{\Sigma}$ when $M \gg 1$ as:

$$\boldsymbol{\mu} \approx \frac{1}{M}\sum_{m=1}^{M}\mathbf{x}_m \tag{3.18}$$

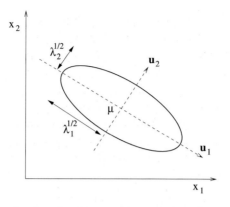

Figure 3.1 A Gaussian function in 2D with mean $\boldsymbol{\mu}$. The ellipse is a contour of constant probability density. The covariance matrix has eigenvectors $\mathbf{u}_1$ and $\mathbf{u}_2$. The corresponding eigenvalues are λ_1 and λ_2.

$$\boldsymbol{\Sigma} \approx \frac{1}{M} \sum_{m=1}^{M} [\mathbf{x}_m - \boldsymbol{\mu}][\mathbf{x}_m - \boldsymbol{\mu}]^{\mathrm{T}} \qquad (3.19)$$

Parametric density estimation is often inappropriate without prior knowledge since any assumed parametric form can be rather arbitrary. In particular, images of faces do not form a well-defined distribution such as a Gaussian. Such a model is generally incapable of capturing the true distribution of face images in an observation feature space.

3.4.2 Non-parametric Models

Rather than adopt an explicit, parametric functional form, non-parametric density estimation makes as few assumptions about the form of the underlying probability distribution as possible. A popular example is the Parzen windows estimation method in which an overall density function, $p(\mathbf{x})$, is estimated by averaging M kernel density functions each of which is determined by one of the M data points. The kernel function is usually a symmetric, unimodal density function such as a Gaussian of fixed variance, i.e.

$$p(\mathbf{x}) = \frac{1}{M} \sum_{m=1}^{M} \frac{1}{(2\pi\sigma^2)^{\frac{N}{2}}} \exp\left(-\frac{\|\mathbf{x} - \mathbf{x}_m\|^2}{2\sigma^2}\right) \qquad (3.20)$$

A disadvantage of this method is that the number of kernel functions and hence the number of parameters grows with the size of the data set. The method essentially *memorises* each of the data points and is therefore expensive in terms of storage. Furthermore, evaluation of a new data point's density will be expensive.

Histograms can also be considered to be a method for non-parametric density estimation. A histogram quantises the observation feature space into regular *bins* of equal volume. The number of bins, K, must be carefully chosen. If K is too small, the histogram will not be able to model the distribution but if K is too large, the amount of data needed to populate the histogram becomes unrealistically large. This is especially true of high-dimensional feature spaces (i.e. dimensionality greater than about ten) such as those typically used in object representation schemes. The value of K must be chosen to address this trade-off. This is a specific example of the so called *bias-variance dilemma* or the *model-order selection* problem. In common with other non-parametric methods such as Parzen windows, histograms scale poorly. In one sense, a histogram can conceivably be considered to be a parametric model with $K-1$ parameters. If K bins are needed for a univariate density model, a similar model in N-dimensions requires K^N bins. The number of bins and likewise the size of the training sample set required grows exponentially with the dimensionality of the observation feature space. Whilst non-parametric methods exhibit good asymptotic behaviour as the data set size tends to infinity, they behave poorly with the relatively small data sets from which estimation must usually be performed.

3.4.3   Semi-parametric Models

A parametric form with a fixed number of parameters is often unrealistically restrictive. On the other hand, the non-parametric approach behaves poorly unless huge data sets are available. In addressing the bias-variance dilemma, simple parametric methods have high bias while non-parametric methods have high variance. Semi-parametric models take the middle-ground and adopt a flexible parametric form in which the number of parameters can be varied depending upon the nature of the true probability distribution. It is important to note that the number of parameters is not determined by the *size* of the data set.

Mixture models are a kind of semi-parametric model which are particularly useful for estimating density functions of unknown structure from limited and often sparse observations. Given K parametric density functions, $p(\mathbf{x}|k)$, $k = 1 \dots K$, a mixture model, $p(\mathbf{x})$, is defined as a linearly weighted summation of these K components, i.e.

$$p(\mathbf{x}) = \sum_{k=1}^{K} p(\mathbf{x}|k)\, P(k) \qquad (3.21)$$

The weights in this summation, $P(k)$, are known as the *mixing parameters* and they sum to unity:

$$\sum_{k=1}^{K} P(k) = 1, \qquad 0 \le P(k) \le 1 \qquad (3.22)$$

Since density functions are *generative models*, $P(k)$ can be regarded as the prior probability of an observation being generated by mixture component k. The component densities in a mixture are usually taken to be of the same parametric form. One of the most commonly used mixture models is a mixture of Gaussian density functions, known as a *Gaussian mixture*. Figure 3.2 shows an example of modelling a complex distribution function in 2D space using a Gaussian mixture.

The number of components in a mixture is set to address the bias-variance dilemma and should typically be much less than the size of the data set ($K \ll M$). Learning is then the process of estimating the mixture model parameters. In the case of a Gaussian mixture, these parameters are the components' means, covariance matrices and mixing parameters. Maximum-likelihood estimation is not possible using a closed analytic form as it was in the case of a single Gaussian. However, an iterative learning algorithm exists which attempts to maximise likelihood. This is the Expectation-Maximisation (EM) algorithm described in Appendix C.

3.5 Unsupervised Learning without Density Estimation

Probability density estimation is especially problematic in high-dimensional feature space and alternative approaches of unsupervised learning are often computationally more feasible. Although they fall short of providing a generative density model, they can be useful for reducing dimensionality or

(a)

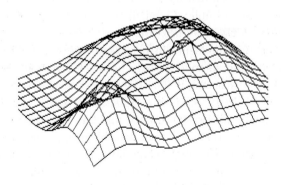

(b)

Figure 3.2 An example of a Gaussian mixture model in 2D space. (a) The fourteen components of the mixture model. (b) The density function given by the mixture model in (a). The values of the mixing parameters $P(k)$ affect the heights of the peaks in the function surface.

clustering data. Many of these other unsupervised learning methods arise as special or degenerate cases of density estimation models.

3.5.1 Dimensionality Reduction

A technique commonly used to reduce dimensionality is principal components analysis (PCA). PCA operates on the assumption that a distribution can be modelled as a Gaussian density function which has negligible variance in several directions. In other words, the data are assumed to lie approximately within a linear subspace of lower dimensionality. This is illustrated in Figure 3.3 for the case where a 3D distribution can be approximated by a 2D Gaussian distribution. The directions of significant variance are called the principal components. They are the eigenvectors of the covariance matrix which have the largest corresponding eigenvalues (see Figure 3.1). The principal components are an orthogonal basis for the subspace. They define a linear transformation of the data that reduces dimensionality. Further details of PCA can be found in Appendix C.

In fact, PCA provides a way to estimate a Gaussian probability density function when the amount of data available would otherwise be considered inadequate to estimate a full covariance matrix. Such a Gaussian function has its covariance matrix estimated by explicitly estimating the principal eigenvectors and eigenvalues and then approximating the remaining less significant eigenvectors [235, 236, 295]. This approach has been taken a step further and used to estimate mixtures of PCA models [335]. These methods will be discussed more fully in the context of visual tasks such as face detection and identification later in the book.

3.5.2 Clustering

Clustering entails assigning each data point in an unlabelled data set to exactly one of K possible classes or *clusters* so that the points in any given cluster are similar to one another. A loss function that penalises dissimilar points within a cluster is used. The result of clustering is to partition the input space into disjoint regions.

A commonly used clustering method is the K-means algorithm [208]. It assigns points at random to K classes and then computes the mean vector for each class. Points are then reassigned to the class with the nearest mean and the means recomputed. This is repeated until convergence.

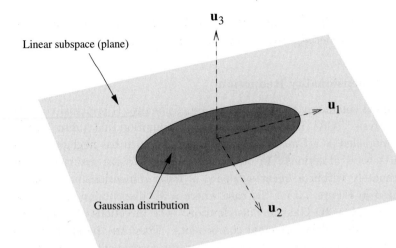

Figure 3.3 A 3D Gaussian distribution and its eigenvectors. The third eigenvector has negligible eigenvalue. Therefore the distribution lies approximately within a 2D linear subspace. The two dominant eigenvectors are called the principal components and are an orthogonal basis for the subspace.

Clustering can be thought of as a special case of a mixture density model. For example, if each data point in a Gaussian mixture is thought of as belonging to the Gaussian function with the greatest probability of generating that point, a clustering is defined. In fact, a mixture of Gaussians with variances tending to zero is effectively a clustering model. While clustering algorithms fail to define a probability density function, they are often computationally efficient and indeed provide useful initialisation for learning a Gaussian mixture.

3.6   Linear Classification and Regression

Linear functions provide a simple and sometimes effective family of functions for inference. They can be written in the form:

$$f(\mathbf{x}) = (\mathbf{w} \cdot \mathbf{x}) + b, \quad \mathbf{w} \in \Re^N, \quad b \in \Re, \qquad (3.23)$$

When $N = 2$, $(\mathbf{w} \cdot \mathbf{x}) + b = 0$ defines a plane and when $N > 2$ it defines a *hyperplane*. The position and orientation of this hyperplane are changed

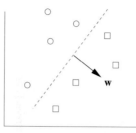

Figure 3.4 A linear classification function that separates two classes of data points.

by adjusting the parameters $\mathbf{a} = [\mathbf{w}\ b]$, where $\mathbf{w}$ is the hyperplane's normal vector. Figure 3.4 shows a simple example in which a binary classification function is implemented to separate two classes of data points. In general, given a data set $(\{\mathbf{x}_m, y_m\},\ m = 1 \ldots M,\ \mathbf{x} \in \Re^N,\ y \in \{-1, +1\})$, a linear classification function $f(\mathbf{x}, \mathbf{a}) = \mathrm{sgn}((\mathbf{w} \cdot \mathbf{x}) + b)$ can be learned by adjusting the parameters. If a linear function exists that classifies the data without error then the data are said to be *linearly separable*. Linear functions can also be used for regression by adjusting the parameters to optimise the 'closeness of fit' to the training data.

3.6.1 Least-squares

We now consider how to learn using linear functions. A classical least-squares method is often used to determine the parameters, $\mathbf{a} = [\mathbf{w}\ b]$, by minimising the empirical risk as given in Equation (3.9). An exact solution exists although numerical difficulties can arise. In practice, a technique such as singular value decomposition (SVD) should be used to determine the parameters [277]. This least-squares method is often effective for learning regression functions. However, better loss functions exist for learning classification functions [27].

3.6.2 Linear Support Vector Machines

There are usually many parameter settings, each defining a different hyperplane, that result in low empirical risk for a given training data set. What is needed is a method for choosing a hyperplane that gives low *generalisation error*. Statistical learning theory suggests just such a method for determining an *optimal hyperplane* [351]. In the case of a linearly separa-

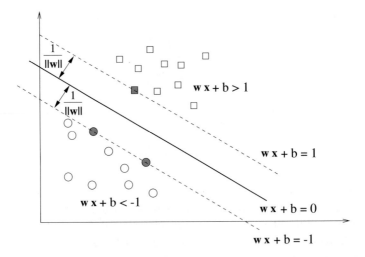

Figure 3.5 The optimal hyperplane, $\mathbf{w}\,\mathbf{x} + b = 0$, separates the classes with maximal margin $\left(\frac{2}{||\mathbf{w}||}\right)$. Support vectors are shown shaded.

ble data set with two classes, the optimal hyperplane is the one giving the largest margin of separation between the classes. This optimal hyperplane bisects the shortest line between the convex hulls of the two classes. It is also orthogonal to this line. A relatively small subset of the data points lie exactly on the margin and these are called the *support vectors*. Note that the optimal hyperplane is completely determined by these support vectors. Figure 3.5 shows a simple example.

A learning machine called a linear support vector machine (LSVM) implements the optimal hyperplane. The support vectors lie on the two hyperplanes $\mathbf{w}\,\mathbf{x} + b = \pm 1$. The margin is therefore $\frac{2}{||\mathbf{w}||}$. This margin is maximised by minimising $||\mathbf{w}||$ subject to the constraint

$$y_m(\mathbf{w}\,\mathbf{x}_m + b) \geq 1, \; m = 1 \ldots M \tag{3.24}$$

Most data sets are not linearly separable and so this minimisation problem needs to be modified to allow misclassified data points. Such a *soft margin classifier* that allows but penalises errors can be obtained by introducing error variables, $\xi_m \geq 0$. The minimisation is then as follows [70]:

Minimise $\qquad \frac{1}{2}||\mathbf{w}||^2 + \kappa \sum_{m=1}^{M} \xi_m \tag{3.25}$

Subject to $\quad y_m(\mathbf{w}\,\mathbf{x}_m + b) \geq 1 - \xi_m, \; m = 1 \ldots M$

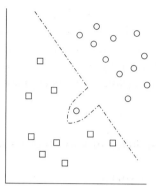

Figure 3.6 The role of the SVM penalty parameter κ.

This results in a hyperplane that minimises the sum of deviations, ξ, while maximising the margin for the correctly classified data. It is a quadratic programming problem which can be solved using standard optimisation techniques or alternatively optimisation methods specifically tailored to support vector machines [150, 271]. In fact, a dual form of this optimisation problem is solved in practice in which the margin is maximised according to a set of Lagrange multipliers $\boldsymbol{\alpha}$:

$$\text{Minimise} \quad \tfrac{1}{2}\sum_{m=1}^{M}\sum_{i=1;i\neq m}^{M} \alpha_i \alpha_m y_i y_m (\mathbf{x}_i\, \mathbf{x}_m) - \sum_{m=1}^{M} \alpha_m \quad (3.26)$$

$$\text{Subject to} \quad \sum_{m=1}^{M} \alpha_m y_m = 0 \text{ and } 0 \leq \alpha_m \leq \kappa,\ m = 1\ldots M$$

The use of error variables, ξ_m, constrains the range of the Lagrange multipliers α_m from 0 to κ. This *penalty parameter*, κ, aims to prevent outliers from affecting the optimal hyperplane (see Figure 3.6).

We have already noted that the optimal hyperplane is determined by the support vectors. In fact, the hyperplane parameters $\mathbf{w}$ are a linear combination of the support vectors:

$$\mathbf{w} = \sum_{m=1}^{M} y_m \alpha_m \mathbf{x}_m \qquad (3.27)$$

where the Lagrange multipliers, α_m, are non-zero only if $\mathbf{x}_m$ is a support vector. The decision function of the optimal hyperplane is thus:

$$f(\mathbf{x}) = \text{sgn}\left(\sum_{m=1}^{M} y_m \alpha_m (\mathbf{x} \cdot \mathbf{x}_m) + b \right) \qquad (3.28)$$

Figure 3.7 shows an example of applying a linear support vector machine to learn the decision hyperplane of a two-class problem.

Note that both learning using Equation (3.26) and classification using Equation (3.28) are performed by computing dot products with the support vectors. Support vector machines for linear regression can be set up in a similar manner [325].

3.7 Non-linear Classification and Regression

3.7.1 Multi-layer Networks

Successful inference is not always possible using only linear functions. A common way to obtain families of non-linear functions is to transform the inputs $\mathbf{x}$ by a set of non-linear functions, $\phi_k(\mathbf{x})$, often called *basis functions*:

$$f(\mathbf{x}, \mathbf{a}) = \sum_{k=1}^{K} w_k \phi_k(\mathbf{x}) + b \qquad (3.29)$$

The basis functions together perform a non-linear mapping, $\Phi : \Re^N \mapsto \Re^K$, from input space to a K-dimensional feature space, i.e. $\Phi(\mathbf{x}) = [\phi_1(\mathbf{x}) \, \phi_2(\mathbf{x}) \, \dots \, \phi_K(\mathbf{x})]^{\mathrm{T}}$. Certain forms of basis function will allow any continuous function to be approximated to arbitrary accuracy using $f(\mathbf{x}, \mathbf{a})$. Note that the parameter set, $\mathbf{a}$, now includes any parameters needed to determine the basis functions, as well as $\mathbf{w}$ and b. Most so-called *multi-layer neural networks* are of this form and in this context the basis functions are often called *hidden units*. Many texts on these types of networks are available [27, 148, 288, 290] so only a brief treatment is given here.

Radial basis functions (RBFs) are commonly used. These include Gaussian functions with covariance matrices of the form $\sigma^2 \mathbf{I}$:

$$\phi_k(\mathbf{x}) = \frac{\exp(-||\mathbf{x} - \boldsymbol{\mu}_k||)^2}{2\sigma_k^2} \qquad (3.30)$$

Alternatively, Gaussian functions with full covariance matrices can be used. In this case, the resulting networks have been called *hyper-basis function* (HBF) networks [273]. A different form of basis function yields other families of functions commonly called *multi-layer perceptrons* (MLPs). These have basis functions of the form:

$$\phi_k(\mathbf{x}) = g(h_k(\mathbf{x})) \qquad (3.31)$$

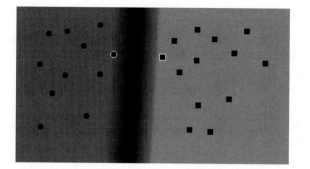

Figure 3.7 The decision hyperplane given by two support vectors for a linearly separable two-class problem.

where h_k is a linear function with the familiar form:

$$h_k(\mathbf{x}) = \mathbf{v}_k \cdot \mathbf{x} + c_k \qquad (3.32)$$

and g is a sigmoid (S-shaped) function such as $g(a) = \tanh(a)$. The parameters to be optimised during learning are now $\mathbf{a} = (\mathbf{w}, b, \mathbf{v}_1, c_1, \ldots, \mathbf{v}_K, c_K)$. When used for classification, a sigmoid function is usually also applied to the output $h_k(\mathbf{x})$.

In order to learn using these non-linear families of functions, methods for optimising the parameters given a finite data set are needed. The *back-propagation* algorithm [253, 299, 366] provides a computationally efficient way to compute the derivatives $\frac{\partial \mathcal{R}_{emp}}{a_0}, \frac{\partial \mathcal{R}_{emp}}{a_1}, \ldots \frac{\partial \mathcal{R}_{emp}}{a_i}$ of an empirical risk function with respect to the parameters. Once these derivatives have been estimated, the parameters can be adjusted in order to reduce the empirical risk using one of many available optimisation schemes. The simplest of these schemes is gradient descent. Other suitable schemes include conjugate gradient algorithms, quasi-Newton methods and, specifically for the least-squares loss function of Equation (3.5), the Levenberg-Marquardt algorithm. Practical use of these algorithms involves several other issues such as parameter initialisation and rules for terminating learning which are discussed elsewhere [27].

These learning algorithms all employ the inductive principle of empirical risk minimisation. Their use tends to be *ad hoc* in many respects including the selection of the number of basis functions (hidden units). Alternatively, learning non-linear classification and regression functions can be based on the principle of structural risk minimisation using support vector machines.

3.7.2   Support Vector Machines

Support Vector Machines (SVMs) have been shown to be an attractive and arguably more systematic approach to learning non-linear functions [252, 271, 306, 307, 351]. Instead of directly minimising the empirical risk calculated from the training data, SVMs use the inductive principal of structural risk minimisation to achieve good generalisation.

The multi-layer networks just described used basis functions to perform a non-linear mapping, Φ, to a feature space before performing classification or regression in this feature space using a linear function. Implementation of the linear function in feature space using a support vector machine would appear to require computation of dot-products $\Phi(\mathbf{x}) \cdot \Phi(\mathbf{x}_m)$ for each support vector $\mathbf{x}_m$ (see Equation (3.26)). However, the potentially computationally intensive mapping Φ does not need to be explicitly evaluated. Instead, a kernel function, $\phi_m(\mathbf{x})$, satisfying Mercer's condition [351] can be used as a substitute for $(\Phi(\mathbf{x}) \cdot \Phi(\mathbf{x}_m))$. Suitable kernel functions include polynomials $\phi_m(\mathbf{x}) = (\mathbf{x} \cdot \mathbf{x}_m)^d$, sigmoidal functions $\phi_m(\mathbf{x}) = \tanh(\mathbf{v}_m(\mathbf{x} \cdot \mathbf{x}_m) + c_m))$ and Gaussian functions $\phi_m(\mathbf{x}) = \exp\left(\frac{-||\mathbf{x} - \mathbf{x}_m||^2}{2\sigma_m^2}\right)$.

This kernel trick means that the computation remains feasible even if the feature space has very high (even infinite) dimensionality. The implicit mapping Φ can be chosen so that a linear function is all that is required in feature space to achieve as low an empirical risk as possible (see Figure 3.8). Learning now entails solving the following optimisation problem:

$$\text{Minimise} \quad \tfrac{1}{2}\sum_{m=1}^{M}\sum_{i=1;i\neq m}^{M}\alpha_i\alpha_m y_i y_m \phi_m(\mathbf{x}_i) - \sum_{m=1}^{M}\alpha_m \quad (3.33)$$
$$\text{Subject to} \quad \sum_{m=1}^{M}\alpha_m y_m = 0 \text{ and } 0 \leq \alpha_m \leq \kappa, \; m = 1,\ldots,M$$

The decision function is now:

$$f(\mathbf{x}) = \text{sgn}\left(\sum_{m=1}^{M} y_m \alpha_m \phi_m(\mathbf{x}) + b\right) \qquad (3.34)$$

The kernel trick can also be used with other methods. For example, a nonlinear version of PCA known as Kernel Principal Components Analysis (KPCA) has recently been introduced by Schölkopf et al. [306]. The basic idea of KPCA is both intuitive and generic.

In general, PCA can only be performed effectively on a set of observations which vary linearly. When the variations are nonlinear, they can always be mapped into a higher dimensional space which is again linear, as

Nonlinear input space   Linear feature space

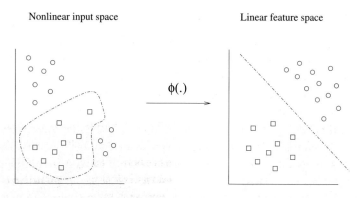

Figure 3.8 Mapping a nonlinear input space into a linear, but higher dimensional feature space.

shown in Figure 3.8. Kernel PCA utilises SVM to find a computationally tractable solution through a simple kernel function which intrinsically constructs a nonlinear mapping Φ from the input space to a high-dimensional feature space in which a linear solution can be found. As a result, KPCA performs a nonlinear PCA in the input space.

Figure 3.9 illustrates two rather complex examples of learning decision boundaries in 2D space using a support vector machine. In the second example, the decision surface obtained using an example-based radial basis function network is also shown for comparison.

3.8 Adaptation

The learning problems discussed so far have assumed a fixed set of observations, $\mathcal{X}$, from which estimation is performed. In other words, the underlying probability distribution is assumed to be fixed and stationary. In a dynamic visual world such an assumption is not always appropriate. Instead, the underlying distribution is often *non-stationary* and the learned model must be adapted continually as new observations are obtained. For instance, each time a face is observed, relevant face models can be updated using on-line learning to reflect any changes in facial appearance. Let us consider a simple one-dimensional Gaussian model with parameters μ and σ in order to illustrate adaptation.

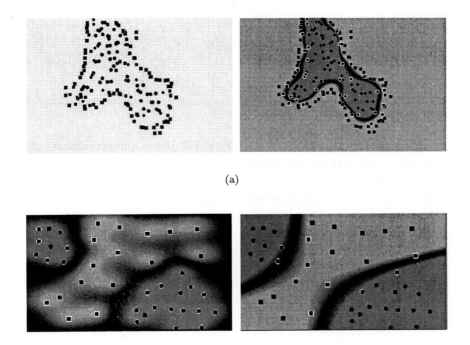

(a)

(b)

Figure 3.9 Examples of nonlinear decision boundaries learned by support vector machines. (a) An example of using SVMs to learn complex nonlinear decision boundaries (right) from a set of sample observations (left) in 2D space. Highlighted square dots denote negative support vectors and circular dots show the positive support vectors. The decision surface is intensity-coded. (b) An example of support vector machines giving good decision boundaries (on the right) compared to the poor result from a more conventional method such as an example-based RBF network (on the left).

Suppose that at uniform intervals of time, $t = 0, 1, 2, \ldots$, a new data point x_t is obtained. At time t, the model can be updated using the following rules:

$$\mu_t = \kappa x_t + (1 - \kappa)\mu_{t-1} \qquad (3.35)$$

$$\sigma_t^2 = \kappa(x - \mu_t)^2 + (1 - \kappa)\sigma_{t-1}^2 \qquad (3.36)$$

where $0 \leq \kappa \leq 1$ controls the time-scale of adaptation. These simple recursive expressions allow the model to adapt without the need to store previous data. They amount to a moving weighted average that weights previous data with exponential decay. This kind of adaptation scheme is often effective but it does introduce a time-lag which can be undesirable in real-time tracking and recognition. Prediction of model parameters based on current and previous data is needed in such cases. We will discuss prediction in the context of tracking in Chapter 7.

3.9 Biological Perspectives

Statistical learning has been introduced in rather general terms. It is informative to ask to what extent such learning might play a role in face recognition by humans and some other mammals. For instance, one might ask the following three questions:

(1) To what extent is face perception innate (hard-wired by evolution) and to what extent is it learned during one's lifetime?
(2) At what age are people first able to recognise a face?
(3) How much prior knowledge is needed in order to efficiently bootstrap learning?

Evidence of face detection, free from other semantic connotations, can be found in newborn infants. Human neonates with essentially no visual experience respond to face-like stimuli and can perform face detection and tracking. This suggests that an unlearned or *evolved* responsiveness to faces is present at birth. In time, interactions between an infant and adults who are close to the child become personal and the mechanisms involved in encoding individual faces are thought to emerge [87, 238]. An early part of this process is a mutual visual involvement of mother and baby where the baby becomes more selectively responsive to the mother's face [54,

113, 254]. Thus, it seems that face detection is an innate capacity which is subject to modification by subsequent experience [139]. Innate, prior knowledge of faces sufficient for detection and tracking is used to *bootstrap* further learning.

Support for models of face recognition processes that incorporate adaptive, statistical learning can be taken from experiments that look into the effects of ethnic group or race upon recognition. Experiments have shown that strategies are acquired for analysing the kinds of faces to which one is most frequently exposed. Tests of Caucasian subjects invariably show a higher rate of identification accuracy for white than for black faces while a trend in the reverse direction has often been found for black subjects [107, 108, 212]. However, white subjects can learn to discriminate more reliably between black faces when trained under laboratory conditions in identifying the relevant features of black faces [83, 214, 215]. Whilst, adults identify faces from other races less accurately than faces from their own race, young children identify other-race and own-race faces with equal accuracy [59, 126]. This can be taken as evidence for statistical learning.

Recent studies have also begun to investigate the development of the neural and cognitive processes related to recognition of familiar faces by human infants. Experiments using *event-related potentials* have shown that six month old infants are able to recognise their mother's face and that neural processes accompanying recognition depend on the difficulty with which mother can be discriminated from an unfamiliar face. The experiments suggest that perceptual analysis or encoding of an unfamiliar face is more protracted when the unfamiliar face looks similar to the known face. When the unfamiliar face and the known face are very different, perceptual analysis or encoding may occur more quickly and may reflect the infant's allocation of attention to the faces [72, 85, 245]. Studies of infants' recognition of briefly familiarised faces also suggest that the neural processes involved in recognising well-known faces may differ from those involved in recognising less well known faces [85].

3.10 Discussion

In this chapter we have introduced in quite broad terms, the notion of statistical learning from sparse data using learning machines. Such algorithms implement functions that approximate probability distributions.

These functions are determined through parameter optimisation in order to minimise a risk functional. In the case of unlabelled data, basic concepts and models for probability density estimation, dimensionality reduction and clustering were introduced. A treatment of more recent developments in statistical learning of functionals involving support vector machines was also given and illustrated. In the case of labelled data, linear and non-linear families of functions for implementing classification and regression functions were described.

Given that we have discussed the need for appropriate representation (Chapter 2) and now the mechanisms available for learning, we shall return to the problems of performing the perceptual tasks required for face recognition in a changing environment (Chapter 1). The essential question we ask is how such vision tasks can be most effectively performed computationally using artificial systems.

In order to understand the different roles of computation, let us start with the notions of sense perception and meaningful perception. One often visually perceives the existence of objects without knowing exactly what those objects are. Such perception of objects does not associate any meaningful explanation to the perceived form and is known as *sense perception* [94]. Visual perception of moving faces, however, is more than sense perception. It entails perceiving facts about existence. Such perception of facts invokes judgments according to knowledge or belief. This constitutes some degree of *meaningful perception.*

In order to examine the computations involved in the perception of moving faces, we have artificially decomposed the overall perceptual process into constituent tasks. In the next Part of this book, we start by explaining the computations and mechanisms broadly related to the sense perception of moving faces before introducing the need for more meaningful perception in the context of face detection and pose understanding. Not until Part IV shall we return to the problems of perceptual integration and perception in context. There we will discuss how modules addressing the different visual tasks can be integrated in order to perform perception in a coherent and closed-loop fashion.

PART II

FROM SENSORY TO MEANINGFUL PERCEPTION

4   Selective Attention: Where to Look

> *What information consumes is rather obvious: it con-*
> *sumes the attention of its recipients. Hence, a wealth of*
> *information creates a poverty of attention and a need to*
> *allocate that attention efficiently among the overabundance*
> *of information sources that might consume it.*
>
> — *Herbert Simon*

An effective perceptual system must exhibit the ability to direct information processing to the most relevant aspects of the perceptual input on the
basis of a coarse analysis of that input. In order to analyse and recognise
human faces in realistically unconstrained environments, focused visual attention can be crucial to the correctness and effectiveness of the desired
interpretation [56]. To this end, motion and colour provide particularly
useful and complementary pre-attentive and knowledge-based visual cues
for focusing attention on people and their faces. Other pre-attentive cues
can be provided by stereo disparity [80] and object surface texture [79].

Humans are almost always moving and their movement is usually significant enough to be easily detectable. However, computing visual motion can be both difficult and expensive. Perceptual grouping of estimated visual motion consistently over time poses even more problems [132,
323]. Motion cues are most readily available with static cameras although
qualitative motion can be computed using moving cameras at extra computational cost.

Colour offers several advantages over motion as an alternative visual
cue although it may not always be pre-attentive and can be regarded as
object-based [361]. Compared to motion, colour enables robustness under
occlusion, scale, rotation in depth and resolution changes [331] and can
often utilise efficient algorithms yielding real-time performance on modest
hardware. For example, in the context of face perception, models of hu-

man skin colour can be used to focus attention on regions of skin which might correspond to faces. Colour models of people's clothing can also be learned on-line to facilitate tracking of subjects [232]. Overall, a robust and computationally effective mechanism for focus of attention is more likely to be based on the fusion of multiple visual cues. Furthermore, the use of higher-level, knowledge-based information such as models of facial appearance and the exploitation of spatio-temporal context enable robust detection and tracking of faces.

For the general purpose of focusing perceptual attention, let us first consider in more detail the possibility of using visual motion and colour information as cues for drawing attention in a visual scene: to bootstrap the task of "where to look". We then describe how these cues can be used to efficiently focus attention on probable face regions through the appropriate use of perceptual grouping, prediction and data fusion. In Chapters 5, 6 and 7 we describe how integration of these cues with models of facial appearance enables robust, real-time detection and tracking of several faces simultaneously in a dynamic scene. A resulting system outputs segmented facial image sequences from scenes containing several people. First, let us start with the problem of computing pre-attentive motion cues and object-based colour cues. How can one compute motion and colour information from images of a given scene?

4.1   Pre-attentive Visual Cues from Motion

Although estimates of the 2D dense motion field in the image, known as *optical flow* fields, can be used to provide strong constraints for perceptual grouping, the computation is intrinsically ill-posed and its consistency suffers under occlusion and fast motion. It is well understood that accurate, quantitative estimation of visual motion is often prohibitively time consuming and computationally difficult [128, 130, 309]. However, qualitative and partial estimation of motion without solving the *aperture problem* [157, 216] is surprisingly good for providing clear pre-attentive cues. In particular, qualitative *local motion* can be estimated and used to seed perceptual grouping and segmentation quite effectively. In the following, we discuss several methods for motion detection and estimation, ranging from simple temporal differencing to spatio-temporal filtering and qualitative estimation of visual motion.

4.1.1   Measuring Temporal Change

Changes in the intensity (brightness) of image pixels are caused by motion, imaging noise and varying illumination. Motion is embedded in this change and cannot therefore be recovered directly. However, if changes in the intensity $I(x, y, t)$ of each pixel did correspond solely to the motion of opaque objects then we could write:

$$\frac{dI(x, y, t)}{dt} = \nabla I \cdot \mathbf{u} + \frac{\partial I(x, y, t)}{\partial t} = 0, \qquad (4.1)$$

where ∇I is the intensity gradient $[I_x \, I_y]^T$ and $\mathbf{u}$ measures the visual motion, i.e. $\mathbf{u} = \left[\frac{dx}{dt} \, \frac{dy}{dt}\right]^T$. This has been called the *constant illumination assumption*. If it holds then some information about local motion can be recovered:

$$\frac{\partial I(x, y, t)}{\partial t} = -\nabla I \cdot \mathbf{u} \qquad (4.2)$$

Localised intensity change at each image coordinate (x, y) provides meaningful information about motion. A crude but often effective approximation can be obtained using simple pixel-wise subtraction of successive images:

$$\frac{\partial I(x, y, t)}{\partial t} \approx I(x, y, t) - I(x, y, t-1) \qquad (4.3)$$

This can be used as a very fast means to provide pre-attentive cues for focusing attention. The absolute difference image emphasises motion in areas with significant spatial texture. However, a halo effect occurs around moving objects due to previously occluded scene background becoming unoccluded. Differencing can be similarly performed between an image and a pre-recorded background image of the scene containing no moving foreground objects. Although, computationally inexpensive, these methods have limitations. In particular, illumination in any scene is almost certainly not constant. Changes in either ambient or directional illumination, reflections and cast shadows can all cause erroneous detection. These methods are also susceptible to noise in the imaging process. One way to reduce the sensitivity to intensity change caused by factors other than motion is to apply *spatial filtering* using a Gaussian function before performing temporal differencing:

$$\frac{\partial I(x, y, t)}{\partial t} \approx \frac{\partial}{\partial t} \left(G(x, y, t) \otimes I(x, y, t)\right) \qquad (4.4)$$

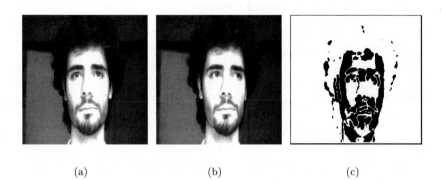

(a)   (b)   (c)

Figure 4.1 The effect of temporal differencing between two successive image frames of a moving subject after Gaussian spatial filtering. (a) Image frame at t_1, (b) frame at t_2, and (c) temporal differencing between the two successive frames. The absolute difference has been thresholded to produce a binary image.

Figure 4.1 shows an example of applying temporal differencing to two successive Gaussian filtered image frames.

4.1.2   Motion Estimation

Motion estimation is best achieved at moving image contours where computations are likely to be most relevant and reliable [128, 130, 151]. This can be effectively achieved by convolving the intensity history of each pixel in a Gaussian smoothed image frame $I(x, y, t)$ with the second-order temporal derivative of a Gaussian function $G(t)$. This yields a sequence given by:

$$Z(x, y, t) = \frac{\partial^2 G(t)}{\partial t^2} \otimes I(x, y, t) \tag{4.5}$$

with the temporal Gaussian derivative filter given by

$$\frac{\partial^2 G(t)}{\partial t^2} = \frac{-2s^3}{\sqrt{\pi}} \left(1 - 2s^2 t^2\right) \exp\left(-s^2 t^2\right) \tag{4.6}$$

where $s = \sqrt{3/(2n^2)}$ is a temporal smoothing constant controlled by the number of image frames taken for the temporal convolution, $4n + 1$, where $n = 1, 2, \ldots$ [98]. Moving object boundaries produce spatial zero-crossings in $Z(x, y, t)$ at image locations in the middle frame of the history used for the temporal convolution [98]. Global illumination changes and even changes in the intensity level of static objects do not result in such zero-crossings. Figure 4.2 shows the effect of applying such a spatio-temporal filter to an image sequence in which two people walk through a rather cluttered scene. Images from the sequence are shown along with the corresponding temporally filtered image $Z(x, y, t)$ and the image of detected temporal zero-crossings.

In fact, the above spatio-temporal filtering method can be further extended to estimate local motion components in the directions of local intensity gradient, known as the *normal flow* [55, 128, 157]. A 3D spatio-temporal convolution operation can be applied to compute a sequence of images of spatio-temporal zero-crossings $Z(x, y, t)$:

$$Z(x, y, t) = -\left(\nabla^2 + \frac{1}{u^2}\frac{\partial^2}{\partial t^2}\right) G(x, y, t) \otimes I(x, y, t) \qquad (4.7)$$

where

$$G(x, y, t) = u\left(\frac{a}{\pi}\right)^{3/2} \exp\left(-a(x^2 + y^2 + u^2 t^2)\right) \qquad (4.8)$$

$$\nabla^2 = \left(\frac{\partial^2}{\partial x^2} + \frac{\partial^2}{\partial y^2}\right) \qquad (4.9)$$

The constant u is a temporal scaling factor and a defines the spatio-temporal convolution size $w = \frac{2}{\sqrt{a}}$. The above operator can be approximated by three one-dimensional operations in x, y and t for computational efficiency [55, 135].

The normal flow can be estimated as the temporal gradient of the zero-crossings computed over at least 3 successive frames $Z(x, y, t)$. Following Buxton and Buxton [55], let $Z_{ijk} = Z(x + i, y + j, ut + k)$ be a three-dimensional neighbourhood at point (x, y, t). A least-squares fitting of Z_{ijk} to a linear polynomial of the form $f_{ijk} = f_0 + f_x i + f_y j + f_t k$ gives:

$$f_x = \frac{1}{18}\sum_{ijk} i Z_{ijk}, \quad f_y = \frac{1}{18}\sum_{ijk} j Z_{ijk}, \quad f_t = \frac{1}{18}\sum_{ijk} k Z_{ijk} \qquad (4.10)$$

where the convolution size w should be set to ≥ 8 if $Z(x, y, t)$ is to be approximately linear over a $3 \times 3 \times 3$ neighbourhood. The spatio-temporal gradient of Z at (x, y, t) estimates the normal flow as:

$$\begin{bmatrix} \dot{x} \\ \dot{y} \end{bmatrix} = \frac{-u f_t}{f_x^2 + f_y^2} \begin{bmatrix} f_x \\ f_y \end{bmatrix} \qquad (4.11)$$

(a) frame t_1 (b) frame t_2 (c) frame t_3

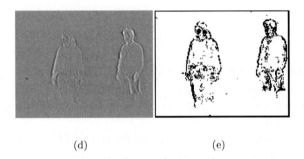

(d)   (e)

Figure 4.2 Robust motion detection. (a)-(c) show image frames from a sequence of two people walking in a cluttered scene. (d) A filtered image $Z(x, y, t)$ using Equation (4.5). (e) The detected temporal zero-crossings.

It is necessary to point out that this spatio-temporal filter measures continuous motion over time. When the ratio of frame rate to visual motion is low, object position changes by more pixels than the number of frames taken into account over time and the computed visual motion field can be poor as a result. In theory, however, given a sufficiently high ratio of frame rate to image motion, normal flow can be used to both improve the consistency of perceptual grouping and to help segment occluding objects with differing visual motions.

4.2   Learning Object-based Colour Cues

Colour provides strong visual cues and plays important roles in various aspects of biological vision. Unfortunately, human colour perception is complex and not fully understood. The colour of an object as perceived by humans depends upon illumination, surface properties, and the sampling of the energy spectrum performed by the sensors in our eyes. Furthermore, it also depends upon our expectations and the spatio-temporal context. Here we consider, computationally, how colour can be used to provide visual cues for focusing attention without any reference to how human colour vision functions. A typical camera provides images of tri-chromatic pixels with Red, Green and Blue (RGB) components. For convenience, we will use the word *colour* to refer to the form of these signals as well as to colour percepts. The RGB values of an imaged surface vary due to the extrinsic factors of illumination, viewing geometry and camera characteristics. For instance, the R value at pixel (x, y) is given as:

$$R(x, y) = \int E(\lambda) S(x, y, \lambda) \, C_R(\lambda) \, d\lambda \qquad (4.12)$$

where $C_R(\lambda)$ is the spectral sensitivity of a camera's red channel, $E(\lambda)$ is the spectrum of the incident illumination and $S(x, y, \lambda)$ is the spectral reflectance of the object surface. Similar equations hold for G and B. The problem of modelling the surface properties, $S(x, y, \lambda)$, consistently in the presence of varying illumination is known as *colour constancy*. This is in general non-trivial and the most effective algorithms are often computationally expensive. Despite these sources of variation, colour is used in human vision in a manner that is largely object-based [361]. Colour models can be learned and associated with specific objects or object features despite the potential sources of variability. In particular, models of skin colour can be used [186, 302, 304, 370]. Colour signals can thus be used as an effective means for perceptual grouping and selective attention. In fact colour has been exploited in machine vision for performing segmentation [285, 318, 369], tracking [229] and object recognition [220, 331].

4.2.1 Colour Spaces

RGB signals reside in a 3D colour space and each RGB pixel is then a point in this space. The pixels of a face image form a distribution in this colour space which can be modelled by estimating a probability density function. Intensity is distributed across the RGB values so that a face's distribution varies with scene brightness. One way to achieve a level of invariance to scene brightness is to convert the RGB signals into a form which makes the intensity explicit. The HSI colour space is one such form. It consists of Hue (H), Saturation (S) and Intensity (I). Hue corresponds to our intuitive notion of "colour" while saturation is the vividness or purity of that colour. A distribution in 2D HS space provides a colour model with a degree of invariance to scene brightness. Pixels with very low intensity or saturation can be discarded because the observed hue becomes unreliable for such pixels. Figure 4.3 shows the distributions measured from three face images in a camera's HS space. In these plots, saturation is zero at the centre and increases along radii while hue is the angle swept out by these radii.

In addition to the extrinsic factors, variation occurs between people and intuitively we might expect large variations between people of different ethnic groups. An individual's facial colour might also vary with temperature (e.g. blushing). It is interesting to notice that despite our own intuition about skin colour being very different for different ethnic groups, the skin of all ethnic groups in fact clusters tightly in a 2D colour space such as HS (see Figure 4.3) [161, 373]. In fact, nearly all the variation due to ethnic group is in the intensity of the signal. This is not so surprising when we consider that the pigmentation in skin is common to all people.

Although colours are sensitive to changes in camera parameters and the spectral composition of the illuminants, for now let us assume that these are relatively stable in a given scene. In Chapter 7 we will consider how colour models can be made adaptive in order to cope with these variations. First we describe how to estimate probability densities in colour space.

(a)

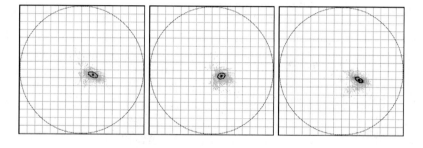

(b)

Figure 4.3 An illustration of tight clustering of skin colour in HS-space for different faces. (a) Sampling skin colour from different faces with different skin-tones. (b) The faces' colour distributions in HS-space. The ellipses correspond to contours of constant probability density estimated by fitting a Gaussian function.

4.2.2   Colour Density Models

When the statistical learning problem of estimating a probability density function was introduced in Chapter 3, methods were categorised as being non-parametric, parametric or semi-parametric. All three of these approaches are possible when performing density estimation in a colour space in order to model the apparent colour distribution sensed from an object.

Swain and Ballard [331] renewed interest in colour-based recognition through their use of colour histograms for real-time matching. Recall that histograms are a non-parametric density estimation technique in which colour space is quantised into K *bins* and the density function is approximated based on the fraction of pixels which fall into each bin. Histograms yield a reasonable estimate when the number of data points (pixels) is very large and the colour space is relatively coarsely quantised. The main limitation of histograms is their arbitrary quantisation of the space in a way which takes no account of the data.

Skin gives rise to a fairly compact, unimodal distribution in colour space. In fact, a simple parametric Gaussian is often sufficient to model the distribution of skin colour. The ellipses in Figure 4.3 denote maximum-likelihood fit Gaussians. In general, however, multi-coloured objects give rise to more complex multi-modal distributions. If a multi-coloured object consists of several distinct and differently coloured patches, then it may be beneficial to decompose the object and model each patch using a separate colour model [220]. Furthermore, if such colour patches are relatively homogeneous, each can be directly modelled using a single Gaussian. However, many objects cannot be thus decomposed. In the absence of any sufficiently accurate parametric model, a semi-parametric approach can be adopted using finite mixture models. Estimation is thus possible in a finely quantised colour space using relatively few data points without imposing an unrealistic parametric form on the colour distribution [229, 285]. These mixture models are useful for modelling the colours of peoples' clothing or the scene background, in addition to skin [232]. *Outlier* points, which can be caused by image noise and specular highlights, have relatively little influence upon a mixture model. Expectation-Maximisation (EM) provides an effective maximum-likelihood algorithm for estimating a Gaussian mixture from a data set (see Appendix C) [27, 287]. Figure 4.4 shows an example of a Gaussian mixture model of a multi-coloured object in HS-space. Once a model has been learned it can be

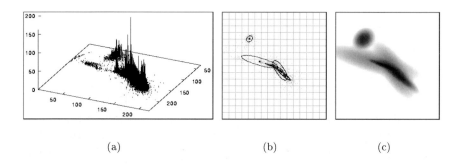

(a)   (b)   (c)

Figure 4.4 A seven component Gaussian mixture model of a multi-coloured object estimated using a constructive EM algorithm. (a) A histogram of the training data. (b) The mixture components. (c) The resulting probability density function.

converted into a look-up table for efficient on-line indexing of colour probabilities.

The resulting mixture model will depend on the number of components, K, and the initial choice of parameters for these components. A simple initialisation procedure can be adopted. For example, a suitable value for K is chosen based upon visual inspection of the colour distribution. The component means are initialised to a random subset of the training data points. All priors are initialised to $\frac{1}{K}$ and the covariance matrices are initialised to $\sigma^2 \mathbf{I}$, where σ is the Euclidean distance from the component's mean to its nearest neighbouring component's mean. However, such an initialisation method is rather *ad hoc*.

Alternatively, a constructive algorithm which automatically selects the number of components and their parameters can be used [284]. A standard technique employed for model training, known as *cross validation*, attempts to find the model order that provides the best trade-off between bias and variance. A number of models of different order are obtained by iteratively splitting Gaussian components during training by minimising an error function for a training set. These models are then evaluated by computing the error function for a disjoint *validation set*. The model with the lowest error for the validation set is considered to exhibit the best generalisation and its order is taken to be optimal. The details of such an algorithm are given in Appendix C. The application of this algorithm to a data set from a multi-coloured object is illustrated in Figures 4.4 and 4.5.

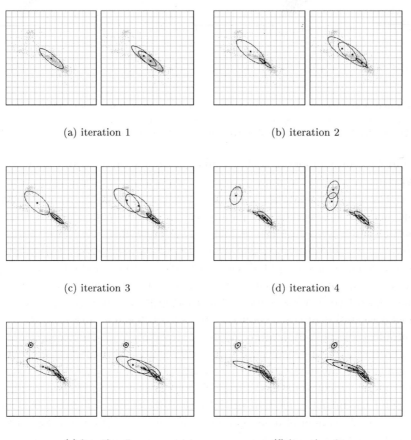

(a) iteration 1   (b) iteration 2

(c) iteration 3   (d) iteration 4

(e) iteration 5   (f) iteration 6

Figure 4.5 Automatic model order selection for the colour distribution of a multi-coloured object. A sequence of pairs of plots illustrate the splitting process, with each pair showing convergence followed by the splitting of a component. In each pair, the plots on the left and right show respectively the distribution before and after the splitting at each iteration.

Instead of using the EM algorithm and cross validation to estimate a skin colour density function, a classification function can be learned using both positive and negative example pixels (i.e. pixels belonging to skin regions and non-skin regions). The problem of model order selection can be addressed by structural risk minimisation using support vector machines. An SVM implemented using Gaussian kernel functions captures the decision boundaries without modelling the full distribution of the colour. Rather than using techniques such as cross-validation to determine the number of Gaussian functions needed, support vectors are automatically determined according to a clearly defined error margin in risk minimisation.

4.3 Perceptual Grouping for Selective Attention

Both motion and colour provide pixel-level visual cues. Object-based selective attention, on the other hand, requires *perceptual grouping* of such pixel-based cues. Perceptual grouping is a process whereby a vision system organises image regions into emergent boundary structures that aim to separate objects and scene background. In general, pre-attentive motion cues give rise to clusters of motion contours which often correspond to entire moving regions of, for instance, human bodies. Object-based colour models, on the other hand, yield regions of pixels with high likelihood. Bottom-up grouping can be performed based on connectivity, proximity and morphological operators. Computational efficiency is obtained by performing grouping on sub-sampled motion and colour probability images and by adopting multi-resolution strategies. Figure 7.4 shows images from a sequence with multiple regions of visible skin corresponding to two moving faces. The probability map produced by a skin colour model is shown along with the regions identified by grouping.

Let us illustrate the grouping problem by describing a method that uses recursive, non-linear morphological operations at multiple scales. This method can be seen as a combination of relaxation and something similar in spirit to geodesic reconstruction [359]. It proceeds as follows.

(1) Compute log probabilities of the foreground (either motion or colour) in the image. This results in a probability image, I^o.
(2) Apply morphological erosion to I^o. This reduces noise and erroneous foreground and yields image Ier.

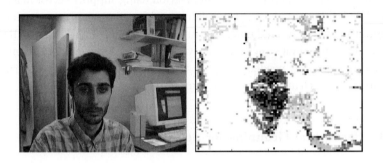

(a)   (b)

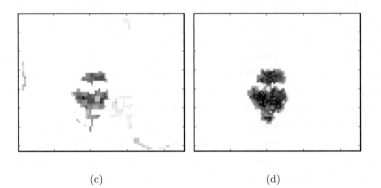

(c)   (d)

Figure 4.6   An example of using morphological operators for perceptual grouping. (a) An image frame from a sequence. (b) Foreground (skin) colour probabilities in the image space. (c) Perceptual grouping of skin-coloured region in the image space using multi-scale morphological operations after 1 iteration. (d) After 4 iterations of morphological operation.

(3) Let $I^* = I^{er}$, then iterate the following operation a number of times:

$$I^* = \frac{1}{2}\left(I^* \otimes \texttt{low-pass-filter} + I^o\right) \qquad (4.13)$$

where $\otimes$ denotes convolution.

Such an operation effectively performs perceptual grouping in the resulting image I^*. An example is shown in Figure 4.6. The iterative process is usually fast with good grouping obtained after a few iterations.

4.4 Data Fusion for Perceptual Grouping

Although grouping of either motion or colour cues often provides reasonable focusing of attention, there are situations under which either cue gives poor results. For example, motion will detect any suitably large moving objects irrespective of whether they are people or not. In crowded scenes with multiple moving people who temporarily occlude one another, motion grouping will not consistently group people as separate regions. Colour, on the other hand, suffers from the fact that many other objects can have colour distributions which strongly overlap those of skin. Typical examples are wooden furniture and cardboard boxes. However, motion and colour are complementary and provide good cues under different conditions. Fusion of these two cues can therefore reduce ambiguity, leading to improved performance and grouping of more tightly constrained regions.

A simple approach to fusion is to fuse the visual cues at the pixel-level before any grouping takes place. A foreground pixel to be grouped can be given by a joint posterior probability $P_{\mathcal{F}}(\mathbf{x} \mid \mathcal{M}, \mathcal{C})$ based on motion ($\mathcal{M}$) pseudo-probability $P_{\mathcal{F}}(\mathbf{x} \mid \mathcal{M})$ and colour ($\mathcal{C}$) probability $P_{\mathcal{F}}(\mathbf{x} \mid \mathcal{C})$ at each pixel $\mathbf{x}$:

$$P_{\mathcal{F}}(\mathbf{x} \mid \mathcal{M}, \mathcal{C}) = \frac{P_{\mathcal{F}}(\mathbf{x} \mid \mathcal{M}) \, P_{\mathcal{F}}(\mathbf{x} \mid \mathcal{C})}{\sum^{\mathcal{V}} P_{\mathcal{F}}(\mathbf{x} \mid \mathcal{M}) \, P_{\mathcal{F}}(\mathbf{x} \mid \mathcal{C})} \qquad (4.14)$$

where $\mathcal{V}$ denotes a vicinity of pixels to $\mathbf{x}$ with significant motion or colour probabilities. Figure 7.4 illustrates a scene in which two people pass while talking and occlude not only one another but also other static skin-coloured objects in the scene. The motion, colour and fused maps are shown along with the resulting regions of attention. Further pixel-level data fusion for perceptual grouping can also include explicit modelling of the background scene. The scene against which any action takes place is usually known and its appearance changes relatively slowly. Therefore, the scene can often be modelled in order to aid perceptual grouping for selective attention. Let us consider how this can be done with both static and moving cameras.

Given a static camera, a background scene pixel's value varies slowly or at least within a predictable range. Most other change can be taken to be due to an object in the scene occluding the background. Detection of such changes therefore provides a useful visual cue. The simplest approaches are based on subtraction of a background scene intensity image from each image in a sequence. This approach has advantages over temporal change detection discussed earlier in that there is no halo effect and poorly textured regions are usually detected. However, the background will usually vary over time due to illumination changes, shadow and camera noise. The background model must therefore be updated [249]. If a colour camera is used this approach can easily be extended by maintaining and updating a statistical model of each pixel's variability in colour space [232, 369].

In the case of moving cameras, the colour of the scene can be modelled using a mixture model and this model can aid focus of attention even in the presence of unknown camera motion. The distributions in colour space formed by multi-coloured scenes are multi-modal and can span wide areas of the colour space. Given estimated probability density functions for both the foreground objects (e.g. skin), $\mathcal{O}$, and the background scene, $\mathcal{S}$, the probability that a pixel, $\mathbf{x}$, belongs to the foreground is given by the posterior probability $P(\mathcal{O}|\mathbf{x})$:

$$P(\mathcal{O}|\mathbf{x}) = \frac{p(\mathbf{x}|\mathcal{O})P(\mathcal{O})}{p(\mathbf{x}|\mathcal{O})P(\mathcal{O}) + p(\mathbf{x}|\mathcal{S})P(\mathcal{S})} \qquad (4.15)$$

The probability of misclassifying a pixel is minimised by classifying it as the class with the greatest posterior probability. A pixel is therefore classified as object foreground if and only if, for example, $P(\mathcal{O}|\mathbf{x}) > 0.5$. The prior probability, $P(\mathcal{O})$, can be set to reflect the expected size of the object within the search area of the scene $[P(\mathcal{S}) = 1 - P(\mathcal{O})]$. Figure 4.7 shows an example in which both the person and the background have been modelled. The two resulting probability density functions are shown as images. The image of posterior probabilities when the prior probabilities are set to $P(\mathcal{S}) = P(\mathcal{O}) = 0.5$ is also shown. This approach has the advantage that foreground and scene models can be acquired independently. Alterna-

(a) foreground   (b) background

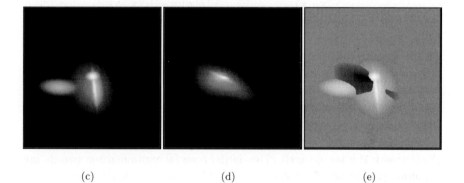

(c)   (d)   (e)

Figure 4.7 Colour mixture models of a multi-coloured foreground (person model) and background (scene model). (a) and (b) show the image data used to build the models. (c) illustrates the probability density estimated by a mixture model for the object foreground and (d) illustrates the density for the scene background. (e) is the combined posterior density in the HS colour space where the bright regions represent foreground whilst the dark regions give the background. The grey areas are regions of uncertainty.

tively, a classification function can be learned directly from foreground and background pixels using, for example, support vector machines.

4.5   Temporal Matching and Tracking

For the purposes of temporal matching and tracking, both motion and colour regions of interest can be modelled as Gaussian distributions in the image plane. Each region is modelled by a mean $\boldsymbol{\mu} = [x\,y]$ corresponding to its centroid and a 2×2 covariance matrix $\boldsymbol{\Sigma}$. In the case of motion, a region is parameterised by the mean and covariance of the coordinates of its temporal zero-crossings. In the case of colour, the mean and covariance are computed using the likelihood values, $p(\mathbf{x})$:

$$\boldsymbol{\mu} = \frac{\sum \mathbf{x} p(\mathbf{x})}{\sum p(\mathbf{x})}, \qquad \boldsymbol{\Sigma} = \frac{\sum p(\mathbf{x})[\mathbf{x} - \boldsymbol{\mu}][\mathbf{x} - \boldsymbol{\mu}]^{\mathrm{T}}}{\sum p(\mathbf{x})} \qquad (4.16)$$

where $\mathbf{x}$ ranges over those image coordinates that have a colour likelihood, $p(\mathbf{x})$, above a threshold. The probabilities are thresholded to reduce the influence of non-skin pixels. Probabilities lower than the threshold are taken to be background and are consequently set to zero in order to nullify their influence on $\boldsymbol{\mu}$ and $\boldsymbol{\Sigma}$.

In many scenarios, the orientation of the regions remains approximately aligned with the image axes. This is the case for motion when people are standing upright and for colour face tracking when the head is upright. In this case, a region's covariance matrix can be modelled as diagonal and each region has just four parameters: $(x, y, \sigma_x^2, \sigma_y^2)$. This low-order region parameterisation facilitates efficient and stable tracking. Obviously, modelling by assuming a Gaussian distribution of moving zero-crossings or colour is a crude approximation. A more detailed shape model could be used to impose additional geometric constraints with additional computational penalties [323]. However, such explicit shape models may neither be necessary nor desirable.

Figure 4.8 shows the bounding boxes obtained by grouping the motion detected in the image frame. In addition, the probable regions of heads are shown as boxes. These head boxes were estimated using the detected motion clusters and heuristics that the heads are uppermost and in proportion to the body.

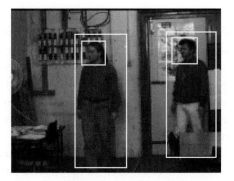

Figure 4.8   An image frame from Figure 4.2 with bounding boxes for the tracked people and their heads over-laid. Outer boxes are based on the grouped temporal zero-crossings. Head boxes are estimated using heuristics about human body configuration.

4.6   Biological Perspectives

The efficacy of focusing visual attention is a lesson learned from biology [305]. This strategy is widely used to cope efficiently with an overflow of sensory data. A useful analogy from human vision is the use of peripheral vision to cover a wide visual field whilst attention is focused on the central, foveal region of the retina. However, even though the outcome of such attention-mediated processing can in many cases be uniquely verified, visual attention is attributed to more than one selection mechanism and is performed in different areas of the brain and for different reasons [305].

Attention theories in biological vision have traditionally relied on studies from behavioural data. More recently such studies have been augmented with neuropsychological and neurophysiological experiments where event-related brain potential modulations are measured in order to investigate the brain activity during the selective attention process [106]. The research carried out focuses on a number of issues: (a) the derivation of computational theories of why we attend to particular regions and how we decide from all the sensory data which ones to focus our attention upon, (b) the nature of primal features used for focusing our attention and the processes underlying their integration, and (c) how attended information is processed. Admittedly many of the conclusions drawn from such experiments are partly speculative but the recent synergy of psychology and neurophysiology research has helped to enhance our understanding of the processes underlying human visual attention.

It is a widely accepted view that mechanisms of selective attention bias the competition of perceptual processing among objects or events in favour of information that is most important for adaptive behaviour [90]. According to the race model developed by Shibuya and Bundesen [316], sensory data are weighted in the first instance according to the sensory evidence that they were generated by a target. Computational theories then attempt to explain how sensory data as part of important objects or events compete for visual processing [106, 160].

The visual system consists of two main visual processing streams. Selection for object recognition is attributed to the ventral pathway and search features include colour, motion and orientation [69, 91, 207]. The computation of spatial pre-cuing or spatial motor-actions is ascribed to the dorsal pathway where knowledge of the spatial location of a target is used for more accurate responses to visual aspects [91]. Visual processing in both streams is task dependent and this type of selectivity has been called "endogenous visual attention" [276].

It is generally acknowledged that the visual environment is maintained across eye movements in trans-saccadic memory. The information that can be stored in trans-saccadic memory is very limited and only attended regions are encoded there for further processing [106]. This is because it appears that attention moves to the saccade target location before the eyes move, thereby increasing the likelihood that objects or events near the saccade location are encoded into trans-saccadic memory at the expense of other visual information [169].

In many cases visual attention also serves as a binding function of visual features of different representations. Irwin and Gordon [169] have shown that because of attention shifts, object attributes such as colour and orientation near the saccade target location are conjoined and stored in trans-saccadic memory. Their results have also shown that there is some evidence of additional benefit gained from spatial pre-cuing.

4.7   Discussion

Although both motion and colour-based visual cues can be used for selective attention, such information alone is often insufficient and computationally under-constrained, especially with multiple objects moving closely. High-level knowledge is needed to overcome such ambiguities in perceptual grouping and selective attention [56, 132]. In the case of selective attention in dynamic face perception, a simple way to assert some form of high-level knowledge, for example, is to assume that a selected region of interest corresponds to a person. Then the location of the head can be estimated relative to the region of interest using simple heuristics. However, such a crude approach can be easily broken down under most conditions. Essentially, explicit knowledge about *what faces look like* is required in order to more accurately focus the attention and verify the presence of a face in terms of its image location and size.

A method is required which can discriminate effectively and efficiently between images of faces and non-faces. What then, are the desired properties of a high-level face model and the objectives that such a model should meet in directing attention? Such methods should ideally be invariant across a range of extrinsic factors such as lighting conditions, spatial scales and viewpoints. They should cope with intrinsic variations including hairstyle, facial expression and the presence or absence of spectacles and make-up. Such a face model can then be used to constrain the ambiguities in perceptual grouping and selective attention. For instance, a grouped motion or colour region which is consistently found to possess two faces should be split into two regions. In the next chapter, we describe various methods for learning a generic face model and in particular, focus on models that use appearance-based representation. The resulting methods provide fast and reliable detection and segmentation of face-like image patterns.

5 A Face Model: What to Look For

The whole is more than the sum of its parts.

— Aristotle, Metaphysica

Despite the fact that a degree of selective attention can be achieved by performing perceptual grouping of pixel-level motion and colour cues, such attention is in general rather crude. In the case of face perception, it provides focus of attention without being able to determine whether faces are actually present within those attended areas of interest. Truly attentive focusing of interest requires more knowledge about faces. Such knowledge is used to guide *perceptual search* in the attended regions of interest in order to determine the actual size and position of any face. We regard this process as the task of *face detection.*

What is a face model and how should we acquire one for face detection? Human faces together constitute a particular and rather special category or class of 3D objects. In fact, a face is only part of the surface of an object and as such it is not even clear how to delineate the boundary of a face. The outline of a face varies with hair-style and cannot be precisely defined although attempts to detect such outlines have been made [140, 300]. The face class exhibits an intrinsic variability which is difficult if not impossible to characterise analytically. Variability in the shape and surface properties of faces is due to factors which include identity, gender, age, hair-style and facial expression. Artifacts such as make-up, jewellery and glasses cause further variation. In addition to all these factors, facial appearance is affected by the observer's viewpoint, the imaging system, the illumination sources and the other objects present. It is because of all these intrinsic and extrinsic variations, many of which cannot be parameterised analytically, that statistical learning from examples is needed in order to characterise and model the face class. The background against which faces are to be detected is unknown and the class of non-face images which can be encountered potentially consists of all other naturally occurring images. The non-linear decision surfaces between images of faces and non-faces are too complex for humans to discover manually. Rule-based approaches have been attempted but with limited success [372]. The source of variation that causes most problems for face detection is pose change. Faces are at least partially occluded by the head from nearly any viewing angle and facial appearance changes dramatically with pose. Let us start by addressing the restricted problem of detecting upright faces in frontal or near-frontal views. The problem of coping with large pose changes will be taken up again in the next Chapter.

5.1   Person-independent Face Models for Detection

Most approaches to face detection fall into one of two categories: they are based on either local features or holistic templates. In the former category, facial features such as eyes and mouth are located and configurational constraints are used to detect plausible face patterns. This is a form of *representation-by-parts* in which a face object is decomposed into parts which are objects in their own right. In the holistic approaches on the other hand, no semantically meaningful subparts of faces are defined and the face is not decomposed. We will now discuss both of these approaches before considering holistic methods in greater detail.

5.1.1   Feature-based Models

One approach to face detection would be to first search for the main facial features such as eyes, noses and mouths. Plausible configurations amongst the detected features could then be identified as faces [53, 141]. The main problem with this approach is that it requires an eye detector, a nose detector and a mouth detector ... ! The problem of detecting faces has been replaced by the problem of detecting multiple, similarly complex and deformable parts. Although configurational constraints will reduce the accuracy required of each individual facial feature detector, we now have multiple detection tasks to perform. The strong configurational appearance of faces must be exploited. For example, facial features can be treated as nodes in a deformable graph [195] or as elements in a statistical model which captures a range of variations in facial appearance [199].

These feature-based methods are characterised by:

(1) Representation by parts (*a priori* semantic knowledge).
(2) Constraints on the spatial configurations of parts.
(3) Use of relatively high resolution images.

While such methods are useful for facial analysis and correspondence in identification, they are not well suited to face detection in complex scenes. Image search becomes expensive since there are now a large number of model parameters to be adjusted. The detection and alignment of facial features are usually performed on images of relatively high spatial resolution. However, in dynamic scenes, face detection often needs to be achieved at much lower resolution. Interestingly, the human vision system is often required and able to effectively detect faces at a resolution as low as 15×15 pixels. Face detection methods which rely on feature detection typically use face images at least 60×60 pixels in size [380]. It would seem inappropriate to adopt an approach that aims to process more information than necessary. Perhaps one of the main limitations with the local feature-based approach is its inability to cope with occlusions due to changes in viewpoint. It is clear that correspondences between certain features do not exist under occlusion and an attempt to establish consistent correspondences between 2D image features across views is intrinsically ill-posed.

5.1.2 Holistic Models

The holistic approach aims to avoid arbitrary decompositions of faces into parts. It treats the detection task as a search for a face image in its entirety [52, 223, 252, 297, 330]. The spatial arrangement of facial features is then implicitly encoded within an *holistic representation* of the internal structure of a face. The holistic approach is characterised by:

(1) No *a priori* decomposition into semantically meaningful facial features.
(2) Use of relatively low resolution images.

It is difficult to handle situations in which a face is partially occluded by other objects using such an approach. It may be possible to address this kind of partial occlusion using robust statistics to treat occluded regions as statistical outliers. Such an approach has yet to be fully explored [28, 86]. However, this potential drawback is outweighed under most conditions

Figure 5.1 A circular or elliptical masking operator can be used to remove most of the hair and background from face images used for training a face model [297, 330].

by the advantages of being able to perform fast and sufficiently reliable detection at low spatial resolution. The feature-based, representation-by-parts approach relies on domain specific knowledge to partially address the problem. However, such heuristics are also potential sources of error. In contrast, the holistic approach need not use such prior knowledge.

In the case of an holistic approach, some of the variations in the face class are addressed by image pre-processing, others by perceptual search in the attended regions of interest and the rest by statistical learning. There are two strategies one can adopt to perform face detection. If a face model can be learned and this model can be matched with specific image regions, face detection can then be based upon the quality of the matches. Alternatively, a classification function which discriminates between faces and non-faces can be learned. In principle, the representation scheme used can be either explicitly 3D or based on 2D views. In practice, 2D view-based statistical models are very attractive as they facilitate learning directly from example images. In particular, *template-based* representation in which image pixels are treated as elements in a high-dimensional vector space, as described in Section 2.4, enables fast matching in dynamic scenes. Detection is then based on a decision function in the image vector space obtained using inductive learning. In order to make learning computationally viable, the dimensionality of the vector space needs to be kept low. In the case of images, however, this is often not the case. Even with only the interior of a face at low resolution, the dimensionality of the face image space is relatively large. For example, Figure 5.1 shows a typical face image used for learning a face model. Here only the interior of the face is used whilst the rest is masked out in order to reduce the influence of hair and background. Nevertheless, the masked image is still a vector of 300 dimensions.

For a more robust representation, there are a number of image pre-processing methods which can be used to reduce the variability of the image vectors in a useful way. For instance, Gabor wavelet and Gaussian derivative filters can be applied to the images in order to yield a more salient representation [286, 371]. Normalising the overall brightness and variance of the images partially removes variations largely due to the intensity of illumination and the imaging system response. A simple shade correction filter can help reduce effects due to directional illumination. Histogram equalisation can also be used [297, 330]. Nevertheless, given that sensory noise and external factors such as changes in lighting cannot entirely be filtered out, even processed images should still be regarded as probabilistic entities.

5.1.3   The Face Class

Let $\mathbf{x} \in \Re^N$ denote an image vector after any preprocessing. It is treated as a random vector generated according to an unknown probability distribution associated with a unique label, *the face class*. Assume that a *supervisor* (e.g. a human) can compute a label y for any image indicating whether or not it is an instance of the face class. Given a set of labeled images $\{(\mathbf{x}_1, y_1), (\mathbf{x}_2, y_2), \ldots (\mathbf{x}_M, y_M)\}$, a learning machine can be trained to compute a classification function $f(\mathbf{x})$ which approximates the supervisor's labeling function with a measure of confidence in its decision. Here we consider how such a decision function $f(\mathbf{x})$ can be learned from examples.

In order to learn a model from example images, it must be pointed out that the choice of training samples is crucial. Ideally, the training data should be representative of the variations such as identity, age, gender, expression, small rotation in depth, facial hair and artifacts such as glasses. Realistically, however, there is a limit to the number of face images that can be used, typically at most a few thousand. More than that makes data collection and preparation impractical.

One can consider that all images fall into two classes in the image vector space: faces and non-faces. Since the non-face class includes all images of anything except faces, it is too broad and complex to sample representatively and most of it is irrelevant, i.e. obviously non-face. The relevant non-face distribution to be considered is sampled from the attended probable face regions rather than the distribution of all images. An intuitive solution to modelling a decision function that separates faces from non-faces is perhaps to model the distribution of the face class by estimating its probability density function. However, while this distribution is less broad, it is still likely that a huge amount of data is required in order to estimate its density sufficiently accurately since the non-faces often closely resemble faces or parts of faces. Alternatively, instead of estimating a density function for the face class, a classification function can be learned. In theory then, there exist at least three different solutions to the problem:

(1) Sample only faces and learn a density-based model of the face class.
(2) Sample from a restricted set containing both faces and non-faces. Estimate density functions for each of these classes and use them to perform MAP classification.
(3) Sample from a restricted set containing both faces and non-faces. Learn a classification function which defines a decision boundary between the two classes.

5.2 Modelling the Face Class

Let us first consider how a generative model of the face class can be learned from example face images by performing density estimation. We assume that faces form an unknown probability distribution in the image space and that this distribution can be modelled by a density function $p(\mathbf{x})$. Given a learning machine capable of implementing a family of densities $p(\mathbf{x}, \mathbf{a})$, the learning problem is to estimate the unknown distribution by a density function $p(\mathbf{x}, \mathbf{a_0})$ through minimising its risk functional in the form of Equation (3.6). Unfortunately, density estimation is rather difficult because the dimensionality of the image space is large. To illustrate the problem, consider face images similar to that of Figure 5.1 with its dimensionality of $N = 300$. Non-parametric density estimation has good asymptotic properties, i.e. it can yield a good estimation given sufficient data. However, the amount of data required is likely to be prohibitive. Furthermore, since non-parametric approaches are effectively memory-based, they typically require the entire training set to be stored and once trained, matching is very slow, requiring comparison with every training vector. On the other hand, even a single parametric Gaussian model would require 45450 parameters to be estimated! This is the phenomenon commonly referred to as *the curse of dimensionality* [18]. In addition to the problem caused by the curse of dimensionality, faces are far more likely to form a rather complex, multi-modal distribution which cannot be accurately modelled using well defined parametric models. A more extensive set of functions are in fact needed, for example, a mixture of Gaussians. This will of course further exasperate

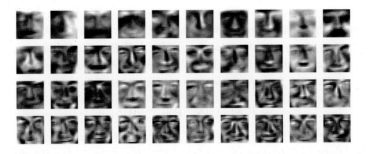

Figure 5.2 The first 40 eigenfaces computed from a training set of more than 5000 frontal view face images.

the problem because the number of parameters is now even greater. A common way to reduce the number of parameters in such Gaussian models is to constrain them to have diagonal covariance matrices. Unfortunately, this assumes that image pixels are uncorrelated which can be a rather poor assumption, especially for face images. Faces are highly structured and pixels are in fact highly correlated both locally and holistically. For this reason, a better way to constrain these parametric models is to first estimate the principal components.

5.2.1 Principal Components Analysis for a Face Model

Principal Components Analysis (PCA) provides a linear method for reducing the dimensionality of a data space and its details are described in Appendix C. Given a set of face images and its covariance matrix, the K dominant eigenvectors $\mathbf{u}_1, \mathbf{u}_2, \ldots, \mathbf{u}_K$ of the covariance matrix form a linear basis spanning a principal subspace. Each of these N-dimensional eigenvectors can be visualised as an *eigenface* image [341]. Figure 5.2 shows some typical examples of eigenfaces computed from a given set of face images. A face image $\mathbf{x}$ can be represented by a K-dimensional coefficient vector $\boldsymbol{\alpha}$ after projection onto the K-dimensional principal subspace:

$$\boldsymbol{\alpha} = \mathbf{U}^{\mathrm{T}}(\mathbf{x} - \boldsymbol{\mu}) \tag{5.1}$$

where $\mathbf{U} = [\mathbf{u}_1\, \mathbf{u}_2 \ldots \mathbf{u}_K]$ is the eigenvector matrix and $\boldsymbol{\mu}$ is the mean vector of the data set [184]. In this way, the dimensionality is reduced from N to K.

Suppose that all face images can be well approximated by projection onto the K-dimensional principal subspace. This implies that faces reside in or close to the principal subspace. Turk and Pentland [341] suggested using a vector's distance from this subspace to determine whether it was a face. This *distance from face space* measurement is given by (Appendix C):

$$d(\mathbf{x}) = ||\mathbf{x} - \boldsymbol{\mu}||^2 - ||\boldsymbol{\alpha}||^2 \qquad (5.2)$$

However, even if the face class can be reasonably approximated in the principal subspace, images of non-faces can also generate (i.e. be projected into the principal subspace and give) small values of $d(\mathbf{x})$. For example, given a vector $\mathbf{x}$ such that $d(\mathbf{x}) = 0$, further vectors with zero distances can be generated by arbitrarily adding eigenvectors $\mathbf{u}_k$ to $\mathbf{x}$. In other words, PCA in itself does not provide an estimate of density.

Moghaddam and Pentland adapted PCA to define a density estimation in order to give a generative model of the face class [235, 236]. The actual likelihood of a new image under the model can be evaluated. This likelihood is low for an image far from the training set even if it is near the principal subspace. The method is closely related to the independently proposed Probabilistic Principal Components Analysis (PPCA) [335] and Sensible Principal Components Analysis (SPCA) [295]. It outperformed PCA in a face detection task [236] and can be regarded as a special case of Factor Analysis (FA). In FA the observation noise matrix is assumed to be diagonal. In PPCA and SPCA the observation noise is assumed to be spherically symmetric. In PCA this noise tends to zero [296].

5.2.2 Density Estimation in Local PCA Spaces

The structure of face space is in general non-linear and multi-modal. It seems unlikely that a Gaussian model is capable of accurate density estimation. Rather than perform a global, linear dimensionality reduction, the face distribution can be modelled as being linear only locally. This suggests using a mixture of locally linear models to perform density estimation.

Sung and Poggio attempted such an approach and modelled the face distribution using six Gaussians [330]. The parameters of these Gaussians were estimated from a data set of about 4000 face images using a modified K-means algorithm based on a normalised Mahalanobis distance:

$$d(\mathbf{x}; \boldsymbol{\mu}, \boldsymbol{\Sigma}) = \frac{1}{2}(d\ln 2\pi + \ln|\boldsymbol{\Sigma}| + (\mathbf{x} - \boldsymbol{\mu})^\mathsf{T}\boldsymbol{\Sigma}^{-1}(\mathbf{x} - \boldsymbol{\mu})) \qquad (5.3)$$

However, this model does not provide a proper density estimate. The likelihood of data under the model is not made explicit. PCA is performed separately on the data under each Gaussian. An image can then be summarised by a 12-vector of normalised Mahalanobis distances in the principal subspaces along with the distances from each subspace. This 12-vector fails to make the likelihood explicit but is useful as input to a classification function (see Section 5.3). In order to perform density estimation using a locally linear model, mixtures of the probabilistic principal component analysers discussed above can be used. Such a model was proposed by Tipping and Bishop [335]. Related discussions can be found in Hinton *et al.* [154, 155].

So far we have described various approaches to modelling the face class in an appearance-based hyperspace. It has become clear that accurate estimation of the face class density function is computationally difficult not least because of the curse of dimensionality. A generative density model of the face class alone suffers from lack of any information about the non-face class distribution. In general, a decision boundary generated by a function estimated from only positive samples of a class may never be effective at separating that class from its neighbouring class, in this case, the faces from the non-faces. For face detection, a decision boundary is better given by a function estimated from both the positive and negative samples of faces and non-faces.

5.3   Modelling a Near-face Class

The class of non-face images encountered while performing face detection, even only within attended probable face regions, is extremely broad. Accurately modelling this distribution by performing density estimation is computationally infeasible given limited data. However, a decision surface which can successfully discriminate faces from non-faces may be entirely determined without having to model most of this non-face distribution. In fact, only those *near-face* images that lie close to the face space and are therefore easily confused with face images need to be considered. Such confusable near-face images can be selected from a more extensive non-face data set using an iterative training method in which images incorrectly classified as faces are included in the training set for future training iterations [52, 233, 297, 330].

Sung and Poggio [330] attempted to model the near-face distribution as six Gaussian clusters similarly to the method they used for modelling the face distribution. However, the model does not explicitly give a density estimation. Instead, it computes a feature vector of distances to each face and near-face cluster. A classification function can then be trained to discriminate faces from non-faces based on these feature vectors. A more complete solution to this problem would require density estimation for both the face and near-face distributions using methods discussed in the previous section. Given these two class-conditional probability densities, a maximum a posteriori (MAP) classification rule can be used.

5.4   Learning a Decision Boundary

Apart from the simple PCA projection, the approaches described so far are all aimed at, in essence, estimating class-conditional densities in order to perform a classification task. However, it is also clear that such an approach is computationally under-constrained given limited data: a problem described earlier as the curse of dimensionality. This is especially true in the high-dimensional image space. If what is required is a decision function which discriminates faces from non-faces, such a function must model a non-linear decision surface in the image space $\Re^N$. The learning problem is then one of classification, achieved by either estimating two density functions or learning a classification function directly. However, learning a decision function through density estimation violates a general principle in learning from sparse data which Vapnik puts succinctly as follows [351]: *"When solving a given problem, try to avoid solving a more general problem as an intermediate step".* This implies that solving two difficult density estimation problems in order to solve a less general classification problem is not a good approach. The estimation of a decision boundary through learning a classification function is in principle a more effective approach to the problem. This is especially true when training data are sparse compared to the dimensionality of the image space. Two approaches introduced in Chapter 3 can be exploited here: multi-layer perceptrons (MLPs) trained using empirical risk minimisation and support vector machines (SVMs). Before describing their use in any detail, let us first consider some of the particular requirements of a face detection method to be used in a *dynamic* vision system.

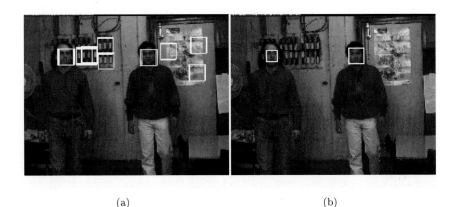

(a) (b)

Figure 5.3 (a) An example output from face detection on a static image using an MLP with just eight hidden units. In this example, image search is only performed at a single fixed scale. There are many false detections. (b) The output using the same MLP when temporal context is exploited. There are no false detections.

5.4.1 Face Detection in Dynamic Scenes

In static images, a classifier used to perform face detection must achieve a very low false-positive rate. This is extremely difficult as there are inevitably sub-images which, when considered out of their spatial and temporal context, appear face-like (see Figure 5.3). The emphasis in learning a classification function for static face detection is therefore placed on minimising the classification error. For example, multiple classifiers can be trained and combined in order to achieve small reductions in classification error rates [297]. Response Operating Characteristic (ROC) curves are used to carefully select appropriate operating points which trade-off false detection rates against the fraction of faces which are classified as non-faces. The number of false-positives can be reduced by discarding isolated detections and merging overlapping ones [297].

In dynamic scenes, however, classification accuracy becomes less critical due to constraints imposed by temporal context. Classification accuracy in individual frames can therefore be traded-off against computational efficiency. Figure 5.4 shows an example of detecting faces in a dynamic scene with very poor lighting and low image resolution. Under such conditions, detection in individual image frames in isolation is

Figure 5.4 Temporal constraints enable robust detection of moving faces in a cluttered scene with very poor lighting and low resolution.

Figure 5.5   Scale normalisation to a fixed resolution of 20×20 pixels.

almost certainly unreliable. In order to detect a face within a probable face region, a multi-scale search is required. This is one of the main
computational overheads. In order to perform face detection in dynamic
scenes the computation is subject to time constraints and classification
must be sufficiently fast. This in general requires a compact classifier
structure. In fact, taking temporal constraints into consideration, it is
possible to design an MLP with as few as eight hidden units that gives
good trade-off between speed and accuracy in dynamic scenes [223, 224,
228]. In order to illustrate these ideas more clearly, let us now describe a
simple but effective method which is used to perform robust detection and
tracking of moving faces in cluttered dynamic scenes. Many aspects of this
method are similar to other face detection systems described elsewhere [52,
252, 297, 330].

5.4.2   Normalisation

Frontal view face images of different people were assembled from various
face databases most of which are publicly available (see Appendix A). The
majority of these face images were from the Usenix face database. Non-face
patterns can be extracted from images of attended regions or other scenes
that do not contain faces. In this case, a database containing 70 images
of indoor and outdoor scenes was used to generate such patterns. In order
to perform effective learning, the training face images should be aligned
as closely as possible with one another. This can be done by normalising
translation, orientation and scale. A common but laborious approach is to
label the positions of facial features by hand and transform the training
images with respect to these features. For example, the line joining the
eyes can be used to normalise for rotation while the distance between its
midpoint and the upper-lip can be used to normalise for scale through either
sub-sampling or interpolation as shown in Figure 5.5 [297]. The training set

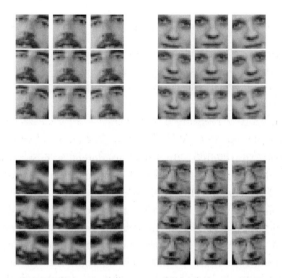

Figure 5.6 Examples from a data set of over 9000 frontal view face images that have been used for training an MLP for face detection. The images shown here were obtained by processing images from the ORL database (see Appendix A). Prior to training, intensity normalisation and masking are also performed.

can also be expanded by rotating the faces through $\pm 10°$ and scaling them to 90% and 110% (see Figure 5.6). Therefore tolerance to small amounts of scaling and rotation in the image-plane can be captured by the classifier.

In order to remove the influence of hair and background noise, an elliptical, binary mask can be applied to the image as shown in Figure 5.1. In this example, the resulting image has 300 pixels. Therefore the classifier aims to learn a decision function that can separate faces from non-faces in a 300-dimensional space. In order to reduce the effects of both directional and global lighting changes, linear shading correction and histogram equalisation can be applied to the face images [297, 330]. However, such computations can be costly, especially in dynamic scenes. An alternative, less expensive approach is to scale each pixel, x_n, by the standard deviation, σ, of the image intensity after subtracting the mean intensity, μ:

$$\text{Intensity Correction}\,(x_n) = \frac{x_n - \mu}{\sigma} \qquad (5.4)$$

5.4.3   Face Detection using Multi-layer Perceptrons

An MLP can be trained using back-propagation on a training set consisting of similar numbers of face and non-face images. Such an MLP takes a 300-dimensional vector as input and produces a scalar output value that can be thresholded to classify the input as either face or non-face. The output value is also used as a measure of confidence in the classification.

Multi-layer perceptrons (MLPs) can be designed to incorporate domain specific information through the use of local receptive field-like connectivity [116, 297, 349]. This is equivalent to fixing some of the weights in the parameter vector to zero. Weight-sharing employed between these receptive field structures has been used to extract local features irrespective of position on the input image [116]. Alternatively, MLPs with square and horizontally elongated receptive field structures can be trained [297]. Although careful design of specific receptive field architectures can achieve good classification, the process is unfortunately rather *ad hoc* and can be over-tuned to specific training data resulting in poor generalisation. The systems can also be costly especially if face detection is to be performed in dynamic scenes. We have found that for dynamic scenes, a fully-connected MLP with as few as 8 hidden units with sigmoid functions is effective for detection and tracking.

Initially, the MLP is trained on equal numbers of face and non-face images. However, the resulting classifier will perform quite poorly. In order to increase classifier accuracy, further training is needed using more carefully selected non-face images that lie close to the desired decision boundary. A process is used which aims to incrementally obtain good samples of near-faces which are difficult both to define and select. This process is as follows. An initial classifier is trained on both a small set of face and a small set of non-face image samples. This initial classifier is then applied to detect faces in a set of large scale images containing no faces. This involves multi-resolution scanning of these images. The patterns erroneously detected as faces in such images are all *false positives* and are used to create a new near-face training set. These near-faces are then used to retrain the classifier. The process is repeated until a sufficiently low number of false positives are detected. Some examples of false positives detected during such an iterative training process are shown in Figure 5.7.

Training an MLP in this way using an algorithm such as back-propagation is rather *ad hoc* in a number of respects. The iterative training

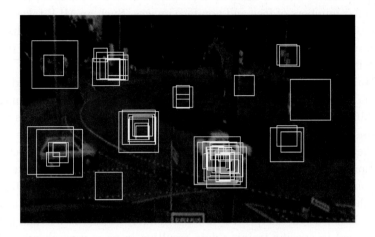

(a)

(b)

Figure 5.7 Multi-scale near-face samples are extracted from non-face images by iterative false positive detections. (a) and (b) show two examples of a large non-face image being scanned for extracting negative training samples.

scheme described is attempting to select those images that lie near the decision boundary since these are the images needed to determine a good classification function. In fact, the images that are needed are the *support vectors*. Support vector machines can be used to obtain a classifier in a more elegant and computationally principled manner.

5.4.4 Face Detection using Support Vector Machines

Let us examine in the following how SVMs can be used to learn a decision function for discriminating faces from non-faces at frontal views [203, 247, 248, 252]. The trained classifier can be used to perform very effective face detection in cluttered scenes. Support vector machines perform structural risk minimisation on sparse training data in order to maximise generalisation on novel observations (see Section 3.7.2). In principle, the process of training an SVM automatically determines the best set of support vectors from a given training set. These support vectors are in fact a subset of the training samples that are closest to the underlying decision boundary (see Section 3.7.2). The potential generalisation capability of an SVM still depends on the quality of the training data. In order to find a set of support vectors that will determine a good approximation to the true decision boundary, a wide range of faces and non-faces must be exposed to an iterative training process similar to that described above for MLP training. This process is illustrated in Figure 5.8 and it is similar in essence to the decomposition training algorithm proposed by Osuna *et al.* [252]. This iterative training process allows the SVM to be effectively trained on a large set of near-face samples while working on a small subset at any one time. The negative support vectors are selected from these near-face images during training. They share strong similarities to faces, as can be seen from the examples given in Figure 5.9 (a). Similarly, new sets of frontal view face images are iteratively fed into the process. Any detection failures are *false negatives* used to adjust some of the positive support vectors identified in the existing training set (see examples in Figure 5.9 (b)). The learning process and the number of support vectors are determined in a principled way by only a few user-adjustable parameters. In SVMs with Gaussian kernel functions, the number of such parameters is typically two: the penalty value for the Lagrange multipliers (κ) and the variance of the Gaussian functions (σ^2).

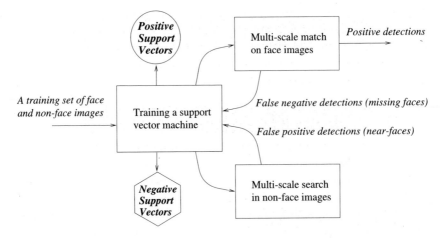

Figure 5.8 An iterative process of training support vector machines in order to find good approximations to true support vectors that separate faces from non-faces.

There can be a number of problems associated with using such face detection models. One of the main problems is that the size of the training data set has to be very large if the model is to be effective. In the example described, more than 18,000 face and near-face images were used for training. This is just for a model of a single, constrained pose! Due to the availability of a large number of frontal view face databases (as described in Appendix A), one can conceivably consider that in the case of the frontal view only, such an approach is acceptable even if the process is necessarily time consuming. The problem becomes much more difficult if not impossible when such a single view-based model is to be extended to multiple views, as discussed in the next Chapter. Such a large amount of training data also makes the training process itself very expensive. This imposes difficulties for model adaptation and online learning through acquiring new data for generalisation to novel views. One simple but effective solution to the problem is to apply dimensionality reduction using PCA to a set of well-aligned training face images. Instead of training SVMs in the image space, SVMs can then be trained in a PCA space of much lower dimensionality. In other words, eigenfaces can be used to reduce the dimensionality by projecting the images into an eigenspace and SVMs can be trained based on their projection coefficients.

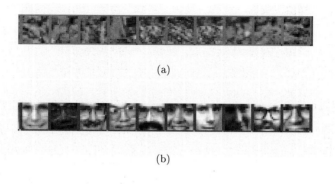

(a)

(b)

Figure 5.9 (a) Typical negative support vectors for the non-face class (after intensity normalisation). (b) Typical positive support vectors for the face class.

Face models can be made to tolerate small variations in viewing parameters such as rotation, scaling and translation in the image-plane by applying such transformations to the training data, as described earlier. However, the greater these variations, the more difficult the learning problem. Instead of trying to learn a decision function which is fully invariant, it is computationally more viable to deal with large variations of this sort using perceptual search and by performing better alignment in the image.

5.5 Perceptual Search

Perceptual search can be conveniently regarded simply as computations required for parameter estimation over space and time. The visual appearance of faces alters with viewing geometry. Holistically, an appearance is determined by the 3D position and orientation of the face relative to the observer. If a face is sufficiently distant from the observer, a *weak-perspective* projection model can be adopted, i.e. scaling followed by parallel projection. In this case, translation, uniform scaling and rotation of a face in the image plane correspond to changes in $3D$ position and rotation about the camera axis. These variations in viewing geometry can all be handled by searching with a fixed-view face detector at a range of positions (x, y), scales (s) and rotations (r) in the image plane. In other words, face detection under weak-perspective consists of finding values for (x, y, s, r).

Figure 5.10 SVM-based near-frontal view face detection in the regions of interest. The SVM used in this example was bootstrapped using 658 images of different faces and a larger number of randomly selected images of non-faces. It was then iteratively trained using a larger number of new face and near-face images as illustrated in Figure 5.8. The trained SVM used 144 positive and 254 negative support vectors.

In fact, weak-perspective projection may not be a good enough model when the face is close to the observer or when the field of view is wide. In this case, an *affine transformation* model that includes shears can be adopted since most of the facial structure is relatively shallow. Affine parameters also provide a means for dealing with modest rotations in depth.

Even with weak-perspective, perceptual search must be performed over four parameters. This search must be restricted in order to ensure computational efficiency. The attended areas of interest from motion and colour cues already provide crude estimates of these parameters. The search can be driven using gradient-based techniques but this often leads to problems of local minima and the face (the global minimum) might not be properly detected. In practice, exhaustive search over an appropriately quantised range of parameter values is more reliable. The level of quantisation used depends on the amount of variation which a face detector can handle. The search can also be guided by temporal constraints as described in Chapter 7.

Probable face regions can usually be scanned at multiple spatial resolutions and during this search, sub-images of appropriate aspect ratio are classified as either face or non-face images. A multi-scale search aims to yield estimates of the position and scale (x, y, s) of a face. In practice, faces are often upright and the image-plane rotation (r) need not be estimated. Invariance to large changes in scale is usually obtained by using the classifier to scan images in a multi-scale pyramid. However, this multi-scale scanning process can be costly if regions of interest are poorly identified in a dynamic scene. Figure 5.10 shows examples of detecting faces in the regions of interest using SVMs. The use of an SVM decision function to perform perceptual search can be very effective at detecting frontal view faces in varieties of novel scenes, coping well with both scale variations and image noise.

In principle, correspondence-based representation would allow search to be performed over shape parameters. In practice, this is unnecessary for face detection and would be computationally expensive. Shape variation is instead handled implicitly by a statistical appearance model.

5.6   Biological Perspectives

Most of the psychophysical experiments on face recognition are concerned with face identification and the recognition of familiar or unfamiliar faces, rather than with our ability to detect faces and disambiguate them from their background. There is, however, experimental work in neurophysiology on the responses of cells to the presence of faces. There have been a number of reports of cells in the temporal lobe of monkeys and even sheep that respond selectively to the sight of faces [263]. The majority of these cells respond to faces in general (across identity and even species) rather than to specific faces. They are highly selective for faces since they do not respond to a great variety of other visual stimuli, or indeed other arousing stimuli. These cells can respond despite changes in the position, scale, orientation and illumination of the face and are therefore able to generalise across such variations. In monkeys, face specific cells respond to both upright and inverted faces while in sheep the response to inverted faces is either substantially reduced or non-existent. It has been suggested that this is because monkeys sometimes hang upside-down in trees. Such invariance to image plane rotation would not therefore be expected in humans.

Cells have also been found which are responsive to only parts of the face such as the eyes and mouth. These cells encode the presence of particular facial features but do not use visual information about the other facial features. Other face-responsive cells require the configurational organisation of the facial features to be correct before they respond. Hence, there are cells which could be acting as holistic face detectors and others which could be performing local facial feature detection. Many of these cells have other interesting properties which will be discussed later in this book.

5.7   Discussion

Once regions of attention have been selected using motion and colour cues, we need firstly to verify that these regions indeed contain objects of interest such as faces and secondly to localise and align these objects. Here we have addressed the task of finding frontal or near-frontal views of faces within attended regions of interest. We adopted a simple template-based holistic representation. Three approaches to learning to identify faces were considered. The first approach tried to model the face class distribution but suffered from lack of knowledge of the distribution of non-face images. The second approach attempted to model a near-face class as well as the face class in order to determine a decision function. Density estimation is problematic in such high dimensional spaces. However, if the only purpose is to learn a classification function then density estimation need not be performed at all. The third approach estimated a classification function directly from face and non-face data. In dynamic scenes, it is suggested that classification accuracy be traded-off in favour of a compact classifier which allows efficient face detection.

In general, face detection requires more than finding frontal and near-frontal views. In fact, face detection is more problematic in an uncontrolled, dynamic environment, not least because as the human head rotates in depth, facial features become occluded. Although it is possible that other classifiers could be similarly trained to detect faces at different poses in order to establish a hierarchical view-based model exhibiting pose invariance, it is unclear how such a scheme can be implemented efficiently.

In the next Chapter, we consider the problem of face rotation in depth. In particular we illustrate how to effectively estimate the 3D pose of a face and how to perform face detection under rotation in depth. In Chapter 7 we extend the problem to using face detection to bootstrap a real-time tracking system and enable robust tracking of faces across different poses.

6 Understanding Pose

*That things depend upon one's point of view is so simple
an idea that it certainly cannot have been necessary to go
to all the trouble of the physical relativity theory in order
to discover it.*

— *Richard Feynman*

Faces do not always appear frontal and upright. In fact, more often than
not, faces undergo large rotation in depth which can occur in either or both
axes out of the image-plane. Such rotations introduce nonlinear transformations (deformations) in the images. Facial features become occluded and the
outline of the face alters its shape causing interference with the background.
The changes in the direction of light reflection from a face due to changes
in its pose, alone cause changes in its appearance. For example, day-time
lighting conditions in normal office environments are rarely symmetric for
the top and bottom hemispheres of the face, while the bias towards the
upper hemisphere is exacerbated by ceiling-fixed light sources during the
night. In general, detecting human faces across views intrinsically requires
a person-independent model that can capture a whole spectrum of very
different facial appearances. This is necessarily a computationally difficult
task.

Let us first consider a rather straightforward extension of the density
estimation approach to modelling frontal views. In principle, a multi-view
face model can also be learned using appropriately aligned face images
at a range of poses. The face class could be modelled by estimating the
density of the entire face space across views using mixture models. A
Gaussian mixture, for instance, could model the face distribution in such
a way that each Gaussian component described a subspace for a specific,
narrow pose range. The problem with such an approach is of course that
a vast number of carefully aligned face images at a large range of different

views are required before anything can be learned. This is impractical if not impossible since obtaining such training data is only realistically possible if a good enough face detector crossing views is available in the first place.

When considering pose change, a useful concept is that of the *view-sphere*. Provided that an observer is sufficiently distant from an observed object, a weak-perspective projection model can be adopted and perspective effects can be ignored. Changes in viewing angle can then be regarded as movement of the observer's viewpoint across the surface of a sphere centred on the object. When the observed object is a face, the centre of this view-sphere could, for example, coincide with the centre of the head. A tessellation of the surface of the view-sphere discretises the continuum of viewing positions into a finite set of poses. For example, discretisation of the viewing angles θ and ϕ into finite intervals of 20° divides the entire surface of the view-sphere into 324 (18×18) regions. A face is completely or almost completely occluded over much of the view-sphere so in fact much of the view-sphere can be ignored. Tessellation of the view-sphere surface suggests an extension to the methods introduced for the frontal view face model (Chapter 5) in which a separate model is learned for each region of the surface of the view-sphere. This amounts to modelling the full nonlinear face space as a collection of linear subspaces with each of these subspaces tuned to a particular pose. If the view-sphere is modelled as a collection of pose-specific subspaces, a mechanism for transforming view-based models between different views is also required. Such an approach aims to model the view-sphere in a piecewise manner and provides pose estimation in addition to face detection.

The role of pose estimation in detection can be regarded as that of focusing model search in face space. This is somewhat analogous to the role of selective attention in image space. Computationally, *understanding pose* involves modelling the face across the view-sphere in order to facilitate both face detection regardless of viewpoint (pose-invariant detection) and pose estimation when necessary.

Let us first examine the nature of the face space across the view-sphere, its bearing on establishing correspondence between neighbouring views and the modelling of its distribution. We must consider whether the face space is piecewise separable and whether images of faces form localised clusters across views in this face space. We will then describe methods for both building *person-specific* and learning *person-independent* face models for pose estimation and face detection across views.

6.1   Feature and Template-based Correspondence

Attempts at obtaining a pose-invariant face model based on maintaining explicit correspondences between local facial features inevitably encounter problems due to self-occlusion, background interference and unreliable feature extraction. They also require high-resolution images of the face and rely upon the ability to locate image features known to correspond to features on the face itself [121, 122, 194, 198]. Self-occlusion restricts such methods to local regions of the view-sphere. It is clear that point-wise dense correspondence is both expensive and may not be possible across large view change since rotations in depth result in self-occlusions which prohibit complete sets of image correspondence from being established. Performing translation, rotation and scaling based on sparse anchor points such as the locations of two eyes or simply the entire face as a template are alternative ways to bring two different views into alignment. A holistic template approach in particular is computationally not only desirable (for real-time performance) but also viable. Although correspondences established with such a template-based approach are only approximate (since they are not point-wise), the vector space formed by faces at a specific view is of low dimensionality [184, 260]. Preprocessing filters can also be used to construct more robust templates and to compensate for inexact correspondences.

6.2   The Face Space across Views: Pose Manifolds

A nodding head undergoes x-axis rotation or *tilt* whilst a shaking head undergoes y-axis rotation or *yaw*. Consider faces rotating in depth from profile to profile, i.e. horizontally about the y-axis. This generates sequences of face images as shown in Figure 6.1 (a). More importantly, in a low-dimensional eigenspace derived using PCA, the projections of these images form a smooth trajectory, as shown in Figure 6.1 (b). It is also true that such characteristics extend to different lighting conditions and all faces. It can be observed in Figure 6.1 (c) that trajectories in 3D eigenspace of the same face rotating in depth under different lighting conditions form a *pose manifold*.

In Figure 6.2, trajectories of different faces from similar head rotations in depth are shown in a 3D eigenspace. In this case, whilst the first principal

(a)

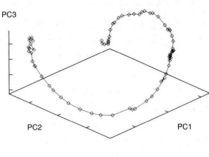

(b)

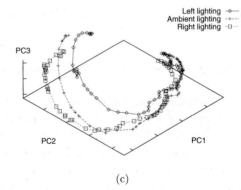

(c)

Figure 6.1 (a) Face images from a head rotation in depth. (b) The distribution of face images from a single head rotation in yaw form a smooth pose trajectory in a 3D eigenspace. (c) Trajectories from the same head rotation but under different directional lighting cluster around a smooth surface: *a pose manifold.*

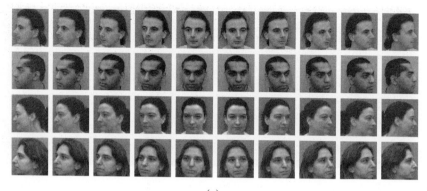

(a)

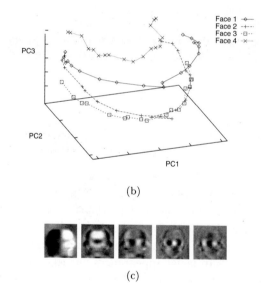

(b)

(c)

Figure 6.2 The distribution of face images from head rotation in depth tends to form a pose manifold even in a low dimensional eigenspace. In this example, (a) faces of four different people rotating in depth form (b) similar trajectories in a 3D eigenspace as they rotate in depth, despite visible differences in lighting, scale and alignment. (c) It is also worth noticing that the higher-order principal components among the first 5 shown here seem to capture finer details in facial appearance.

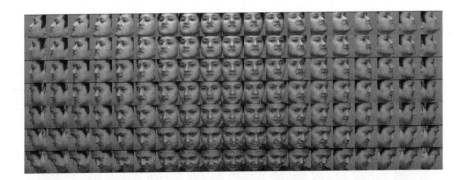

(a)

(b)

Figure 6.3 (a) Examples of face images that cover a large section of the view-sphere from $-90°$ to $90°$ horizontally (yaw) and $-30°$ to $30°$ vertically (tilt). (b) Reconstructed images of a face across yaw using the first 20 eigenfaces of a face view-sphere database.

component (PC1) divides poses from profile-to-profile into two almost symmetric parts centred at the frontal view, the second principal component (PC2) captures more detailed information by dividing the manifold into localised view-based regions. In fact, higher order principal components tend to capture finer details in facial appearances due to other intrinsic and extrinsic variations such as identity and lighting. The effects of higher-order principal components are further illustrated in Figure 6.2 (c) where the 3rd, 4th and 5th principal components all capture increasingly finer changes in facial appearance caused by head rotation in depth.

Let us now consider the more general case in which face images are generated by head rotations about both the y-axis (yaw) and the x-axis (tilt). The face images now cover a large section of the view-sphere as shown in Figure 6.3(a). The pose manifolds produced by such rotations will be more complex and of a higher intrinsic dimensionality than manifolds

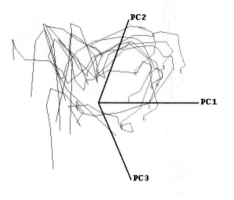

(a)

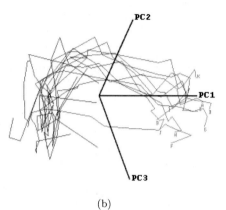

(b)

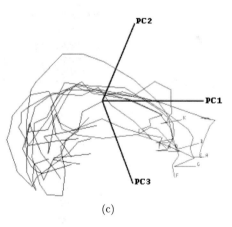

(c)

Figure 6.4 An example of pose manifolds from a set of 10 people rotating their heads from profile to profile, at (a) 60° tilt, (b) 90° tilt and (c) 120° tilt respectively.

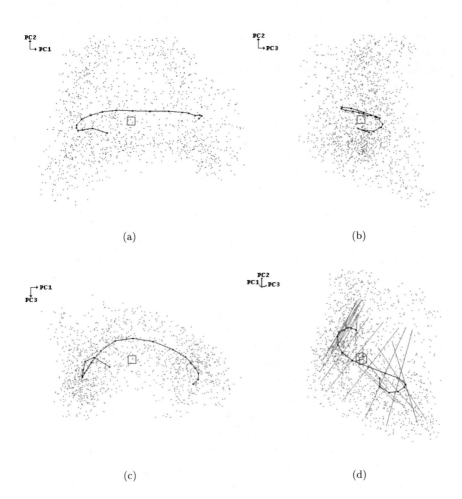

(a)   (b)

(c)   (d)

Figure 6.5 (a) Frontal, (b) side and (c) top views of face pose manifolds across the pose sphere. The trajectory in each view is the mean distribution of the manifold in yaw. (d) A tangential view with superimposed directions of maximal variance along the manifold across yaw.

produced by yaw alone. This can be seen in Figure 6.4. The volume swept out by this manifold can be visualised more clearly by plotting the mean at each yaw angle along with the directions of largest variance at regular intervals along this mean trajectory. This is shown in Figure 6.5. The shape of this manifold is more akin to a *solid tube* or volume function than a thin plate surface, through which face images *flow* from one end to the other as their corresponding yaw angles increase from $-90°$ to $+90°$.

6.3   The Effect of Gabor Wavelet Filters on Pose Manifolds

In general, pose manifolds in PCA space are sensitive to illumination conditions, scale, translation or rotation in the image-plane [71, 260]. In order to isolate the effect of pose change, we can apply image preprocessing to reduce other effects such as illumination change. In addition, it is interesting to examine the effects of any local, directional image features upon pose manifolds. One approach for such preprocessing is to use *Gabor wavelet* filters (see Appendix C). Such filters are multi-scale and selective to specific directional changes in the image. They can therefore be used to obtain invariance to scale change and to investigate the effect of locally oriented image features upon pose manifolds. In addition, they achieve a certain amount of localised normalisation for illumination. Figure 6.6 (b) shows an example of a face image filtered using Gabor wavelets. In this case, wavelets parameterised by 3 spatial frequencies and 4 orientations ($0°$, $45°$, $90°$, $135°$) are applied to a face image. Similar effects can also be obtained using Gaussian derivative filters [286]. However, Gabor wavelets are *complex*, consisting of an odd and even kernel. The Gabor-filtered image can be decomposed into magnitude and phase components. Figure 6.6 (c) shows the magnitude responses for the same image. It can be seen that at lower frequencies, faces are smoothed to a larger extent resulting in less sensitivity to small translations in the image-plane and greater correlation between nearby images in a sequence. However, using excessively low frequencies results in loss of relevant spatial structure as can be seen in the first row of Figure 6.6 (c).

In order to investigate the effect of the local intensity normalisation performed by Gabor wavelets, the magnitude responses at the different orientations are superimposed. An example of such a superimposed magnitude image is shown in Figure 6.7 (b). Figure 6.7 (d) was obtained from filtered

(a)

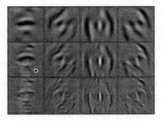

(b)

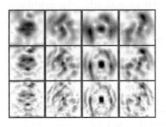

(c)

Figure 6.6   (a) A face image. (b) Its Gabor wavelet responses at three spatial frequencies and four orientations. (c) Its Gabor wavelet magnitude responses.

images of this type. One can observe that compared to the pose manifold shown in Figure 6.1, the pose distribution in the 2nd principal component dimension is more linear and also less variable in the 3rd dimension.

In order to examine the effect of local, directional features upon pose manifolds, one can also construct a composite face representation by concatenating the magnitude responses of the Gabor wavelets at different orientations. Figure 6.7 (c) shows such a composite face representation formed by concatenating responses at four orientations and then sub-sampling by a factor of four. Each eigenvector derived from this composite representation can be visualised as a composite eigen-image consisting of four oriented sub-images. The magnitude of each pixel in such an eigen-image can be envisaged as a measure of the variability of the response of one complex Gabor kernel centred at the corresponding position in the original image. In particular, the magnitudes of the first eigen-image would indicate *where* in the image-plane *which* orientations encode the most information about pose.

Figure 6.7 (e) shows the pose manifold of the face images using composite Gabor representation. Compared to both the pose manifold of intensity images in Figure 6.1 and that of superimposed, filtered images in Figure 6.7 (d), this manifold is well linearised. The pose angles are symmetrically distributed along two lines (the discontinuity at the frontal view is an artifact due to the fact that the profile-to-profile sequences were created by mirroring a profile-to-frontal view sequence about the vertical axis).

We can conclude that face rotation out of the image plane about the y axis and rotation across the pose sphere in general form smooth manifolds in the face space of reduced dimensions obtained using PCA. Furthermore, pre-processing with local, oriented filters such as Gabor wavelets helps to simplify these manifolds in a way that should facilitate pose understanding. Let us now consider two different ways to model a pose distribution in face space in order to both estimate pose and perform effective face detection across views. First, we consider a scheme for person-specific pose estimation.

6.4 Template Matching as Affine Transformation

Performing pose estimation entails the recovery from each face image of a six dimensional state vector $\mathbf{q} = [x\,y\,s\,\theta\,\phi\,r]^{\mathrm{T}}$, where (x, y) is the image-

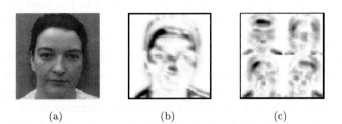

(a)   (b)   (c)

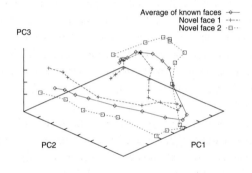

(d)

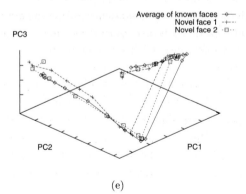

(e)

Figure 6.7 (a) Normalised intensity image. (b) Superimposed magnitude responses. (c) Composite Gabor representation of equal dimensionality. (d) Pose manifold in 3D space from superimposed Gabor magnitude responses of faces rotating in depth. (e) Pose manifold of face images using composite Gabor wavelet responses.

plane position of the face, s is its scale or projected size, (θ, ϕ) is the head's rotation in depth and r is the rotation of the head in the image-plane. The image transformations induced by changing the values of the parameters x, y, s and r can all be approximated using affine transformations in the image-plane. Rotations in depth (θ, ϕ) result in non-linear transformations. It should be possible to estimate all six parameters. In a simple case, assuming that the scale and image-plane orientation can be determined (e.g. the head is upright), pose estimation can then be regarded as the problem of computing four parameters: the image-plane coordinates (x, y) and the rotation in depth (θ, ϕ). A relatively straight-forward way to recover these four parameters is to treat the problem as a correspondence problem. In other words, performing view alignment by establishing correspondences between face images across views. Firstly, Gabor wavelet filtering can be performed on input images. Alternatively, for real-time performance on modest hardware, simpler orientationally selective filters can be used. Secondly, model face templates can be designed so as to exclude the background to as great an extent as possible without the need for specially shaped masks for each pose. Such templates contain most of the visible interior facial region and are of fixed size. The hair is largely excluded in order to avoid difficulties with unpredictable and changing hairstyles. The templates for the different poses need to be spatially aligned in order to obtain a smooth manifold in image space.

A face can be detected and its pose estimated using template matching based on a similarity measure. One obvious choice is to use a Euclidean metric (L_2 norm) as an indicator of dissimilarity:

$$h(\mathbf{x}, \mathbf{y}) = \frac{1}{||\mathbf{x} - \mathbf{y}||} = \frac{1}{\sqrt{((x_1 - y_1)^2 + \ldots + (x_N - y_N)^2)}} \tag{6.1}$$

If images are already intensity-normalised and therefore have zero-mean and unit variance, then this is a useful similarity function which provides invariance to overall intensity and the contrast effects caused by camera gain. Alternatively, Pearson's correlation coefficient can be used without prior image normalisation:

$$h(\mathbf{x}, \mathbf{y}) = \frac{\sum_{n=1}^{N} (x_n - \mu_{\mathbf{x}})(y_n - \mu_{\mathbf{y}})}{\sqrt{\sum_{n=1}^{N} (x_n - \mu_{\mathbf{x}})^2} \sqrt{\sum_{n=1}^{N} (y_n - \mu_{\mathbf{y}})^2}} \tag{6.2}$$

where $\mu_{\mathbf{x}}$ and $\mu_{\mathbf{y}}$ are the mean intensity values of $\mathbf{x}$ and $\mathbf{y}$ respectively.

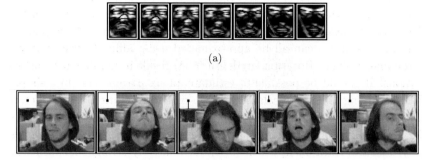

(a)

(b)

Figure 6.8 (a) Templates at $10°$ intervals used to estimate θ. (b) Tracking and estimating x-axis rotation using the 7 templates shown in (a). The last image shows an example of the pose estimation breaking down under large y-axis rotation. The needle in the upper-left corner of each image indicates the estimated head rotation.

Given an image and an appearance model, a matching function is maximised over the search intervals to determine the position and pose of the face. Each evaluation of the matching function, h, involves a comparison between a model view, $\mathbf{y}$, at pose (θ, ϕ) and a sub-image, $\mathbf{x}$, extracted from the input image at location (x, y). Here, $\mathbf{x}$ and $\mathbf{y}$ are the image representations obtained after filtering. This can be thought of as a search in a 4D state space for the state values that maximise a matching function. Each evaluation of this function is essentially a template match between a sub-image of the input and a model view at a particular pose. Maximising this function simultaneously recovers the head's position and pose. The use of oriented filters, whether Gabor wavelets or simpler oriented filters, aids this process, as shown in Section 6.2. Experiments show that without such filtering performance typically degrades drastically after periods of minutes due to changes in illumination conditions. Performance using filtered images did not noticeably degrade over a period of several weeks [226].

It is worth pointing out that horizontally oriented filter kernels respond strongly to the mouth, nostril area, eyes and eyebrows. The responses are most sensitive to x-axis head rotation and are therefore suited to estimating θ. Since these filters respond to the main facial features, they are also useful for detecting and tracking the face. Figure 6.8 (a) shows 7 horizontally

Figure 6.9 A set of 21 horizontally filtered templates.

filtered templates at intervals of 10°. Figure 6.8 (b) shows example frames from a head being tracked using these templates. The estimates of θ are in good agreement with human perception and are not adversely affected by small amounts of y-axis rotation. The last frame in Figure 6.8 (b) shows the pose estimation breaking down for large ϕ. Certain facial expressions cause changes in pose estimates. For example, lowering the eye-brows results in too large an estimate of θ. This expression made the face appear foreshortened as if tilted backwards. Conversely, raising the eyebrows often resulted in too small a value for θ. Human perception of θ may be susceptible to similar effects. A larger set of horizontally filtered templates useful for estimating tilt is shown in Figure 6.9.

Vertically oriented filter kernels respond strongly to the sides of the head and nose. Their response is sensitive to y-axis rotation making them useful for estimating ϕ. A suitable interval between these templates is found to be 15°. Figure 6.10 (a) shows a set of 7 templates in the range ±45° which can be used to estimate ϕ. Figure 6.10 (b) shows example frames during tracking and pose estimation using these templates. The estimation of ϕ is in good agreement with human perception and shows a significant amount of invariance to θ. In order to match both θ and ϕ with good precision, the vertically and horizontally filtered images can be combined to provide sensitivity to rotations around both the x and y axes. The appearance

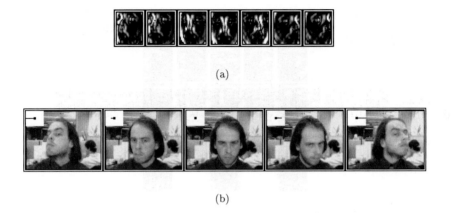

(a)

(b)

Figure 6.10 (a) Templates at 15° intervals used to estimate rotation about the y-axis. The template in the centre is from a frontal view. (b) Estimating y-axis rotation using the 7 templates shown in (a). The needle in the upper-left corner of each image indicates the estimated head rotation.

model can be extended by modelling a wider range of pose angles. Data captured using an electro-magnetic sensor to provide pose ground-truth can be used to evaluate accuracy (see Appendix A).

The template matching described so far measures the head pose (θ, ϕ) using nearest neighbour matching, i.e. the pose label associated with the best matching template is used as the measurement. A more general method is to interpolate over the matching scores of a set of templates. Radial basis function (RBF) networks provide one possible approach to achieving this interpolation [27, 273].

6.5 Similarities to Prototypes across Views

Given a face image database of multiple views of different people, a generic view-based appearance model can be learned for recognising and tracking head pose in a person-independent manner. Here we describe methods for constructing models using small sets of prototype images of different people across the view-sphere.

A simple way to obtain view-based appearance models is to compute an average image template at each pose using filtered face images. Figure 6.11

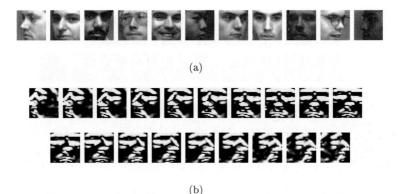

(a)

(b)

Figure 6.11 Examples of mean templates at different yaw angles. (a) An example view of each of 11 subjects used for computing the mean templates. (b) Average horizontally-filtered templates for views from profile to profile.

shows some of the mean templates computed by averaging filtered views of 11 different people. Better appearance models can be constructed using linear combinations of view-based prototypes. In general, an image $\mathbf{x}$ at a given view can be decomposed as a linear combination of prototypes $\{(\mathbf{x}_1, \mathbf{x}_2, \ldots, \mathbf{x}_K)\}$ at that view:

$$\mathbf{x} = \sum_{k=1}^{K} \alpha_k \mathbf{x}_k \tag{6.3}$$

The coefficients $\boldsymbol{\alpha} = (\alpha_1, \alpha_2, \ldots, \alpha_K)$ can be computed using singular value decomposition to minimise:

$$E_{rec}(\mathbf{x}) = \left\| \mathbf{x} - \sum_{k=1}^{K} \alpha_k \mathbf{x}_k \right\| \tag{6.4}$$

A more sophisticated approach can also apply pose modular eigenspaces to represent filtered images, giving more robust and computationally more effective templates for correspondence (Figure 6.12). However, rather than use a linear combination of views, an image can be represented as a vector of similarities to prototype views [100]. We exploit this approach to construct view-based appearance models.

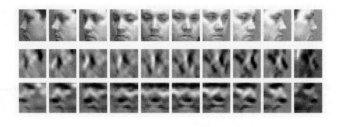

(a)

(b)

Figure 6.12 Computing orientationally filtered face appearance templates in pose modular eigenspaces across the pose-sphere. (a) Vertically (middle) and horizontally (bottom) filtered images of a face across yaw (top). (b) Reconstructed face templates for both vertically (top) and horizontally (bottom) filtered images across yaw using the first 20 eigenvectors from each pose modular eigenspace.

Let a face image, $\mathbf{x}$, be represented as a vector, $\boldsymbol{\alpha} = (\alpha_1, \alpha_2, \ldots, \alpha_K)$, of similarities to a set of prototype faces $\{\mathbf{x}_1, \mathbf{x}_2, \ldots, \mathbf{x}_K\}$ at the same pose, where

$$\alpha_k = h(\mathbf{x}, \mathbf{x}_k) \qquad (6.5)$$

and h is a similarity function. A suitable form for h is Pearson's linear correlation coefficient. Alternative template matching functions are also applicable here [134, 218]. Each component of the similarity vector indicates how alike the input image is to a prototype face image. The L_2 norm of a similarity vector $\boldsymbol{\alpha}$ provides an overall measure of similarity between a novel input image and the prototype faces. This can be used to estimate the pose of the input image by finding the pose which maximises this value.

Similarly to the composite Gabor wavelet representation shown in Figure 6.7 (e), manifolds of similarity vectors of faces to prototypes vary ap-

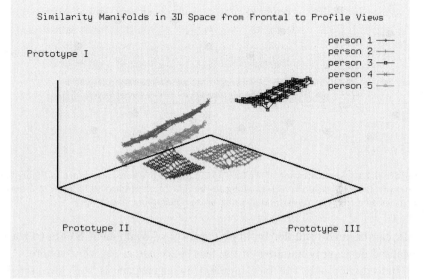

Figure 6.13 An example of a set of 5 faces represented by their similarity to 3 prototypes across pose. Their similarity vectors vary approximately linearly and form clearly class separable manifolds.

proximately linearly across views. Furthermore, different identities tend to be quite separable (see Figure 6.13). This is computationally attractive both for tracking faces across views and for pose estimation. Its class separable nature offers clear advantages over PCA-based representation in identification, as we shall exploit later in Chapter 9.

6.6 Learning View-based Support Vector Machines

As described in Chapter 5, SVMs can be used to learn a nonlinear decision function that is effective for frontal view face detection. One wishes to extend the computation to multiple poses across the view-sphere. A difficulty with this is of course the lack of good training samples. The notion of *progressive learning* illustrated in Figure 5.8 becomes important. An initial SVM learned from a small set of face images will not provide sufficient accuracy for modelling faces across views. It can however be used to acquire a larger database of negative examples for retraining the model. The learning

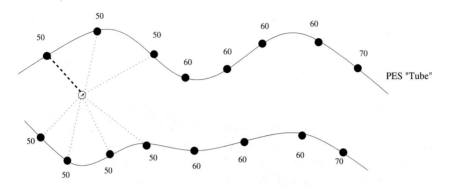

Figure 6.14 An illustration of the face pose manifold in eigenspace shown in Figure 6.5 with yaw-labelled support vectors along its margin (dark circles). The pose of a novel face (white circle) can be estimated using nearest neighbour matching.

task can be made simpler by applying a set of component SVMs to learn localised decision boundaries of the face space across the view-sphere.

Indeed, not only the face manifold in eigenspace is well localised in both tilt and yaw (as shown in Figure 6.5), the distribution of support vectors are also localised and view-dependent. Experiments have shown that by dividing the face pose manifold into five neighbouring sub-ranges in yaw, a set of five component SVMs can be trained using a single global negative data set of 6,000 samples, of which 1666 were estimated as negative support vectors across the pose sphere. However, only 36 of these are shared across two or more component SVMs [248]. This strongly suggests that the negative support vectors are well localised to each yaw segment.

For face detection across the pose sphere, the component SVMs can be arranged into a linear array to form a composite SVM decision function. Furthermore, such a view-based composite SVM face model can also be applied to pose estimation across views. Given that support vectors are localised along the face pose manifold, they are pose labelled and can be used to perform pose estimation using simple nearest neighbour matching as illustrated in Figure 6.14.

Experiments have shown that a view-based, composite SVM face model can perform both face detection across views and pose estimation with re-markable accuracy and speed [247, 248]. Such an SVM was trained using just over 2000 face images and 6000 near-faces across the view sphere between $-90°$ to $+90°$ in yaw and $-30°$ to $+30°$ in tilt. Figures 7.15 and 7.16 show some examples of both multi-view face detection and pose estimation on novel faces using this face model. These computations are all performed at near frame rate with modest hardware.

6.7   Biological Perspectives

Perrett and co-workers have studied many cells in the superior temporal sulcus of monkeys which are responsive to views of the head but which do not respond to other control objects [262, 263]. The majority of these cells were selective for pose with different cells responding maximally to different views. Although cells were tuned to a whole range of views (y-axis rotation), there was an overall statistical preference for four views: frontal, back and profiles, compared with intermediate views. These view-specific cells were broadly tuned and on average reduced their response to half when the head rotated 60° away from the preferred view. There were also cells tuned for x-axis rotation and these generalised across y-axis rotation i.e. a cell responding to a raised head did so whether the head was frontal, profile or back. There are cells which respond only to left profile or only to right profile, confirming that these cells are involved in visual analysis rather than setting up some emotional response which would be the same for the two profiles. These pose-specific cells were also able to generalise their responses across changes in image-plane orientation, scale and illumination. There are also face-selective cells which respond to all poses of the head. It was suggested that these pose-invariant cells might pool the responses of the different pose-specific cells. In other words, the cells might together constitute a multi-view based representation of the 3D face.

A further intriguing finding is that cells responsive to frontal views were found to clump together while cells responsive to profile views were found in other distinct clumps. There are also clumps of cells processing other types of information in the same area of the brain so this brain area is not face-specific. However, the clumping does indicate a distinct anatomical substrate for face processing.

6.8   Discussion

The problems of pose-invariant face detection and pose estimation are intimately related. We have argued that explicit pose estimation is in itself

useful. This will be borne out when we consider other visual tasks later
in the book. Appearance-based representation and in particular, template-
based representation is both effective and sufficient for performing detection
and pose estimation. Pose manifolds were visualised and investigated using
principal components analysis. We have demonstrated that template-based
schemes, especially if templates are filtered using Gabor or similar oriented
kernels, enable effective and robust pose estimation to be performed in
real-time using very moderate computing resources.

Like most living objects in the natural world, humans and their faces
are essentially *dynamic objects* in the sense that they are almost always
in motion, reacting to both internal and external change and events. Our
perception of faces inevitably involves a sense of time and continuity in order
to take advantage of spatio-temporal context. This often involves a process
of prediction and anticipation. Perception of objects and faces in particular
should not and cannot merely be a mental act on *isolated snapshots* of the
visual world. It is not difficult to consider, for instance, that the consistency
and robustness in both perceptual grouping and face detection across the
view-sphere will be greatly improved if temporal continuity and prediction
are used to provide additional constraints in the process [19, 117, 135,
223, 280]. In the next chapter, we examine the nature of spatio-temporal
information that can be used in face perception over time. In particular,
we describe methods for temporal prediction and adaption of models which
can be applied to track detected faces over space and time.

7   Prediction and Adaptation

Time is defined so that motion looks simple.

— *John Archibald Wheeler, Gravitation*

Our behaviour dictates that we are inevitably almost always in motion. A dynamic scenario imposes constraints on the expected motion and appearance of the people to be tracked and recognised. Such a phenomenon implies that *dynamic perception* of humans is necessary if we are to account for the nature of their behaviour and intent. What then is dynamic perception? Let us start with an example scenario and explore its implications for the perception of moving faces.

Suppose a static camera is observing a corridor or narrow passage between rooms. In this environment people invariably walk almost directly towards or away from the camera. Unless they meet someone or are otherwise distracted they tend to move at a fairly constant speed.

An example of a girl in such a scenario can be seen in Figure 7.1 (a). The motion of the face in this sequence was examined by manually locating the eyes and the centre of the upper lip in each frame. Figure 7.1 (b) shows the vertical and horizontal translation of these facial feature points over 145 frames of the sequence. Although the girl walked with approximately constant speed, the motion of the face in the image exhibits acceleration as the girl approaches. The face moves up the image because the camera is mounted below head-height. The vertical acceleration appears to be smooth. However, this will depend on the temporal scale considered.

In Figure 7.2 vertical position is shown for every frame between 100 and 130. The discontinuities due to the oscillatory walking action can be clearly seen approximately every 10 frames (the time for one stride). Figure 7.2 (c) shows how the scale of the face, measured as vertical distance between eyes and mouth, increases over time.

(a)

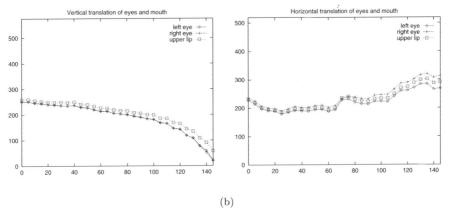

(b)

Figure 7.1   (a) Frames from an example sequence of a girl walking towards a static camera. (b) The trajectories of the eyes and mouth over 145 frames.

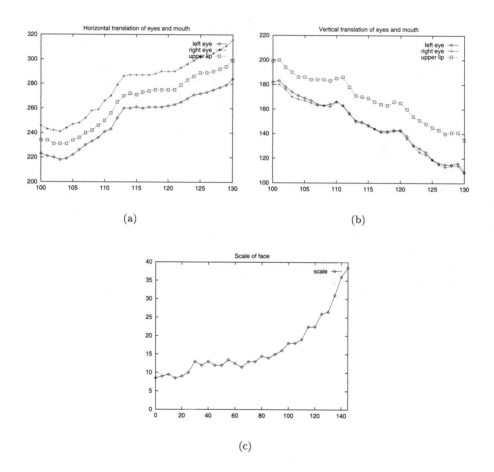

Figure 7.2 (a) Horizontal and (b) vertical trajectories of the eyes and mouth over 30 frames. (c) The scale of the face over 145 frames (i.e. vertical distance from eyes to mouth).

In addition to faces, consider tracking the centroid, scale and aspect ratio of a human body. The centroid will again translate with accelerations in the image depending on the geometry of the ground-plane and camera. The centroid, scale and aspect ratio will all be affected by changes in body posture due to actions such as crouching or pointing. For instance, in a typical teleconferencing scenario, people gesture and communicate with head and body movements which are difficult to predict without high-level knowledge.

In the preceding chapters we have discussed focus of attention, face detection and face pose estimation with the emphasis placed on determining the spatial position and orientation of faces in a given visual scene. Here we consider the use of temporal information and describe how by exploiting spatio-temporal context, faces can be detected and tracked efficiently and robustly in dynamic scenes. Dynamic filtering is used to track the position and orientation of faces based on noisy image measurements. Prediction is used to narrow down the search space for matching leading to increased computational efficiency and improved accuracy.

We begin by describing the spatio-temporal trajectory exhibited by a moving person as a first-order Markov process under which salient *phases* or states of the movement can be explicitly modelled over time. Under this framework temporal changes are treated as state vector transformations according to the probabilities associated with each state. First-order Markov processes that combine prior information and observations can be modelled using Kalman filters [31, 34, 36, 181], Hidden Markov Models (HMM) [131, 283, 289] and *Con*ditional *Den*sity propag*ation* (Condensation) [136, 170, 171].

7.1   Temporal Observations

Kalman filters, HMMs and Condensation provide useful techniques for object tracking and have been used quite widely in computer vision. Their recursive nature makes them well suited to real-time applications and their ability to predict provides further computational efficiency by reducing image search.

The actual state vector $\mathbf{q}_t$ of the object or region being tracked at time t is unknown. The goal of tracking is to estimate this state from noisy observations. At each time frame, t, a vector of noisy observations, $\mathbf{x}_t$, is usually measured from the object or region being tracked. For example, in the case of the Gaussian clusters grouped from motion or colour, each cluster has four observations: the image co-ordinates of the centroid (x, y), the scale (s) and the aspect ratio (a):

$$\mathbf{x}_t = [x_t \, y_t \, s_t \, a_t]^{\mathsf{T}} \tag{7.1}$$

Here we convert the two variance parameters (which represent the spatial extent of the region) into scale and aspect ratio. This is motivated by the fact that the variance parameters are highly correlated while s_t and a_t can in general be modelled as independent random processes.

Alternatively, we can consider tracking near-frontal upright faces, this gives rise to three observations in each frame, namely the position and scale of the face in the image:

$$\mathbf{x}_t = [x_t \, y_t \, s_t]^{\mathsf{T}} \tag{7.2}$$

Similarly, in order to track upright faces rotating in depth, at least five observations are useful, namely the position and scale in the image as well as the rotations in depth about the horizontal and vertical axis:

$$\mathbf{x}_t = [x_t \, y_t \, s_t \, \theta_t \, \phi_t]^{\mathsf{T}} \tag{7.3}$$

If instead we wish to estimate the affine motion of a face then $\mathbf{x}$ is a six-dimensional vector.

7.2 Propagating First-order Markov Processes

We would like to build a system that can track a face based on a finite sequence of ordered observations $\mathcal{X}_T = \{\mathbf{x}_1, \ldots, \mathbf{x}_t, \ldots, \mathbf{x}_T\}$ where $\mathbf{x}_t$ denotes the observation vector $\mathbf{x}$ at time t. Furthermore, we would like to predict the observations as this will constrain matching in the next frame, making tracking efficient and reliable. Markov processes can be used to describe statistical dynamic systems with temporal history by a sequence of states.

Let us assume that the conditional probability of state $\mathbf{q}_t$ given $\mathbf{q}_{t-1}$ is independent of its former history $\mathcal{Q}_{t-2} = \{\mathbf{q}_1, \mathbf{q}_2, \ldots, \mathbf{q}_{t-2}\}$, i.e.

$$p(\mathbf{q}_t|\mathbf{q}_{t-1}) = p(\mathbf{q}_t|\mathcal{Q}_{t-1}) \tag{7.4}$$

Furthermore, let us also assume that a conditional observation probability $p(\mathbf{x}_t|\mathbf{q}_t)$ is independent of the observation history $\mathcal{X}_{t-1} =$

$\{\mathbf{x}_1, \ldots, \mathbf{x}_{t-2}, \mathbf{x}_{t-1}\}$ and is therefore equal to the conditional observation probability given the history, i.e.

$$p(\mathbf{x}_t|\mathbf{q}_t) = p(\mathbf{x}_t|\mathbf{q}_t, \mathcal{X}_{t-1}) \tag{7.5}$$

One can then *propagate* the state probability $p(\mathbf{q}_t|\mathcal{X}_t)$ using Bayes' rule as follows:

$$p(\mathbf{q}_t|\mathcal{X}_t) = \int p(\mathbf{x}_t|\mathbf{q}_t)\, p(\mathbf{q}_t|\mathcal{X}_{t-1}) \tag{7.6}$$

where $p(\mathbf{q}_t|\mathcal{X}_{t-1})$ is the prior from the accumulated observation history up to time $t-1$ and $p(\mathbf{x}_t|\mathbf{q}_t)$ is the conditional observation density. The prior density $p(\mathbf{q}_t|\mathcal{X}_{t-1})$ for accumulated observation history can be regarded as a prediction taken from the posterior at the previous time step, $p(\mathbf{q}_{t-1}|\mathcal{X}_{t-1})$, and the state transition probability, $p(\mathbf{q}_t|\mathbf{q}_{t-1})$:

$$p(\mathbf{q}_t|\mathcal{X}_{t-1}) = \int p(\mathbf{q}_t|\mathbf{q}_{t-1})\, p(\mathbf{q}_{t-1}|\mathcal{X}_{t-1}) \tag{7.7}$$

In the case of Kalman filters, state probability is modelled by a single Gaussian density. This Gaussian density is propagated over time and its mean is taken to be the most probable state. In Condensation, Equation (7.7) is implemented using factored sampling and the posterior $p(\mathbf{q}_t|\mathcal{X}_{t-1})$ is approximated by a fixed number of state density samples [170]. The prediction is more accurate as the number of samples increases but there is a corresponding increase in computational cost.

In a hidden Markov model sequences are modelled by assuming that the observations depend upon a discrete, *hidden* state, q_t. The HMM hidden states are indexed by a single multinomial label that can take one of K discrete values, $q_t \in \{1, \ldots, K\}$. Each of the hidden states has its own conditional probability density function $p(\mathbf{x}|q_k)$. The conditional probability of hidden state q_t given q_{t-1} is independent of its former history $\mathcal{Q}_{t-2} = \{q_1, q_2, \ldots, q_{t-2}\}$. The state transition probabilities $P(q_t|q_{t-1})$ for an HMM can be specified by a single $K \times K$ transition matrix. It can be shown that both Kalman filters and HMMs are special cases of Condensation.

7.3   Kalman Filters

A Kalman filter models the state probability density function $p(\mathbf{q}_t)$ as a single Gaussian function. Therefore, at each time t, a mean $\boldsymbol{\mu}_t$ and a covariance matrix $\boldsymbol{\Sigma}_t$ are estimated to define this Gaussian. The most probable state at time t is then taken to be $\mathbf{q}_t = \boldsymbol{\mu}_t$ while $\boldsymbol{\Sigma}_t$ characterises the uncertainty of this estimate.

The Gaussian density function is propagated over time by fusing predictions of its parameters and predictions of the observations with the actual observations $\mathbf{x}_t$. This fusion process weights predictions and observations according to their estimated uncertainties. The weighting factors used are known as the *Kalman gain*, $\mathbf{K}_t$. The update equations used to propagate the Gaussian density function have the following form:

$$\boldsymbol{\mu}_t = \boldsymbol{\mu}_t^* + \mathbf{K}_t(\mathbf{x}_t - \mathbf{x}_t^*) \tag{7.8}$$

$$\boldsymbol{\Sigma}_t = \boldsymbol{\Sigma}_t^* - \mathbf{K}_t \mathbf{H} \boldsymbol{\Sigma}_t^* \tag{7.9}$$

where $\boldsymbol{\mu}_t^*$, $\boldsymbol{\Sigma}_t^*$ and $\mathbf{x}_t^*$ are predictions and $\mathbf{H}$ transforms a state vector into an observation vector, i.e. $\mathbf{x}_t = \mathbf{H}\mathbf{q}_t$. Further details of the Kalman filter are given in Appendix C. In order to use a Kalman filter to propagate a Gaussian density function, one needs to know how to predict the Gaussian's parameters. In other words we need to define $p(\mathbf{q}_t|\mathbf{q}_{t-1})$.

If the state of the object being tracked is inherently unpredictable or if the state is expected to remain constant then we can simply model its state as constant and treat any change in state as random (unmodelled) noise [77, 227]. In this case the Gaussian state density is predicted as follows:

$$\boldsymbol{\mu}_t^* = \boldsymbol{\mu}_{t-1} \tag{7.10}$$

$$\boldsymbol{\Sigma}_t^* = \boldsymbol{\Sigma}_{t-1} + \mathbf{G}_{t-1} \tag{7.11}$$

where $\mathbf{G}$ is a constant matrix that accounts for unmodelled change.

If we extend the state vector by also estimating the first derivatives, we can perform prediction that takes into account the rate of change. This is done by extending the state vector to: $\mathbf{q} = [q_1, \dot{q}_1, q_2, \dot{q}_2, \ldots q_K, \dot{q}_K]^{\mathsf{T}}$. Details of higher-order prediction of the Gaussian density function are given in Appendix C.

7.4   Propagating Non-Gaussian Conditional Densities

Since Kalman filters are based on a single Gaussian state density which is
unimodal, they cannot represent simultaneous, multiple hypotheses. Condensation, on the other hand, does not make such a strong parametric assumption about the form of the state density, $p(\mathbf{q}_t)$, and can therefore track
multiple, ambiguous targets simultaneously over time [170]. However, based
on the accumulated history of the current observations $\mathcal{X}_t$ alone without
any prior knowledge, the state propagation density $p(\mathbf{q}_t|\mathbf{q}_{t-1})$ is usually
given as the previous estimations plus arbitrary Gaussian noise. Conse-
quently, meaningful estimation of the history accumulated prior $p(\mathbf{q}_t|\mathcal{X}_{t-1})$
can only be obtained by propagating a very large sample set of conditional
densities over time [29]. As a result, the prediction can be both expensive
and sensitive to observation noise. In order to reduce the required number
of samples for the propagation and also to cope with noise and variance in
observation, priors on temporal structures learned from training examples
should be used.

7.4.1   Learning Priors using HMMs and EM

One solution to the problem of over-sampling in Condensation is to
learn and impose *a priori* knowledge of both observation covariance
and the underlying state transition structure over time in order to constrain ambiguities in the sampling and propagation of observation conditional state densities. This is the notion of propagating observation
conditional densities *with priors* (based on *landmarks*) over time [136,
363]. An HMM serves this purpose well. In other words, an HMM can
be used to learn the prior knowledge of both observation covariance and
state transition probabilities between a set of sparse and discrete landmark
locations in the state space in order to constrain the ambiguity in continuous propagation of conditional state densities over time. An HMM can
be trained to capture both the observation covariance and the transition
density distributions between a set of most significant landmarks of a given
set of observation sequences. Details for training an HMM model are given
in Appendix C.

   Let us define the Condensation state vector at time t as $\mathbf{q}_t = \{q_t, \lambda\}$,
given by the current hidden Markov state q_t for a model λ. An HMM model
$\lambda(\mathbf{A}, \mathbf{b}, \boldsymbol{\pi})$ is fully described by a set of probabilistic parameters as follows:

(1) $\mathbf{A}$ is a matrix of state transition probabilities where element a_{jk} describes the probability $P(q_{t+1} = k \mid q_t = j)$ and $\sum_{j=1}^{K} a_{jk} = 1$.
(2) $\mathbf{b}$ is a vector of observation density functions $b_k(\mathbf{x}_t)$ for each state k where $b_k(\mathbf{x}_t) = p(\mathbf{x}_t \mid q_t = k)$.
(3) $\boldsymbol{\pi}$ is a vector of initial probabilities of being in state k at time $t = 1$, where $\sum_{k=1}^{K} \pi_k = 1$.

By training HMMs on a set of observed trajectories, *a priori* knowledge on both the state propagation and conditional observation density can be estimated by assigning the hidden Markov state transition probabilities $p(q_t = k \mid q_{t-1} = j)$ of a trained model λ to the Condensation state propagation densities of

$$p(\mathbf{q}_t \mid \mathbf{q}_{t-1}) = p(q_t = k \mid q_{t-1} = j, \lambda) = a_{jk} \qquad (7.12)$$

Similarly, the prior on the observation conditional density $p(\mathbf{x}_t \mid \mathbf{q}_t)$ is given by the Markov observation densities at each hidden state

$$p(\mathbf{x}_t \mid \mathbf{q}_t) = p(\mathbf{x}_t \mid q_t = k, \lambda) = b_k(\mathbf{x}_t) \qquad (7.13)$$

The Markov observation density at each Markov state $b_j(\mathbf{x}_t)$ is used to provide the prior knowledge about the observation covariance. As a result, the process of both sampling and propagating Condensation states is made both more focused (guided) and robust against observation noise [136, 363].

7.4.2   Observation Augmented Density Propagation

Recognition can be made more adaptable and robust if the current observation vector is also taken into account before prediction. Let us consider the state propagation density $p(\mathbf{q}_t \mid \mathbf{q}_{t-1})$ in Equation (7.7) to be augmented by the current observation, $p(\mathbf{q}_t \mid \mathbf{q}_{t-1}, \mathbf{x}_t) = p(\mathbf{q}_t \mid \mathbf{q}_{t-1}, \mathcal{X}_t)$. Assuming future observations have no effect on past states, $p(\mathbf{q}_{t-1} \mid \mathcal{X}_t) = p(\mathbf{q}_{t-1} \mid \mathcal{X}_{t-1})$, the prediction process of Equation (7.7) can then be replaced by

$$\begin{aligned}
p(\mathbf{q}_t \mid \mathcal{X}_t) &= \sum_{\mathbf{q}_{t-1}} c_t \, p(\mathbf{q}_t \mid \mathbf{q}_{t-1}, \mathbf{x}_t) \, p(\mathbf{q}_{t-1} \mid \mathcal{X}_{t-1}) \\
&= \sum_{\mathbf{q}_{t-1}} \kappa_t \, p(\mathbf{x}_t \mid \mathbf{q}_t) p(\mathbf{q}_t \mid \mathbf{q}_{t-1}) p(\mathbf{q}_{t-1} \mid \mathbf{x}_{t-1}) \qquad (7.14)
\end{aligned}$$

where $k_t = \frac{1}{p(\mathbf{x}_t|\mathbf{q}_{t-1})}$ and

$$
\begin{aligned}
p(\mathbf{q}_t|\mathbf{q}_{t-1}, \mathbf{x}_t) &= \frac{p(\mathbf{x}_t, \mathbf{q}_t|\mathbf{q}_{t-1})}{p(\mathbf{x}_t|\mathbf{q}_{t-1})} = \frac{p(\mathbf{x}_t|\mathbf{q}_t, \mathbf{q}_{t-1})p(\mathbf{q}_t|\mathbf{q}_{t-1})}{p(\mathbf{x}_t|\mathbf{q}_{t-1})} \\
&= \frac{p(\mathbf{x}_t|\mathbf{q}_t)p(\mathbf{q}_t|\mathbf{q}_{t-1})}{p(\mathbf{x}_t|\mathbf{q}_{t-1})}
\end{aligned} \tag{7.15}
$$

Given that the observation and state transitions are constrained by the underlying HMM, the state transition density is then given by

$$
p(\mathbf{q}_t|\mathbf{q}_{t-1}, \mathbf{x}_t) = p(y_t = j|y_{t-1} = i, \mathbf{x}_t) = \frac{a_{ij}^\lambda b_j^\lambda(\mathbf{x}_t)}{\sum_{n=1}^N a_{in}^\lambda b_n^\lambda(\mathbf{x}_t)} \tag{7.16}
$$

The observation augmented prediction unifies the processes of innovation and prediction in Condensation given by Equations (7.6) and (7.7). Without observation augmentation, Condensation performs a *blind prediction* based on observation history alone. Augmented prediction takes the current observation into account and adapts the prior to perform a *guided search* in the state space for prediction. This process not only improves accuracy but also reduces the number of samples needed for propagation and therefore improves recognition efficiency [136, 363]

7.5   Tracking Attended Regions

The number of people in a scene is not usually known *a priori*. In general, people can enter (or leave) the scene or become fully occluded (or unoccluded) at any time. Therefore, it is often desirable to dynamically initialise, maintain and terminate tracking of multiple regions of interest. Separate non-overlapping regions of interest are located using perceptual grouping (see Chapter 4). Once a region is being tracked, prediction is used to constrain the grouping process. Nevertheless, grouping can be inconsistent with regions temporarily splitting and merging. Each region can be tracked using a state vector of the form $\mathbf{q} = [x\, y\, s\, a]^\mathsf{T}$. Let $p_m(\mathbf{q})$ denote the state probability density estimated for the mth region. We would like to maintain a temporally consistent list of regions' state densities: $\mathcal{Q} = \{p_1(\mathbf{q}), p_2(\mathbf{q}), \ldots, p_m(\mathbf{q}), \ldots\}$. Let us consider one method for achieving this aim. At time $t+1$, a new frame is captured and grouping must be performed based on the pre-attentive cues and the predicted list $\mathcal{Q}_{t+1}^*$. If we use a Kalman filter, the state densities are Gaussian and the covariance matrices estimate uncertainty. The predicted uncertainties can be used to define search windows within which grouping is performed. Grouping is also then performed on the remainder of the image to check for new regions. This results in a new list of observed groups $\mathcal{X}_t = \{\mathbf{x}_1, \mathbf{x}_2, \ldots, \mathbf{x}_m, \ldots\}$. The list $\mathcal{Q}_t$ is now updated by associating its groups with those in list $\mathcal{X}_t$ and applying the appropriate update rules given by Equations (C.30) and (C.31) (see Appendix C). The association of groups is achieved using time-symmetric matching [322]. Firstly, each group in $\mathcal{Q}_{t+1}^*$ is matched with the most similar group in $\mathcal{X}_t$ (forward matching). Secondly, each matched group in $\mathcal{X}_t$ is matched uniquely with the oldest candidate match in $\mathcal{Q}_{t+1}^*$ (reverse matching). In this manner, groups are consistently tracked even if they are sometimes erroneously split into several smaller groups.

In order to perform forward matching we need to define similarity between groups. When each group is modelled as a Gaussian we can use a test of equality of the means of two Gaussians [24]. Accurately tracking the motion and form of an articulated and deformable object such as a clothed human body is a difficult research problem. However, our aim here is not to delineate, characterise or analyse human actions or gestures. Rather, it is to track the position and extent of the body and head consistently enough to allow focusing of attention for alignment and analysis of the face. This aim is well served by simple, low-order region models such as Gaussian regions which yield efficient and reasonably robust focus of attention over time.

A region is ignored as noise by higher-level processes until it has been detected and tracked for κ_1 consecutive frames. At this point the group is assigned a *persistence*, κ_2, and will be maintained even in the absence of a matching group for up to κ_2 frames. This allows objects to be tracked for short periods of time despite grouping errors or an absence of image evidence. The parameters κ_1 and κ_2 can be determined by hand and depend upon the expected frame rate.

For selective visual attention, motion is used as one of the common cues (Chapter 4). Regions of motion can be grouped and modelled as Gaussians. However, in individual frames, motion estimation is often noisy. Temporal filtering and prediction become necessary for robust tracking. Figure 7.3 (a) shows an example in which motion regions are tracked using a zeroth-order Kalman filter for the aspect ratio (a_t) and a 2nd-order Kalman filter for the centroid and scale (x_t, y_t, s_t). In this way, multiple people are successfully tracked as they move through a scene. However, when people occlude one another, they can still be grouped together mistakenly as a single region if motion as a cue is used alone.

Similarly to motion, colour models are used for focusing attention on skin-coloured regions and colour mixture models allow multi-coloured regions such as clothing to be modelled. Grouped colour regions can be tracked similarly to the motion regions. However, in many scenarios the face and hands move quite unpredictably so a zeroth-order temporal predictor is in fact usually employed to track region centroids. Figure 7.3(b) illustrates some of the advantages of colour-based tracking. A single skin-coloured region corresponding to a face is tracked against a cluttered background while the camera pans and zooms out. The tracker's ability to deal with changes in scale, large rotations in depth and partial occlusion are all clearly demonstrated. In Chapter 4, it was shown how motion and colour cues can be fused to yield grouped regions corresponding to moving, appropriately coloured regions. Figure 7.4 shows tracking based on these fused regions. The resulting system tracks faces and hands when they are in motion.

7.6   Adaptive Colour Models

We have seen how colour mixture models can be used to perform real-time tracking given reasonably constrained illumination conditions. However, the apparent colour of an object depends upon the illumination conditions, the viewing geometry and the camera parameters, all of which can vary over time. Approaches to colour constancy attempt to reconstruct the incident light and adjust the observed reflectance accordingly [118]. In practice, these methods are only applicable in highly constrained environments. Instead, we can use a stochastic approach for modelling colour dynamically in which colour mixture models adapt to accommodate changes in the viewing conditions. This facilitates robust, real-time tracking under variations in illumination, viewing geometry and camera parameters. The assumption made is that the number of components needed in the mixture will not change over time due to the viewing conditions, rather the parameters of the fixed number of components are adapted. Alternative approaches are possible in which components are added and deleted adaptively [278].

Figure 7.5 illustrates a colour mixture model of a person's colour distribution adapting over time. At each time frame, a new set of pixels is

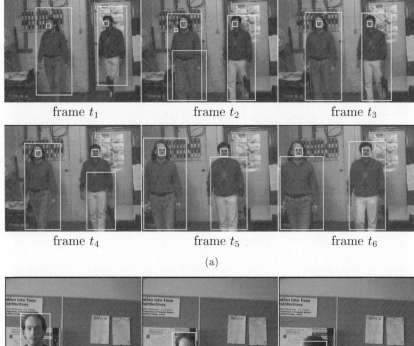

(a)

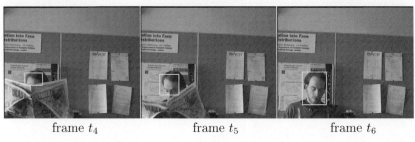

(b)

Figure 7.3 (a) Two people are tracked based on motion cues using time-symmetric matching with Kalman filtering and prediction. The face regions have been estimated using a multi-layer perceptron. (b) A face can be robustly tracked under partial occlusion against a cluttered background.

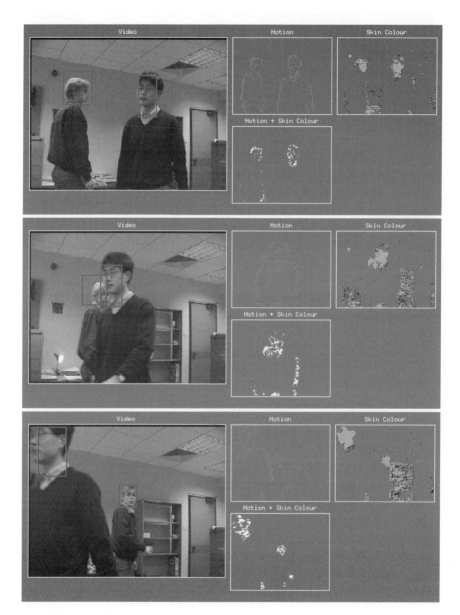

Figure 7.4 An example of tracking multiple faces and coping with total occlusion using motion and colour fusion.

Figure 7.5 An example of a Gaussian mixture colour model adapting over time. Left: face regions overlaid on the image frames. Interlacing is evident due to fast camera motion. Right: colourmaps showing the corresponding colour distributions in HS-space. Ellipses show the Gaussian components.

sampled from the tracked region and can be used to update the mixture model. These colour pixel data are assumed to sample a slowly varying non-stationary signal. Details of an adaptive colour mixture model are given in Appendix C.

7.7 Selective Adaptation

An obvious problem with adapting a colour model during tracking is the lack of ground-truth. Any colour-based tracker can lose the object it is tracking due, for example, to occlusion. If such errors go undetected the colour model will adapt to image regions which do not correspond to the object. In order to alleviate this problem, observed log-likelihood measurements can be used to detect erroneous frames. Colour data from these frames are not used to adapt the object's colour model.

The adaptive mixture model seeks to maximise the log-likelihood of the colour data over time. The normalised log-likelihood, L, of the M data points $\mathcal{X} = \{\mathbf{x}_1, \ldots \mathbf{x}_M\}$, observed from the object, $\mathcal{O}$, at time t, is given by:

$$L_t = \frac{1}{M} \sum_{\mathbf{x} \in \mathcal{X}} \log p(\mathbf{x}|\mathcal{O}) \qquad (7.17)$$

At each time frame, L_t is evaluated. If the tracker loses the object there is often a sudden, large drop in its value. This provides a way to detect tracker failure. Adaptation is then suspended until the object is again tracked with sufficiently high likelihood. A temporal filter is used to compute a threshold and adaptation is only performed when L_t is above threshold. The median, ν, and standard deviation, σ, of L are computed for the T most recent above-threshold frames. The threshold is set to $\nu - \kappa\sigma$, where κ is a constant.

In the following, we give a number of examples of applying such an adaptive colour model and highlight its advantages over the fixed models described earlier. In all the experiments described here, $\kappa = 1.5$ and $T = 2f$ where f denotes the frame rate in Hz. This implementation ran on a standard 200MHz Pentium PC platform with a Matrox Meteor frame-grabber. It performed tracking at approximately $f = 15$Hz.

Figure 7.6 illustrates the use of a mixture model for face tracking and the advantage of an adaptive model over a fixed model. In this sequence

(a)

(b)

Figure 7.6 (a) Frames from a sequence in which a face was tracked using a non-adaptive model. The apparent colour of the face changes due to (i) varying illumination and (ii) the camera's auto-iris mechanism which adjusts to the bright exterior light. (b) The same sequence tracked with an adaptive colour model. Here, the model adapts to cope with the change in apparent colour.

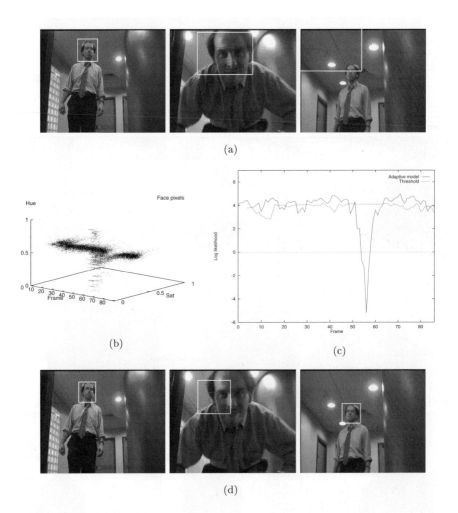

Figure 7.7 An example of erroneous model adaptation. (a) Sample images of a sequence at frames 45, 55 and 75. There is strong directional and exterior illumination in the scene. The walls have a fleshy tone. At around frame 55, the subject rapidly approaches the camera which is situated in a doorway, resulting in rapid changes in illumination, scale and auto-iris parameters. In this case, the model is allowed to adapt in every frame, resulting in failure at around frame 60. (b) A plot of the hue-saturation distribution over time. (c) Normalised log-likelihood measurements and the adaptation threshold. (d) Selective model adaptation applied to the sequence shown in (a).

Figure 7.8 Tracking a fast moving subject under changing lighting conditions using an active camera with pan/tilt actuators and a zoom lens. An adaptive skin colour model was used and tracking was performed at frame-rate on a standard 300MHz PC.

<table>
<tr><td>frame t_1</td><td>frame t_2</td><td>frame t_3</td></tr>
</table>

<table>
<tr><td>frame t_4</td><td>frame t_5</td><td>frame t_6</td></tr>
</table>

<table>
<tr><td>frame t_7</td><td>frame t_8</td><td>frame t_9</td></tr>
</table>

<table>
<tr><td>frame t_{10}</td><td>frame t_{11}</td><td>frame t_{12}</td></tr>
</table>

Figure 7.9 An example of tracking a subject with dark skin tone using an adaptive colour model.

the illumination conditions coupled with the camera's auto-iris mechanism resulted in large changes in the apparent colour of the face as the person approached the window. Towards the end of the sequence the face became very dark, making hue and saturation measurements unreliable. In Figure 7.6 (a), a non-adaptive model was trained on the first image of the sequence and used to track throughout. It was unable to cope with the varying conditions and failure eventually occurred. In Figure 7.6 (b), the model was allowed to adapt and successfully maintained lock on the face.

Figure 7.7 illustrates the advantage of selecting when to adapt. The person moved through challenging tracking conditions, before approaching the camera at close range (frames 50-60). Since the camera was placed in the doorway of another room with its own lighting conditions, the person's face underwent a large, sudden and temporary change in apparent colour. When adaptation was performed in every frame, this sudden change had a drastic effect on the model and ultimately led the tracker to fail when the person receded into the corridor. With selective adaptation, these sudden changes were treated as outliers and adaptation was suspended, permitting the tracker to recover.

Figures 7.5 and 7.8 depict the tracking of a subject moving quickly through strong lighting changes and across a wide range of views. An adaptive skin colour model can cope with large extrinsic variations and poor resolution as well as different skin tones (see Figure 7.9).

7.8 Tracking Faces

The use of MLP and SVM-based face models was introduced for face detection in dynamic scenes (Chapter 5). A face detection process can be bootstrapped using tracked regions of attention. Furthermore, once a face is detected, it can be tracked from frame to frame using correlation. At each frame, a template of the face is stored and used to search for the face in the next frame. The face model is then used to verify that the located template match is indeed still a face. If the face becomes obscured for several consecutive frames resulting in an absence of high confidence face detections, the tracker can lose lock on the face. Recovery then needs to be performed using the face region estimated from the motion/colour tracker.

Figure 7.10 (a) shows an example sequence of a girl being tracked as she approaches the camera. The girl's motion was successfully detected

(a)

(b)

Figure 7.10   (a) A girl is tracked for recognition as she approaches the camera. Bounding boxes for the Kalman filtered motion region and the associated tracked face region are shown overlaid on every 15th frame. The face is shown centred and normalised in scale every 5th frame. (b) Two people are tracked as they walk along a corridor.

and a Kalman filtered region established within the first 15 frames of the sequence. The face was then reliably tracked with the exception of a few frames. At about frame 70 the girl turned her face suddenly to her left and the tracker lost her face. This resulted in inaccurate face boxes with lower confidence values. The tracker had recovered lock on the face by frame 85. A sequence of accurately segmented face images was obtained by simply discarding any images with confidence values below a threshold of 0.99.

Figure 7.10 (b) shows an example of the system tracking two people as they approach along a corridor. This scene has multiple interior and exterior sources of illumination. There are additional difficulties caused by the reflected motion on the polished floor as well as moving shadows. However, the people are successfully tracked with many frames of the sequences yielding accurate face segmentations. Three frames from the sequence are shown. In the first, the facial resolution is very poor and face tracking is not always accurate. The motion region for the person on the right-hand-side is artificially elongated due to motion reflected in the floor but this does not prevent correct localisation of his face. In the second frame shown, feedback from the face detector (MLP) has been used to prevent the two people being grouped as a single moving object. The confidence in the face detections is low because the faces are far from their frontal views. However, the resulting face images are still well centred as a result of recent high confidence detections. In the third frame shown, one of the people has just walked out of the field of view. The system still attempts to find a matching motion region for a few more frames in case the person has ceased to move.

7.9   Pose Tracking

If pose estimation is based on feature-based correspondence, those features can be tracked over time [7, 8, 14, 221, 231]. On the other hand, if appearance-based templates are used, matching all model views at all possible poses in each frame can be prohibitively expensive. Furthermore, face views at different poses can be confused with one another, leading to false maxima. Therefore, temporal continuity assumptions are used. One simple but effective method is to define search intervals for each of the parameters in pose estimation. These search intervals are centred on the expected parameter values which are obtained using prediction. It is im-

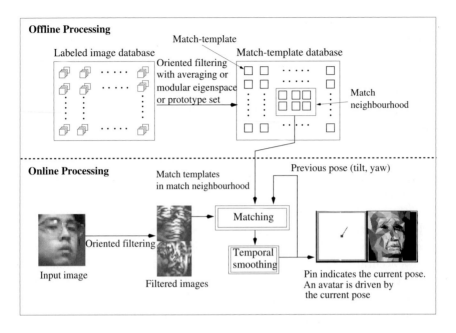

Figure 7.11 A pose tracking system.

portant to set the width of these search intervals appropriately. If search intervals are decreased then frame-rate increases but the correct match might be excluded. Conversely, if search intervals are increased, frame-rate drops and false maxima become more likely. Furthermore, a face model consists of views labelled with poses at discrete intervals so the pose estimates provided by the matching process are similarly quantised. This quantisation becomes especially apparent if the pose estimates are used to drive a synthetic head, or *avatar*, since the avatar motion will be discontinuous. In this case, it is helpful to smooth the pose estimates using a temporal filter. For example, tilt can be estimated as

$$\tilde{\theta}_t = (1 - \kappa)\tilde{\theta}_{t-1} + \kappa\theta_t \tag{7.18}$$

where $\tilde{\theta}_t$ is the smoothed tilt estimate at time t, θ_t is the tilt measurement provided by matching, and κ controls the amount of smoothing ($0 \leq \kappa \leq 1$). Figure 7.11 illustrates the design of a pose tracking system.

In the case of full six degrees of freedom pose estimation, the search can be centred on the state

$$\mathbf{q}_t^* = [x_t \, y_t \, s_t \, \theta_t \, \phi_t \, r_t]$$ (7.19)

predicted for that frame. If scale and image-plane rotation are assumed to be approximately constant, the extent of the search space around $\mathbf{q}_t^*$ is then initialised to

$$\mathbf{s}_0 = [d_x \, d_y \, 0 \, d_\theta \, d_\phi \, 0]$$ (7.20)

If no strong match is found in a frame, the search space is expanded:

$$\mathbf{s} = \mathbf{s} + [\Delta d_x \, \Delta d_y \, 0 \, \Delta d_\theta \, \Delta d_\phi \, 0]$$ (7.21)

Whenever a strong match is found the search space is then reinitialised: $\mathbf{s} = \mathbf{s}_0$. Only a subset of the template is typically used in any given frame thereby increasing the frame-rate and improving robustness. In general, increasing the number of templates used makes a false match more likely. However, decreasing the number of templates makes finding no good match a more probable outcome. The search parameters d_θ and d_ϕ are set to address this trade-off. A further trade-off exists in setting d_x and d_y. Large values slow down the achievable frame-rate which in turn increases the visual motion between frames. Small values allow faster frame-rates but might not allow the face to be found. In the simplest version of the system, the predicted state $\mathbf{q}_t^*$ for frame t can be just the estimated state for frame $t-1$. This approach permitted successful tracking. Alternatively, a Kalman filter can be used to dynamically adjust the search space.

7.9.1 Person-specific Pose Tracking

A person-specific model can be based on template images of an individual face. Such a model can be used to perform pose tracking as outlined above. Some example frames showing tracking using this technique are shown in Figure 7.12. Here, in order to match both θ and ϕ with good precision, the vertically and horizontally filtered images are combined to provide sensitivity to rotations around both the x and y axes. Two ways in which to combine them are:

(1) Both vertical and horizontal responses are used to perform matching and pose estimation in each frame.

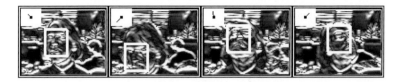

(a)

(b)

Figure 7.12 (a) A head is tracked using templates filtered with a horizontally oriented kernel. The best matching templates' bounding boxes are shown overlaid on a filtered sequence. (b) An unfiltered sequence is shown here for visualisation. The pin diagram indicates estimated pose.

(2) The vertical and horizontal responses are "interlaced" in time. Matching is performed using vertical responses in the odd numbered frames and horizontal responses in the even numbered frames.

7.9.2 Person-independent Pose Tracking

Given a database of multiple views of different people, a generic, view-based appearance model can be learned for tracking head pose in a person-independent manner. In practice, the number of examples available at each view is small. However, appearance models based on mean templates or on similarity to a limited number (in tens) of prototype faces at multiple views can be adopted [99, 100, 101, 102, 103].

A face image $\mathbf{x}$ at pose $\boldsymbol{\gamma} = [\theta \ \phi]$ is then represented as a vector of similarities to a set of prototype faces at the same pose , $\boldsymbol{\alpha}_i^\gamma = (\alpha_1^\gamma, \alpha_2^\gamma, \ldots, \alpha_K^\gamma)$, where

$$\alpha_k^\gamma = h(\mathbf{x}, \mathbf{x}_k^\gamma) \tag{7.22}$$

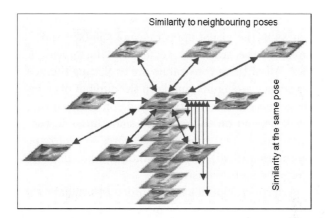

Figure 7.13   Similarity measures at different neighbouring poses and at a specific pose over time.

and h is a similarity function such as Pearson's linear correlation coefficient given in Chapter 6 (Equation 6.2). Given that face images at the frontal view can be readily detected, let a vector, $\boldsymbol{\alpha}$, of similarities to prototypes for a detected face image at the frontal view be measured. Pose recognition and tracking can then be performed as follows. A sub-image extracted from the input image frame at location (x, y) is compared to each of the prototypes at pose $\boldsymbol{\gamma}$ to yield a vector of similarity values $\boldsymbol{\alpha}$. A search over these states is performed so as to maximise:

$$H_t(\boldsymbol{\gamma}) = ||\boldsymbol{\alpha}_t^{\gamma}|| + \kappa_1 \, h_1(\mathbf{x}, \mathbf{x}_{t-1}) + \kappa_2 \, h_2(\boldsymbol{\alpha}_t^{\gamma}, \boldsymbol{\alpha}_{t-1}) \qquad (7.23)$$

where $||\boldsymbol{\alpha}_t^{\gamma}||$ is the L_2 norm of the similarity vector at pose $\boldsymbol{\gamma}$ at time t. Function $h_1(\mathbf{x}, \mathbf{x}_{t-1})$ is the similarity measure between the detected face images at the same pose over two successive time frames (Figure 7.13). Function $h_2(\boldsymbol{\alpha}_t^{\gamma}, \boldsymbol{\alpha}_{t-1})$ is given by the projection (dot product) of the similarity vector measured at the previously estimated pose to that of the currently likely pose, i.e.

$$h_2(\boldsymbol{\alpha}_t^{\gamma}, \boldsymbol{\alpha}_{t-1}) = \frac{\boldsymbol{\alpha}_{t-1} \cdot \boldsymbol{\alpha}_t^{\gamma}}{||\boldsymbol{\alpha}_t^{\gamma}||} \qquad (7.24)$$

Maximising $H_t(\boldsymbol{\gamma})$ imposes two constraints. The first term maximises the magnitude of similarity in a neighbourhood centered at the likely pose at time t. It therefore performs a generic face matching at the likely pose at time t. The search process already imposes temporal constraints on the position and pose of the face. The second term in Equation (7.23) penalises changes in the visual appearance of the face and the third term penalises change in the similarity vector, i.e. in appearance relative to the prototypes. All of these constraints are exploiting temporal continuity. Together they reduce ambiguity and keep the number of erroneous matches low. The constants κ_1 and κ_2 control a trade-off between these factors and their values will depend on the expected smoothness in the pose change, variation in appearance and similarity measures to prototypes at different views. The norm used ($\|\boldsymbol{\alpha}\|$) was the L_2 norm although other norms could be used and may be more robust.

We have performed experiments in order to evaluate the appearance models' ability to estimate pose. The models used were (i) a person-specific model consisting of views of a single person's head, (ii) an average head model learned from views of 11 different people, (iii) a model based on similarity to prototypes in which 11 different people were used as the prototypes, and (iv) a view-based composite SVM as described in Section 6.6. Matching with the person-specific and the average head models was performed using Equation (7.23) with κ_2 set to zero. Matching with the similarity-based model was performed using Equation (7.23) with $\kappa_2 = 1.0$ and κ_1 set to zero. Testing was performed on sequences of people used to learn the models and then on sequences of novel people. Figures 7.14, 7.15 and 7.16 show a few examples of detecting the presence and tracking 3D pose of moving faces using a person-independent model and a view-based composite SVM model. The tracked pose was compared with the ground-truth provided by an electro-magnetic sensor. The mean absolute pose error (m.a.e.) over some 1300 frames from different sequences of different people moving in a pose range of $\pm 90°$ yaw and $\pm 30°$ tilt is shown in Table 7.1. It should be noted that the true face tilt in the test sequences occasionally exceeded the modelled $\pm 30°$ range (see the last example in Figure 7.14). Therefore, system error rates for operation within the modelled pose range are in fact better than those reported in Table 7.1. The errors under the column heading "known people" were obtained by running the system on sequences of people whose faces were used to learn the appearance model. The errors under the heading "novel people" were obtained on sequences of people not in the database. These give an indication of the ability to generalise to previously unseen people. It is worth pointing out that the ground-truth measured by the magnetic sensor has a m.a.e between $2.5°$ to $3.5°$.

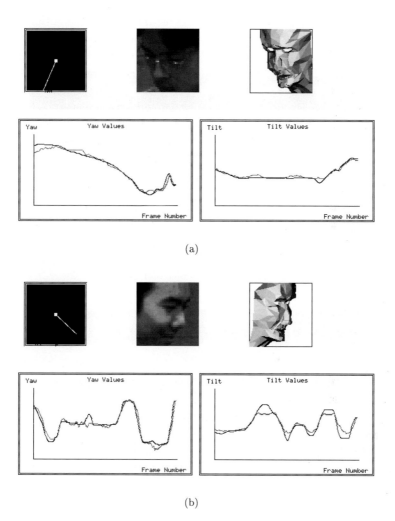

Figure 7.14 Face pose tracked by a person-independent face appearance model. The upper row of each screen-dump shows a pin diagram indicating the current pose estimate, the current matched input image and a simple avatar being controlled by the pose estimates. The lower row of each screen-dump shows plots of the estimated yaw (on the left) and tilt (on the right) over time. In these examples, the subjects wore an electromagnetic sensor so that pose ground-truth could be obtained. These ground-truth data are plotted in grey along with the pose estimates (in black) for comparison.

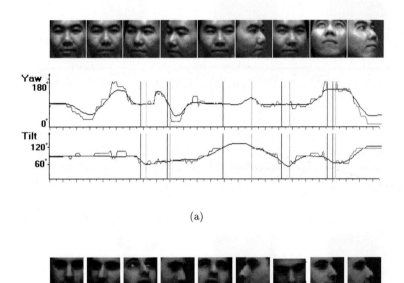

(a)

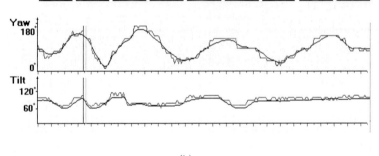

(b)

Figure 7.15 Detection and tracking of novel faces across views using a view-based, composite SVM. The pose in both tilt and yaw is tracked and shown as the grey plot under each example face. The ground-truth measured independently using an electro-magnetic sensor is shown in black. The mean error in the pose estimation is approximately 10° in yaw and 8° in tilt. The vertical lines along the pose plot over time indicate image frames where face detection failed.

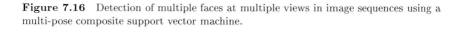

Figure 7.16 Detection of multiple faces at multiple views in image sequences using a multi-pose composite support vector machine.

Table 7.1 Generalisation to novel people in pose recognition and tracking. These m.a.e measures have between 2.5° to 3.5° noise due to the noise in the ground-truth provided by the magnetic sensor.

Appearance model	Known people		Novel people	
	ϕ m.a.e.	θ m.a.e.	ϕ m.a.e.	θ m.a.e.
Person-specific	9.4°	6.3°	24.6°	12.9°
Mean templates	5.7°	4.5°	11.7°	10.7°
Similarity measures	7.3°	3.7°	6.1°	6.1°
Composite SVM	9.2°	6.4°	10.2°	7.9°

While the person-specific method performed well on the learned person's head, it was not able to generalise well to other people. The average model also performed well on learned people and was able to generalise better to novel people. The best performance was obtained by the multiple prototype model which was able to generalise to novel people with a mean absolute pose error of only 6.1°. The use of horizontal and vertical filters makes the person-specific templates sensitive to small changes in features on the face. In the average model, the small differences between different peoples' facial features are blurred together and the model generalises better as a result. The method based on similarity to multiple prototypes was consistently more accurate than the other models.

7.10   Biological Perspectives

Evidence of the ability of humans to track and predict motion patterns is drawn from our everyday performance of many visual and visuomotor tasks. Such visual behaviour depends on oculomotor behaviour and our cognitive ability to interpolate spatio-temporal information.

Studies of oculomotor behaviour are broadly concerned with two classes of eye movements: (i) saccadic eye movements which are high-velocity eye rotations used to bring images of chosen objects to the fovea and (ii) smooth eye movements which are slower, continuous movements designed to track smooth motion of retinal images produced either by the motion of objects or by motion of the eye itself.

Traditionally, oculomotor behaviour had been believed to be a low-level, reflexive aspect of eye-movement control. Recently, methodological developments that allow eye movements to be studied during performance of increasingly more complex and naturalistic tasks show that cognitive processes, expectations, selective attention and learning become as or more important than sensory cues. Therefore, biological vision is both active and purposive in nature which indicates that cognition may play a much more important role than previously attributed [192]. Moreover, the operation of even apparently low-level and involuntary aspects of oculomotor control begin to depend on the cognitive demands of the task as a whole, be it reading, searching or reaching for objects in space.

We know for example that human beings can make accurate and precise predictions about the future paths of moving objects [256]. Smooth pursuit, the smooth eye movements when an object is moving, require sensory cues, particularly the motion of images on the retina, to track the motion of objects in the outside world. However, expectation and selective attention account to a large extent for the ability of smooth eye movements to maintain a stable retinal image in the presence of object motion. Because smooth pursuit cannot be initiated or suppressed voluntarily, it has always appeared to be a sensorimotor reflex under the control of stimulus motion on the retina. Despite its involuntary nature, pursuit characteristics depend on the ability to predict the future path of a moving target and to attend to the target and ignore its background. The eye is truly anticipating future motion, using what the subjects know about upcoming events based on interpretation of both auditory and visual symbolic cues. Thus, pursuit is effective because it takes advantage of the ongoing cognitive activity and shows evidence of prediction and anticipation [191].

7.11   Discussion

We have considered how temporal continuity and prior or learned motion models can be used to perform tracking. The notion of propagating state-space density functions over time was described. Kalman filters can be used to propagate unimodal Gaussian densities and thus perform probabilistic tracking in a way which deals with uncertainty in the observations and the motion models. Condensation propagates multi-modal densities and thus maintains multiple hypotheses about the state. It can therefore deal robustly with visual distractions albeit with an associated increase in computational expense. Finally, hidden Markov models interpret spatio-temporal patterns using discrete transitions between a set of sparse states.

The use of such modelling and filtering techniques was demonstrated in the context of three of the visual tasks discussed earlier, namely focus of attention, face detection and pose estimation. In other words, they were used to *track* regions of attention and the image position, scale and pose of faces. Additionally, the importance of model adaptation was illustrated in the context of colour cues. In particular, adaptive mixture models were used to cope with varying illumination conditions during tracking.

The spatio-temporal constraints used have been quite general in nature and thus are applicable to a wide variety of scenarios. However, in specific applications with constrained scenes many more constraints can be brought to bear. For example, expectation of where to find a person is constrained by the environment. The motion trajectories are often also highly constrained by the environment. Gong and Buxton [132] demonstrated an elaborate adaptive segmentation algorithm based on Bayesian belief networks. We will have more to say on spatio-temporal context when we discuss perceptual integration in Chapter 11.

In this Part, we have described methods for focus of attention, face detection, pose estimation, tracking people and tracking faces. The common purpose here has been to recover the pose and position of each face in the scene in a robust and consistent manner. These processes yield sequences of segmented facial images labelled with confidence parameters and estimates of face pose. This requires the ability to recognise which objects in a scene are faces. Psychologists sometimes refer to this as *entry-level recognition*. In contrast, the next Part of this book is concerned with the problem of discriminating between different people's faces. We refer to this as *face identification*.

Face identification is difficult because while all faces have similar structure there are numerous sources of variation between images of the same face. The variation between images of a face caused by illumination, pose, aging and expression changes is often greater than the variation that would be caused by a change of identity (see introduction in Chapter 1).

In order to perform identification, we need a computational mechanism for learning representations of individuals' faces. These representations must then be matched to novel face images in order to identify them. It is necessary to find a way to generalise from previously observed images of a face in order to identify it under novel viewing conditions. In the next Part, we begin in Chapter 8 with the assumption that all faces to be learned and identified are observed in upright frontal view. In Chapter 9, we relax this assumption and consider how to deal with changes in pose. In Chapter 10, we further explore the use of temporal information when performing identification of faces over time from image sequences.

PART III

MODELS OF IDENTITY

8 Single-View Identification

It is the common wonder of men, how amoung so many million faces, there should be none alike.

— *Thomas Browne, Religio Medici*

Having focused on the problems of computing visual cues such as motion and colour, detecting faces in cluttered scenes and tracking the changes of a face and its 3D pose over time, let us now consider the problems of modelling the identity of a person's face through learning and subsequently recognising it as being of that person in novel images. Initially, we consider the simplified task of identification from an isolated static image of a face when one, a few or even many images of that face have been previously observed. In other words, we shall ignore the problem of pose variation and assume for the moment that all faces are observed at approximately the same pose. In the examples used here, this will be the frontal view. It is worth pointing out that other fixed, single views can also be used and indeed, a three-quarters view (45° yaw) may be more informative. Learning facial identities from frontal views has certain practical advantages such as the availability of sizeable frontal view face image databases.

8.1 Identification Tasks

What computation is required when performing a face identification task? Figure 8.1 illustrates schematically the four identification tasks defined in Chapter 1. In these diagrams, face images are represented as points in a hypothetical multi-dimensional face space. For illustrative purposes, this face space is only two-dimensional and is assumed to contain all possible face images and to exclude all non-face images. Each of the four plots illustrates a different identification task, in order of increasing difficulty.

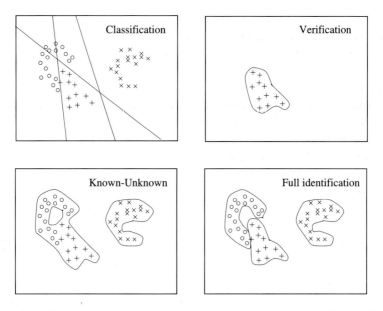

Figure 8.1   Plotted in a hypothetical *face space* are example images of three different faces. Suitable decision boundaries are shown for the four identification tasks.

Classification: In the first task, it is assumed that only a fixed number of different, known faces will be encountered. In this case, in order to identify which of the faces is being observed in a novel image, it is enough to learn a classification function that aims to separate a finite set of known faces. The illustration shows an example in which three lines (or hyperplanes in higher dimensions) are used to separate three faces.

Verification: In the second task, the identity of a face is provided. The task is to determine whether this claimed identity is the true identity of the face.

Known-Unknown: In the third task, a face must be classified as either known or unknown. Although such a task may appear to be simpler than the face classification task, the discriminant function required is in fact more complex because of the need to account for the unknown face population. Face verification can be regarded as a special case of this task in which the known class consists of just one face.

Full identification: Finally, in full identification it is necessary to decide if a novel face is known and if so to determine its identity.

It is worth pointing out that the face space has high dimensionality and visualisation in only two dimensions would in fact reveal little or no structure. Nevertheless, this figure serves to illustrate computational differences between the identification tasks which should be quite generic even if face distributions are realistically a lot more complex. How well different faces are separated in the face space will depend upon the representation scheme used to model the face space. However, it is likely that each identity will form strongly non-convex regions in the face space. Furthermore, regions of different identities are likely to overlap significantly. A face identity could even form several separate regions in face space due to discontinuous changes in appearance (e.g. removal of spectacles).

8.2   Nearest-neighbour Template Matching

First let us consider a straightforward approach to face identification. Its limitations will help to motivate other more sophisticated methods to be described in the rest of this chapter. This naive approach is as follows:

> An individual face is represented by simply *storing all the available images of it*. A face is then identified from a novel image by comparison with each of the stored face images. It is *identified as the face with the most similar stored image*, provided that *a sufficiently similar image can be found in the stored set*.

In order to use this approach it is necessary to formalise the notion of being similar, or *similarity*. A function $h(\mathbf{x}_1, \mathbf{x}_2)$ which measures the similarity of two images $\mathbf{x}_1$ and $\mathbf{x}_2$ is needed. Suitable functions were introduced in Chapter 6 in the context of template-based pose estimation. These were based upon Pearson's correlation coefficient (Equation 6.2) or Euclidean distance (Equation 6.1). However, there are many rather obvious limitations to such an approach using either of these similarity measures. To name a few:

(1) Identification involves a potentially large indexing problem in which case many high-dimensional images must be compared in order to find a good match. Such exhaustive search in high-dimensional space simply may not be computationally feasible in practice.

(2) The representation used is extremely inefficient in terms of memory, consisting as it does of storing all images of all faces.

(3) The approach does not perform computation to model the underlying uniqueness (identity) of a face from its images. It is therefore poor at generalising from stored images of a face to novel images of that face under different imaging conditions. In other words, given a novel image of a face, a sufficiently similar image in the stored set is quite likely never to be found.

Methods of this form are known as *nearest-neighbour* template matching [48, 120]. Their limited generalisation ability means that the training data (the stored images of all the faces to be identified) must densely sample the continuum of possible imaging conditions including lighting, expression and so on. Many image samples are needed per face for this approach to work. Although its computational inefficiency can be addressed to some extent by dedicated implementations using custom VLSI hardware [125], such solutions are both limited and expensive.

8.3   Representing Knowledge of Facial Appearance

The simplistic approach just described does not make use of the powerful constraint that all the images encountered are of faces. A key to obtaining a more accurate and efficient model is to encode and exploit prior knowledge of faces and the ways in which they vary. What is needed is a way to acquire and represent prior knowledge of faces that allows new faces to be encoded and subsequently identified by comparison to the encoded representation. A further requirement is that the representation be amenable to change and learning. One would like to be able to update one's knowledge of faces as more faces are observed. One would also like to be able to update knowledge of a particular face as new images of it are acquired. Prior knowledge of faces is both *statistical* and *structural*. Let us examine each of these, concentrating first on statistical modelling.

An image with N pixels defines a vector in an N-dimensional image space. However, images of the real world occupy only a small fraction of this space. Furthermore, position-aligned and scale-normalised images of upright faces occupy an even smaller fraction of this space. Such face images populate a space with an intrinsic dimensionality much lower than N. This is true because faces are all similar in appearance and possess significant statistical regularities. In theory, a complete description of how faces populate image space can be obtained from a probability density function. However, this is both unknown and in general computationally rather difficult to estimate due to the curse of dimensionality. In practice, a model has to be learned from a relatively small number of example face images. In Chapters 5 and 6, statistical models of facial appearance were learned and used to perform face detection. Here we are interested in learning similar models for the purposes of identification. Several criteria are considered in determining both the representation and the model. They include:

(1) Low dimensionality
(2) Separability
(3) Sparseness and topography

Many algorithms have been suggested for learning representations which attempt to satisfy these various criteria by analysing the statistics of a set of example images. When applied to a set of images of many different faces, they can be used to represent statistical knowledge of faces in general.

In addition to modelling a generic face, statistical models of particular faces can also be learned. Images of a particular face occupy a small fraction of the face space. Again, a probability density function provides the most complete description of the variation in the images of that face but this is unknown. Short of a full density function, a statistical representation of identity can still be learned from example images of a face.

Recall that statistical models of facial appearance for performing face detection use entirely image template-based representations in which each face image is simply represented as a multi-dimensional vector without explicitly encoding any shape information. Whilst this template-based representation has been shown to be sufficient for face detection, it may not be for identification. In particular, one may argue that shape information needs to be modelled in order to cope with facial deformation and subtle changes between different faces. However, modelling such structural information only comes at a price, as we shall see in Section 8.6. In the interests of simplicity of exposition, we focus for the moment on a template-based representation and bear in mind that statistical techniques employed here can also be used in combination with a representation of structure [66]. This will become more apparent in the context of modelling identities across multiple views in the next Chapter.

8.4   Statistical Knowledge of Facial Appearance

Consider the problem of representing statistical prior knowledge of faces based on a training set of M aligned face images. These training images randomly sample the distribution of face images. As discussed in the context of frontal view detection, computing density functions in an N-dimensional image space is clearly impractical where $M \ll N$. There are perhaps two types of simple technique one can employ to address the problem. The dimensionality of the image space can be reduced to some extent by subsampling and the training set size can be increased by generating virtual samples by, for example, mirroring the face images about their axis of symmetry. However, a more general treatment of this problem should be adopted through statistical learning. Instead of performing the computation in the original image space, some form of feature extraction or clustering can first be applied to derive a more compact representation in a feature space of lower dimensionality. Indeed, such feature extraction or clustering is both desirable and possible for images of most object classes. In particular, this is true for face images because the intrinsic dimensionality of the face space is in fact much lower than that of the image space since faces are all similar in appearance and possess significant statistical regularities. Needless to say, low dimensional representation facilitates efficient storage and matching and makes further statistical modelling and learning more computationally tractable.

8.4.1   Low Dimensionality: Principal Components Analysis

Many algorithms have been suggested for learning low-dimensional representations from an unlabelled set of examples. They were introduced earlier in the context of face detection in Chapter 5. It is perhaps not surprising that Principal Components Analysis (PCA) has been widely adopted to capture the face space in a low-dimensional feature space: the eigenspace. Provided that careful alignment and intensity normalisations are performed, PCA can also be used as a simple low-dimensional linear representation for face identification [341]. Essentially, PCA makes the assumption that the probability density function is significantly non-zero only in a low-dimensional linear subspace, the eigenspace. An eigenspace is computed by estimating the eigenvectors of the covariance matrix of a training set. The eigenvectors corresponding to the largest eigenvalues are taken as the principal components of an eigenspace and capture the main modes of global variation in the training data set. These principal components are also known as *eigenfaces*. Figure 5.2 shows some examples of eigenfaces. A more complete description of PCA is given in Appendix C.

Although eigenfaces are able to capture some statistical knowledge of faces, the number of eigenfaces to retain is chosen rather empirically. One commonly used criterion is to retain enough of the dominant principal components to capture at least 95% of the variance in the training set. The higher order principal components are therefore discarded. This is based on the assumption that face images form a linear subspace of low dimensionality [184].

Computationally, PCA yields a matrix $\mathbf{U} = [\mathbf{u}_1 \mathbf{u}_2 \ldots \mathbf{u}_K]$ whose columns are the K most significant eigenvectors of the training data's covariance matrix, corresponding to the K largest eigenvalues ($\lambda_1, \lambda_2 \ldots, \lambda_K$). A novel face image, $\mathbf{x}$, is represented by linear projection onto the K-dimensional eigenspace given by a coefficient vector

$$\boldsymbol{\alpha} = \mathbf{U}^{\mathsf{T}}(\mathbf{x} - \boldsymbol{\mu}) \qquad (8.1)$$

where $\boldsymbol{\mu}$ is the mean image of the training set. Geometrically, this projects the novel face image, $\mathbf{x}$, onto the eigenfaces of a training set yielding a low-dimensional representation for that face. Typically, K is between 30 and 50 which is one or two orders of magnitude lower than the dimensionality of the image space. Identification can now, in principle, be performed based on these low-dimensional coefficient vector representations rather than using the images. However, meaningful identification can only be performed if linear projections of different faces to the eigenfaces are separable. This is illustrated by a simplified example shown in Figure 8.2. In a 2D image space (imagine if you will that images have only two pixels) a pair of eigenfaces are used to represent faces. Images of two different faces are plotted

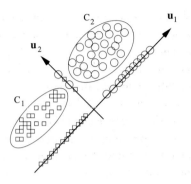

Figure 8.2 Samples from two classes are plotted in a 2D image space. Projection onto the first eigenface ($\mathbf{u}_1$) retains maximal overall variation. In this case the projection also preserves separability while projection onto the other eigenface ($\mathbf{u}_2$) results in the classes becoming confused.

and form two separable clusters (c_1 and c_2). The eigenface $\mathbf{u}_1$ gives the axis of maximal variation in the training data. In this example, projection onto this eigenface preserves separability and reduces the dimensionality from two to one. However, projections of different faces onto eigenfaces are not always separable. In this example, projections onto the second eigenface ($\mathbf{u}_2$) would have resulted in the two classes becoming confused. In general, projections onto the eigenfaces do not preserve class separability.

Identification using PCA

The most straightforward approach to identification as introduced earlier is nearest-neighbour matching. We can now perform such a computation in a PCA space. It is reasonable to expect that the advantages of performing nearest-neighbour matching in low-dimensional eigenspace are computational effectiveness and efficiency. For example, the similarity function given by Equation (6.1) can take two projected images $\boldsymbol{\alpha}$ and $\boldsymbol{\beta}$ as arguments and $h(\boldsymbol{\alpha},\boldsymbol{\beta})$ can then be used as a measure of similarity between the two original face images.

An alternative similarity measure uses the *Mahalanobis distance* so that variations along all axes are treated as equally significant. This is arguably better for discrimination [71]. The Mahalanobis distance is defined as:

$$d(\boldsymbol{\alpha},\boldsymbol{\beta}) = \sum_{k=1}^{K} \lambda_k^{-1}(\alpha_k - \beta_k)^2 \qquad (8.2)$$

Equivalently, we can use an Euclidean metric after applying a *whitening transformation* to the projection coefficient vector to give the representation equal variance along each principal component axis [205]:

$$\boldsymbol{\alpha}_{\text{whitened}} = [\frac{\alpha_1}{\sqrt{\lambda_1}} \ \frac{\alpha_2}{\sqrt{\lambda_2}} \ \cdots \ \frac{\alpha_K}{\sqrt{\lambda_K}}]^{\text{T}} \qquad (8.3)$$

It is important to point out that PCA can be used either to represent prior knowledge of faces in general or to represent a specific set of faces to be identified. This distinction is usually not made explicit in the literature. In the first case, PCA is performed on a very large set of face images which are subsequently discarded. The eigenfaces are retained as prior knowledge of faces and can then be used to encode faces for subsequent identification. This is a *generic* PCA. In the second case, the faces which need to be identified are those whose images are used when performing PCA. In this case, the eigenfaces are *specific* to the particular set of faces of interest.

Computationally, if all the eigenvectors are retained as the eigenfaces and nearest-neighbour Euclidean matching is used, the method is equivalent to template matching as introduced in Section 8.2 [48]. However, if only the first few most significant eigenvectors are retained as the eigenfaces, the Euclidean metric becomes approximate [71, 243] and its matching accuracy decreases. Therefore, it is perhaps not surprising that empirical experiments have shown that the use of *specific* PCA is no more accurate than correlation-based template matching [17]. However, if Mahalanobis distance is used to perform equal variance weighted matching, its accuracy can exceed that of template matching [71].

Let us reconsider the four identification tasks introduced earlier (Section 8.1). The task of classification considers a closed set of faces and for this task specific PCA is more suitable. The other three tasks require knowledge of all faces so a generic PCA is required.

When the identities in the database change, a specific PCA eigenspace will need to be updated. Similarly, a generic eigenspace could be adapted over time to reflect changes in the environmental conditions and target population. Recomputation of the eigenspace using PCA is computationally expensive and would require all the images to be stored. Fortunately, it is possible to update the eigenspace incrementally as new images are obtained [51, 60, 88, 145]. There also exist techniques for merging and splitting eigenspace models to allow groups of people to be added or deleted from a database [146]. However, such techniques raise questions of fidelity since the representational accuracy of the eigenspace is reduced when such methods are used in a repetitive manner.

Critique of PCA

The use of PCA to reduce the dimensionality of the feature space in which recognition is performed has addressed some of the problems with the template matching approach introduced earlier. For instance, the memory requirements are reduced. Indexing in low-dimensional space is also much more efficient. However, there are still three rather critical issues which require our attention:

(1) PCA assumes that face images form a low-dimensional linear subspace. This assumption is at best approximate and at worst grossly inaccurate. Face images in general are not exactly linear combinations of a small orthogonal basis set. If they were, averaging two face images would result in a third face. This is not generally the case because of differing facial structure, rotations in depth and misalignment of facial features caused by affine transformations. It is perhaps unsurprising to discover that the resulting averaged image would often have more than two lips (see Figure 2.2). However, it can be a reasonable approximation provided that adequate position and view alignment are performed to the images before PCA is applied. The use of more detailed correspondence between face images can improve the accuracy of this assumption (see more discussions in Section 8.6).

(2) PCA captures global modes of variation and the resulting representation is not amenable to further processing. Perhaps the most significant limitation of PCA is that it does not distinguish between image variations due to changes of identity and other sources of variation. While the principal components capture the main modes of global variation in the training set, these are not entirely due to changes in identity. In practice, if the examples in the training set have varying illumination, the first few eigenvectors predominantly encode these variations in illumination conditions. Effective PCA is heavily reliant on careful selection and preprocessing of the training data. Which of the principal components are most useful for identification depends critically on the training set used.

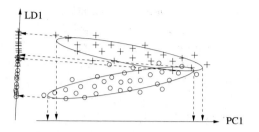

Figure 8.3 An example of images of two faces plotted in a hypothetical 2D feature space. Projections onto the principal component vector (PC1) result in significant overlap between the two face classes. In contrast, projections onto a linear discriminant vector (LD1) can retain good separability.

(3) Due to the nature of PCA, information about identity is somehow distributed over all the eigenvectors. The projection coefficient vectors $\boldsymbol{\alpha}$ are not well clustered by identity. In other words, PCA projection-based representation does not necessarily give good class separability. This is illustrated in a two-class problem shown in Figure 8.3. In this example, the principal component is PC1. It can be seen that projection onto the principal component can result in significant overlap between the two faces, making identification impossible.

8.4.2 Separability: Linear Discriminant Analysis

In order to have better identification, it is necessary to distinguish image variation due to identity from variation due to other sources such as illumination and expression. Consider a set of images of C different faces $\mathcal{X} = \{\mathcal{X}_1, \mathcal{X}_2 \ldots, \mathcal{X}_C\}$ where $\mathcal{X}_c$ denotes a set of images of the same face, c. Given such a data set in which each image is labelled with an identity, it is possible to model the statistics of variation both within and between identities. In particular, a method known as Linear Discriminant Analysis (LDA) can be used to define a linear transformation similar to that of PCA given by Equation (8.1). However, LDA aims to both reduce dimensionality and at the same time maximise the separability of different faces [17, 111, 204, 332]. The essential idea of LDA is to define a transformation (projection) which maximises the variation between different faces, known as *between-class variation*, while minimising the variation between images of the same face, known as *within-class variation*. A simple illustration is shown in Figure 8.3 where LDA transformation is able to retain class separability between two different faces whilst PCA fails. Example images of two faces are plotted in a hypothetical 2D image space. Ellipses indicate the covariance matrix for each face. Note that the variability due to identity is less than the variability due to other factors. As a result projection onto the principal component vector PC1 results in significant overlap between the two face classes. However, projection onto a linear discriminant vector LD1 results in good separation between the faces.

Whilst performing PCA is about computing eigenvectors through solving a standard eigen-problem, performing LDA is about computing a set of linear discriminant vectors by solving a generalised eigen-problem. If the covariance matrix for PCA characterises the 'scatteredness' of a training set $\mathcal{X} = \{\mathcal{X}_1, \mathcal{X}_2 \ldots, \mathcal{X}_C\}$, one can alternatively measure both a *within-class scatter matrix* ($\mathbf{W}$) and a *between-class scatter matrix* ($\mathbf{B}$) for the same training set, provided that the data set consists of sufficiently large numbers of samples, $\mathcal{X}_c$, for each individual face class:

$$\mathbf{W} = \sum_{c=1}^{C} \sum_{\mathbf{x} \in \mathcal{X}_c} (\mathbf{x} - \boldsymbol{\mu}_c)(\mathbf{x} - \boldsymbol{\mu}_c)^{\mathrm{T}} \tag{8.4}$$

$$\mathbf{B} = \sum_{c=1}^{C} M_c (\boldsymbol{\mu}_c - \boldsymbol{\mu})(\boldsymbol{\mu}_c - \boldsymbol{\mu})^{\mathrm{T}} \tag{8.5}$$

where M_c ($\gg 1$) is the number of samples of class $\mathcal{X}_c$, $\boldsymbol{\mu}_c$ is the sample mean for class $\mathcal{X}_c$, and $\boldsymbol{\mu}$ is the sample mean for the entire data set $\mathcal{X}$. Given $\mathbf{W}$ and $\mathbf{B}$ of $\mathcal{X}$, *linear discriminant vectors* $(\mathbf{u}_1, \mathbf{u}_2, \ldots, \mathbf{u}_K)$ are the generalised eigenvectors of $\mathbf{W}^{-1}\mathbf{B}$ with the largest eigenvalues $\lambda_1, \ldots, \lambda_K$. In theory, there can be at most $C-1$ non-zero eigenvalues and therefore discriminant vectors for a data set consisting of C face classes. Realistically, however, the number of computable discriminant vectors is likely to be less than the number of face classes in the training set ($K < C$). Like eigenfaces, these discriminant vectors are images, also known as *Fisherfaces*. It is worth pointing out that unlike eigenfaces obtained using PCA, Fisherfaces are not orthogonal and independent. Therefore they are not optimal in terms of information compression although they yield better class discrimination. More details about performing LDA can be found in Appendix C.

Given a discriminant matrix consisting of Fisherfaces as its columns, $\mathbf{U} = [\mathbf{u}_1\mathbf{u}_2\ldots\mathbf{u}_K]$, a novel face image, $\mathbf{x}$, can be represented by linear projection:

$$\boldsymbol{\alpha} = \mathbf{U}^\mathrm{T}\mathbf{x} \qquad\qquad (8.6)$$

Recall that one rather crucial assumption to be met if LDA is to be performed is that the training data set must consist of a sufficiently large number of samples for each individual face class ($M_c \gg 1$). However, such an assumption does not usually hold and it is not then computationally viable to perform LDA directly on a set of face images. This is because the curse of dimensionality can easily result in the within-class scatter matrix, $\mathbf{W}$, being singular. To overcome this problem, PCA and LDA can be used together. LDA only needs to be performed in a low-dimensional eigenspace obtained by first applying a global PCA to the training data set.

Critique of LDA

After projections onto linear discriminant vectors, a nearest-neighbour classifier with a Euclidean metric can be used to perform identification. However, given that many examples of each face are required to be made available for performing LDA, it can be argued that instead of LDA, it is now both feasible and desirable to explicitly estimate nonlinear statistical models of identity. This is because the use of LDA will not in general preserve the separability of different face classes. Only linearly separable classes will remain separable after the linear projection and images of different faces are not always linearly separable. Identification using LDA is essentially still based on linear classification.

As with PCA, LDA can be performed in either a *generic* or *specific* manner. In generic LDA, linear discriminants are computed for a large set of representative face images of any identity. These images are then discarded and the discriminant vectors retained as prior knowledge of different faces. In specific LDA, the data set contains *only* images of a small set of specific faces which are subsequently to be identified. Specific LDA has been shown to be effective for the classification task. However, it is not clear how it performs in the generic case on large numbers of faces. In other words, it is not clear to what extent LDA allows prior experience to be exploited in order to generalise to novel viewing conditions in identification.

8.4.3   Sparseness and Topography: Local Feature Analysis

One limitation of both PCA and LDA is that the principal components are global in that they are computed based on images as holistic patterns. It can be argued that local representation is more desirable since it offers robustness to changes in localised image regions and is more amenable to further processing. Local feature analysis [259] derives kernels from the pixel-wise correlations of the principal components and results in a local, topographic representation. Independent components analysis [65] is a generalisation of principal components analysis which decorrelates higher-order statistics of the images. Both methods tend to produce sparse representations and could provide improved face representations for recognition.

8.5   Statistical Knowledge of Identity

So far we have described a number of ways to measure the similarity of two face images. For instance, similarity can be defined directly between two images using a correlation coefficient (Equation 6.2) or an Euclidean metric after intensity normalisation (Equation 6.1). Alternatively, after projection onto eigenfaces, similarity can be defined using either Euclidean or Mahalanobis distance (Equation 8.2). Similarity can also be defined using Euclidean distance after projection onto Fisherfaces. There are of course further possibilities. These include the use of other norms such as the L_1 norm which may be more robust. Any of these similarity measures can be used to perform nearest-neighbour identification. In this general approach, the identity of a face image is determined as that of the most similar stored face image. The similarity of the nearest neighbour can be used as a measure of confidence in the identification. Furthermore, placing a threshold on this measure enables faces with no good matches to be categorised as unknown. While it can be surprisingly effective, nearest-neighbour identification has a number of drawbacks:

(1) All previously observed images of every face must be represented and stored.
(2) Matching involves a large indexing problem.
(3) Generalisation is limited.
(4) The method is susceptible to noise.

The extension to K-nearest neighbours in which identification is based on the K nearest images $(K > 1)$ can improve accuracy. It does not, however, address the first two drawbacks.

8.5.1 Identification Tasks Revisited

Let us now reconsider the four identification tasks defined at the beginning of this Chapter. Given many example images of a face represented in a low-dimensional feature space, one aims to estimate a statistical model of identity of the face. A best possible statistical characterisation of a facial identity is its probability distribution in the feature space. Given a representation of sufficiently low dimensionality, one can argue that it becomes feasible to estimate the density function for a face from those example images of that face. This approach enables identity models to be learned and updated independently of one another. The identification tasks are then addressed in terms of class-conditional density estimation, where each face constitutes a class, c. Let α denote a low-dimensional representation of a face image $\mathbf{x}$. Assuming that a class-conditional density $p(\alpha|c)$ can be estimated from a set of examples of a face, the identification tasks can then be defined in terms of class-conditional densities as follows.

Face classification: The face classification task is a *C-class classification problem* in which all C classes can be modelled. Given a collection of representative samples for each of the C face classes, the probability of misclassifying a face is minimised by assigning it to the class, c, with the largest posterior probability $P(c|\alpha)$ given by Bayes' theorem

$$P(c|\alpha) = \frac{p(\alpha|c)P(c)}{p(\alpha)} \tag{8.7}$$

where $p(\alpha)$ is the unconditional density of α, $p(\alpha|c)$ the class-conditional density and $P(c)$ the prior probability for class c. The denominator $p(\alpha)$ is for normalisation and need not be evaluated in order to maximise posterior probability [96].

Face verification: Face verification is treated as a *two-class classification problem*. The two classes c_0 and c_1 correspond to the cases where the claimed identity is true and false respectively. In order to maximise the posterior probability, $\boldsymbol{\alpha}$ should be assigned to c_0 if and only if

$$p(\boldsymbol{\alpha}|c_0) > \frac{p(\boldsymbol{\alpha}|c_1)P(c_1)}{P(c_0)} \qquad (8.8)$$

Density $p(\boldsymbol{\alpha}|c_1)$ represents the distribution of all faces other than the claimed identity c_0. In general, this can be difficult to estimate. On the other hand, if a simple assumption is made such that it is constant over the relevant region of space, falling to zero elsewhere, Inequality (8.8) is then equivalent to thresholding $p(\boldsymbol{\alpha}|c_0)$. A more acceptable assumption is that density $p(\boldsymbol{\alpha}|c_1)$ is smaller in regions of face space where $p(\boldsymbol{\alpha}|c_0)$ is large. Now, if $p(\mathbf{x}|c_1)$ is chosen to be a monotonically decreasing function $f(p(\boldsymbol{\alpha}|c_0))$, Inequality (8.8) is still equivalent to thresholding $p(\boldsymbol{\alpha}|c_0)$. In this case, the threshold takes the form

$$g^{-1}\left(\frac{P(c_0)}{P(c_1)}\right), \quad \text{where} \quad g(z) \equiv \frac{f(z)}{z} \qquad (8.9)$$

Since g is monotonic, g^{-1} is unique [26]. Utilising sample images of c_0, it is feasible to perform verification by thresholding $p(\boldsymbol{\alpha}|c_0)$. However, in order to achieve more accurate verification, as in the case of face detection described in Chapter 5, negative samples (images from class c_1) need to be used in order to better estimate the decision boundaries. In addition, only those negative samples which are close to c_0 are relevant here. This can be achieved by an iterative learning process in which incorrectly classified images of c_1 are selected as negative samples. Face images used to learn a generic face model for detection as described in Chapter 5 can also be used to provide a source of negative examples for identity verification [223].

Known-Unknown: This task can also be treated as a two-class classification problem. The two classes c_0 and c_1 correspond to the cases where the subject is and is not a member of a known group $\mathcal{C}$, respectively. The methods discussed above for face verification can then be similarly applied to this task. Alternatively, an identity verifier can be modelled for each known person. If the numerator in the threshold of Inequality (8.8) is the same for all verifiers then they can be simply combined.

Full identification: This task can be performed by combining the classification task with the known-unknown task. Alternatively, C identity verifiers can be used.

8.5.2 Class-conditional Densities for Modelling Identity

Let us now consider the problem of computing class-conditional densities for identification. Given a set of examples of a face $(\alpha_1, \alpha_2, \ldots, \alpha_M)$, its class-conditional density $p(\alpha|c)$ can be estimated in a number of ways depending on the nature of the training data set available. Intuitively, one may consider estimating a single parametric density function using relatively few parameters. If such a function can indeed be computed, it would enable identification to be performed rather efficiently. For example, a single Gaussian density model can be adopted requiring estimation of a mean vector, μ_α, and a covariance matrix, Σ_α. Identification using such a model aims to measure similarity to a face based on Mahalanobis distance. Given that the available number of example images of a face (often less than ten) can still be relatively small compared to the dimensionality of its feature vector α (often in tens), the model may still need to be further simplified in order to reduce the number of parameters estimated. For example, the covariance matrix can be constrained to be diagonal or even radially symmetric. In the case of radial covariance, only a single variance parameter, σ_α^2, needs to be estimated in addition to the mean. An even simpler model can be obtained when $\sigma_\alpha^2 \to 0$. In this case, only the class mean needs to be estimated from the data and identification is then reduced to *nearest-mean* classification. Alternatively, probabilistic PCA can be used to estimate within-class density functions [237].

However, the distribution of a face in image space is unlikely to be accurately modelled by a single function such as a Gaussian. For example, a face can populate more than one region of image space due to certain binary properties of faces such as the presence or absence of glasses [25]. The distribution of a face in its low-dimensional feature space after linear projections such as PCA and LDA is also unlikely to be Gaussian. In fact, faces in general are more likely to populate at least one and possibly several highly non-convex regions in the face space. An appropriate model for class-conditional densities needs to be sufficiently general in order to capture these highly non-convex distributions. It is also important to allow for a range of model complexity in order to model faces of which a relatively small amount of sample images are available initially. As more data are collected, the model can then be adapted to capture the underlying distribution more accurately. A sensible approach to the problem is to use Gaussian mixture models [230]. For identification tasks, other methods such as nearest-neighbour and nearest-mean emerge as special cases of using Gaussian mixtures. A class-conditional Gaussian mixture takes the form of a mixture of K components

$$p(\boldsymbol{\alpha}|c) = \sum_{k=1}^{K} p(\boldsymbol{\alpha}|k)P(k) \qquad (8.10)$$

where $\boldsymbol{\alpha}$ is the low-dimensional feature space representation of an image and K is the number of mixture components used for class c. Similarly to the colour mixture models described in Chapter 4, although far more difficult to compute due to much higher dimensionality, $p(\boldsymbol{\alpha}|c)$ can be estimated using the Expectation-Maximisation (EM) algorithm (see Appendix C). The number of parameters in the model can be reduced by constraining the form and the number of Gaussian mixture components. It is important to point out that despite the potential simplicity of a mixture component, the range of face distributions that can be captured by a mixture model is complex. This is because the complexity of a face distribution is captured by the *mixture complexity* rather than the complexity of each individual component. Support vector machines introduced in Section 3.7.2 can be readily applied here to systematically determine the mixture complexity of a Gaussian mixture model for a given training data set. Empirical experiments have shown that modelling identities using mixture models can be rather effective provided an appropriate mixture complexity is carefully chosen [230].

Non-parametric, kernel density estimation might also be employed. For example, a mixture of radial Gaussians with one Gaussian centred on each training sample could be used to exhaustively represent the training set [159]. While this density estimation process is computationally straightforward, it suffers from similar efficiency problems to the nearest-neighbour approach. Such a model requires all examples to be stored and compared during identification.

8.6   Structural Knowledge: The Role of Correspondence

Until now we have concentrated on estimating statistical models from images of faces under the assumption that image alignment has been performed adequately. This alignment is affine and achieved by translation, image rotation, scaling and possibly also shearing transformations. However, the statistical models of identity also need to cope with more general, nonlinear changes which cannot be addressed by affine alignment. These include changes of shape between different faces and facial deformation due to changes of facial expression. While an image template-based representation is sufficient and rather effective for face detection, it is not necessarily optimal for identification.

Let us now consider the problem of modelling general 2D shape variation explicitly. Modelling changes in the 2D shape of faces allows us to extend the linear assumptions upon which many of the statistical models are founded and therefore enables such models to cope with nonlinear changes in facial appearance. There is of course a price to pay for such a simplification of the statistics and that is the need to establish correspondence. The essence of modelling 2D shape and changes in shape can be regarded as the problem of establishing point-wise or sparse correspondence between different images. When faces are set in good correspondence, they can be more accurately modelled in linear spaces. In particular, statistical models such as PCA and LDA are more accurate [23, 74, 206]. However, solving the correspondence problem is computationally non-trivial.

8.6.1 Beyond Alignment: Correspondence at a Single View

Matching 2D face shapes even at a single view (pose) requires solving the correspondence problem at that view. Let us first consider establishing correspondence between images of the same face at a single view: *Given two images of a face taken at different times, determine which pairs of image points correspond to the same point on the face.* Although the pose is fixed so that no self-occlusion due to rotation in depth occurs, there are still several situations in which image points have no correspondence (see Section 2.5 for detailed discussion). Even when correspondence exists, it is difficult to establish because of: (1) facial deformation due to changing facial expression, and (2) changes in illumination conditions altering the local appearance.

If establishing correspondence between two images of the same face seems difficult, the problem in general is perhaps more challenging because correspondence is required between images of *different* faces. This implies that we first define a correspondence between 3D points on the two faces. The image correspondence problem then becomes: *Given two images of*

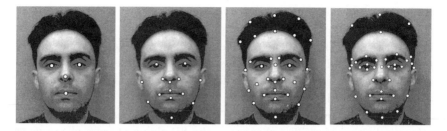

Figure 8.4 Examples of facial feature points selected for establishing correspondence between face images.

two different faces, determine which pairs of image points correspond to "corresponding" points on the two faces. Although the overall structure of two faces is likely to be the same (i.e. two eyes, one nose above a mouth and so on), the fine scale structure will differ. Clearly, it is difficult to define correspondence at all points on the faces, even at a single-view.

Even though dense correspondence cannot always be defined, attempts have been made to establish such correspondences between face images. The methods used tend to be based on computing optical flow. They are inevitably computationally expensive and usually require human intervention in order to ensure acceptable performance [354]. The computational difficulty and the expense of computing dense correspondence during matching and identification are prohibitive for real-time identification. These methods are useful however for face synthesis applications and computer graphics. Fortunately, dense correspondence is not a requirement for accurate identification using statistical models. In fact, correspondence between faces can be more reliably established with less computation at some intermediate level where there is consistent common structure. Such sparse correspondence would certainly lead to improved identification accuracy.

Figure 8.4 shows different sets of typical facial feature points adopted for correspondence by various face identification algorithms. In the first example, correspondence is established between just four landmark features: the eyes, nose and mouth [260]. The other three examples used fourteen [199], thirty-one [367] and thirty-six [75] landmark feature points respectively.

8.6.2   Combining Statistical and Structural Models

If it is deemed acceptable for models that capture prior knowledge of faces to be learned off-line, it is then feasible to establish correspondence between training images with human intervention. This usually involves the tedious task of hand labelling the feature point positions on each training image. The training images are warped into a standard shape which brings the feature points into alignment. Usually, the average shape is used. Suitable warping techniques have been developed in the computer graphics community. Two methods which have been successfully used are Bookstein's algorithm based on thin plate splines [199] and linear interpolation [71].

After warping to a standard shape, each example can be represented as a shape vector and a shape-free texture vector [66, 76]. The elements of the shape vector are the 2D image co-ordinates of the landmark points. The elements of the texture vector are the intensity values of the warped, shape-free image. Statistical models are then learned using these shape and texture vectors as examples. Faces can be more accurately modelled in linear spaces if such a representation is adopted instead of image templates.

The computational difficulty now is to perform matching since this requires on-line correspondence to be established between model and image. The use of an average, standard shape avoids the need to compute many correspondence maps. However, matching still entails a relatively expensive search over parameters of variations in shape and texture. The match can be based on models of the local appearance of the landmarks [367] or along curves joining the landmarks [104, 199].

For real-time identification, however, establishing even a small set of feature correspondences between faces can still be highly problematic, especially at low image resolution. Alternatively, affine alignment can in fact be rather effective for distinguishing between a small group of people at a single view. In this case, training examples are automatically aligned by a face detection and tracking process. The need for tedious human intervention in establishing correspondence is avoided and model building is therefore a fast process. The matching process is computationally efficient, enabling real-time performance.

8.7 Biological Perspectives

Although human faces share similar appearance characteristics compared to other objects in our surroundings, our ability to differentiate between these highly similar visual objects is remarkably good [38]. We can cope with changes in lighting, background, expression and partial occlusion. There is also evidence to suggest that discrimination between faces is better than for other homogeneous categories of familiar items, such as houses or canine faces [303, 375]. Furthermore, memory for faces under laboratory conditions is generally found to be more accurate than the recognition of other kinds of familiar objects [35, 107].

So what computation does face identification in human vision really involve? Although evidence from psychophysical and neurobiological experiments and cognitive models of face recognition show that face identification is a combination of independent processes that involve the encoding of features, the retrieval of such information from memory and the recognition of a face, their bearings on computational and engineering solutions are far from clear. Understanding the process and assessing humans' ability in identifying faces are difficult yet intriguing tasks. They involve the analysis of complex and interacting perceptual and cognitive functions. In cognitive terms, there are two distinct identification processes:

(1) Deciding from the visual appearance of a subject's face whether they are known or unknown [38].

(2) Recalling semantic information associated with a face such as a name, an occupation or other forms of semantic interpretation which are associated with the social and behavioural identities individuals have adopted in the environment they inhabit [38, 109].

Studies of adults with neurological impairment have shown that people who have difficulty identifying familiar faces are often still able to correctly match photographs of unfamiliar faces. This suggests that unfamiliar faces may be processed differently from well-known faces [376, 377]. The resolution required for face identification is not necessarily high. Humans can perform effective identification using images of spatial resolution as low as 18×24 pixels [9].

It is imperative to point out that the human process of identifying a known individual involves more than just faces. In addition to faces, visual cues relating to people's height, gait, build and familiar clothing also contribute to identification in our social interactions. Body gestures, contextual knowledge and expectation provide powerful cues for human recognition.

Neurobiological studies suggest that about 10% of the face-selective cells found in monkey temporal lobe show sensitivity to identity [263]. This sensitivity arises in two ways: cells either respond to particular characteristic facial features of an individual or to some configuration of the features of that individual. These findings seem to be consistent with the idea of gnostic or "grandmother" cells. In such a scenario, a specific cell responds only to the visual appearance of one's grandmother! It is more likely that populations of cells together code for such complex stimuli although many individual cells within such a population could be highly selective for grand-mother. As pointed out by Perrett *et al.* [263] the difference between pop-ulation and gnostic coding is a somewhat false dichotomy. Furthermore, it has been found that small populations of cells often carry sufficient infor-mation to identify particular faces. These results were taken as evidence for sparse population coding of faces. Cell populations in anterior inferotem-poral cortex code information relating to the physical properties of faces whereas cell populations in the superior temporal polysensory area relate to other aspects such as familiarity [379].

In future studies, it may be informative to determine how the neural processes involved in recognising the face change as the face becomes more and more familiar. It might also be revealing to present objects other than faces to determine whether the neural processes involved in recognising familiar objects are similar or dissimilar to those involved in recognising familiar faces. It may be particularly informative to investigate these ques-tions with infants of different ages [85].

8.8 Discussion

Four identification tasks were defined: face classification, face verification, known-unknown and full identification. All but face classification require consideration of the class of unknown people and as a consequence identities should be modelled in a generic face space rather than a face space which is specific to the set of known people.

Face identification tasks in realistic scenarios are characterised by the availability of sequences of many sample images under sensory conditions which may include low resolution, large scale variation, changing illumina-tion, mis-alignment and partial occlusion. Therefore, identification based upon isolated images under realistic sensory conditions is highly inconsis-tent and unreliable. In dynamic environments, visual recognition of poor quality images is compensated by accumulation of evidence over time. For example, to recognise the face of a moving person is much easier and more robust over hundreds of face images of a person acquired in a few seconds rather than relying on a few snapshots which can be highly noisy and even incomplete. The task of recognising *few identities with many samples* under poor conditions suggests alternative methods to either PCA or LDA.

Both PCA [71, 260, 341] and LDA [17, 111, 332] based recognition typically adopt a nearest neighbour or nearest mean match in the face space. However, given a large training set containing hundreds of relatively poor samples of a class, a better model of class identity in the face space is its class-conditional density function. In order to recognise different identities, one estimates the class-conditional density of each identity and the overall inter-class Bayesian decision boundaries in the face space [230]. In particular, mixture models of appropriate order can achieve greater accuracy in an identification task than nearest mean and are more computationally efficient than nearest neighbour matching.

The need for establishing a greater degree of correspondence becomes greater when view variation becomes significant and larger numbers of faces must be identified. This is especially so if the number of example images is relatively small. In this case it becomes difficult to estimate reliable statistical models from template-based representations. There is obviously a trade-off here between the statistical and structural modelling. The greater the degree of correspondence used, the more tractable the statistics and the harder the structural matching.

In order to perform face recognition in general, an additional problem arises: that of understanding faces from multiple views. Compared to single-view face identification, it is notoriously more difficult to identify faces of moving people in natural scenes when faces are observed under continuously changing viewpoint. Face images of the same subject from different viewpoints are significantly more dissimilar than images of different people appearing in the same view. Head rotation in depth introduces nonlinear transformations in the image plane which cause difficulties for identification by correspondence. Such effects not only make the task of establishing correspondence more difficult, they also introduce additional complexity into the statistical distribution of face identities. How then can we model and identify faces under significantly different views? In the next chapter, we describe view-based methods for modelling and identifying faces across multiple views.

9 Multi-View Identification

Where's the face
One would meet in every place?

— John Keats, Fancy

It has been stressed from the outset that the appearance of a person's facial image depends upon many intrinsic and extrinsic factors including age, facial expression, illumination conditions and viewing geometry. Although an effective face recognition method needs to overcome all of these variations, perhaps the most difficult and commonly encountered factor is change of viewing geometry. It is far from sufficient to consider identification as merely concerned with isolated, static face images at some fixed pose (3D view) such as the upright, frontal view. Identification needs to be performed *in the presence of* (although it *need not be invariant to*) large pose variation. As a face rotates in depth, significant self-occlusion occurs. In fact, face images of the same person obtained from different viewpoints are usually significantly more dissimilar than images of different people viewed at the same pose.

So far we have focused on face models that can be learned from a population of upright, frontal view face images. These models are used to encode a representation of a new face at the same pose and novel images of that face can then be identified. Such an approach essentially treats faces as two-dimensional patterns. One may consider that in order to perform identification using images from a range of viewing angles in 3D space, the underlying three-dimensional nature of a face must also be taken into account in some way. Similarly to the problem of 3D pose estimation (Chapter 6), modelling 3D information for identification has traditionally been tackled by attempts to construct rather detailed 3D geometrical models of faces using model parameters to capture detailed shape variations between different faces. However, such an approach is, computationally, both expensive and difficult. In fact, for the purpose of identification, psychophysical and neurophysiological studies strongly suggest an alternative view-based approach more akin to that adopted earlier for pose estimation. Some of these findings will be highlighted at the end of this chapter. Let us first examine more closely the task of identifying faces at different poses using view-based methods which utilise learnable appearance models rather than explicit 3D structural models. This raises the following issues:

(1) Given certain 2D views of a face, a mechanism is required to encode a representation which subsequently allows that face to be identified when seen from significantly different viewing angles. We might ask whether a profile view contains sufficient information to allow subsequent identification of, say, a frontal view. Experimental evidence suggests that overlapping of visible surfaces between views is often sufficient to support identification [250]. How then can generalisation across large pose changes be realised?

(2) Conceptually, one may consider explicit pose estimation to be unnecessary for facial identification. For example, generalisation across pose might be achieved by interpolating between the responses of modules tuned to respond to prototype faces in a pose-invariant manner [99, 103]. However, since facial appearance variation due to pose is much greater than that due to identity, identification can be significantly simplified if pose is made known [134, 292, 294].

(3) The ability to estimate and predict the pose of a face and the ways in which it changes over time can impose temporal continuity in estimating the identity of the changing images of a face.

In the remainder of this chapter, we consider two different but complementary ways to address the problem of identification at significantly different views using 2D information alone. It is important to point out that, for now, the different views are not assumed to be temporally ordered, as they would be if taken from a sequence of a head rotating in depth. We shall return to the temporal dimension of identification later in Chapter 10.

We first explore an approach in which facial identities are modelled by learning from examples of each face at a whole range of poses. This requires a large number of learning samples but it should allow faces to be identified provided that they have already been observed and modelled at a similar pose. Secondly, we ask whether faces can be identified at poses significantly different from any at which they have previously been observed. This is clearly a more general and harder identification task. We review some theoretical basis for such generalisation across pose. We also describe a method that explores how the requirements for dense correspondence can be relaxed in order to derive a computationally viable approach to the task of associating facial identities across pose.

9.1 View-based Models

Recall that our treatment of the problem of fixed-view identification began by considering a simplistic nearest-neighbour approach in which each face was represented by simply storing all available images of it (Chapter 8). Limitations of this approach were the large indexing problem, large memory requirements and poor generalisation, making it both inefficient and ineffective. If the nearest-neighbour approach is also contemplated for identification at multiple views, the limitations associated with the fixed-view case are only further exacerbated. This is because the amount of variation in both shape and texture of facial appearance is now much greater resulting in additional difficulties.

In the image space, the distribution of faces at different views (poses) forms a nonlinear subspace (see face space introduced in Chapter 6). Compared with the problem of identifying faces at a fixed-view, it is therefore insufficient for multi-view identification to merely apply linear projections using either PCA or LDA and model identities in the resulting low-dimensional linear space. Instead, the task of identification requires a nonlinear transformation (identification function) that either captures individual face distributions (density models) or the boundaries of such distributions (classification functions) in the image space. Whilst capturing a single generic face model across views for face detection and pose estimation using density models is difficult, it is perhaps computationally even less feasible to model the face space sufficiently accurately for identification in this way. This is despite the fact that the face space remains intrinsically of much lower dimensionality than image space and consists of a large number of redundant sub-dimensions (null subspaces). In general, in order to remove null subspaces, a linear projection such as PCA can be applied before nonlinear modelling is introduced. However, since the projection to the lower dimensional eigenspace is linear, the resulting distribution of face images in the eigenspace remains nonlinear. Such dimensionality reduction can nevertheless improve computational tractability.

Tessellation of the view-sphere surface using a collection of subspaces (Chapter 6) suggests an extension to the methods introduced for fixed-view identification (Chapter 8). A separate model can be learned for each region of the view-sphere. Provided that pose can be estimated for view index-ing, a face viewed from any pose can then be encoded using the relevant model and subsequently identified at that pose. Such an approach to multi-view identification has been applied to the eigenface method using multiple, pose-specific eigenspaces [260]. It amounts to modelling the full nonlinear face space as a collection of linear subspaces with each of these subspaces tuned to a particular pose. Thus, it indirectly provides a view-invariant face model for identification. The number of different poses which need to be modelled in order to achieve view-invariant identification depends on the representation and matching strategy used. The use of viewing angle intervals of more than 25° to 30° is largely ineffective.

There remains a severe limitation: A face can only be identified at a given pose if it has previously been observed and encoded at that same pose. In other words, the face must already be *familiar*, having previously been seen, at the whole range of poses before this form of pose-invariant identification can be performed. This raises the question how a relatively *unfamiliar* face that has only been observed at a few poses can be identified when subsequently observed at other significantly different poses. In gen-eral, pose-invariant identification requires a way to *generalise across pose*.

If correspondences can be established between points in a set of 2D views of a (rigid) object, linear combinations of these views can be used to interpolate novel views between them [310, 346, 347]. Such an interpolation can also be performed simply using radial basis function networks [272]. This type of object-based interpolation to recognition is only accurate if precise correspondence can be established. Its use is therefore limited by self-occlusion to small pose changes and by imprecision to objects that are relatively distinct [242]. When considering a particular object in isolation, correspondence across large pose change is not feasible and the shared 3D structure of all faces suggests that such an approach is unlikely to provide a mechanism for generalising face identification across pose. Instead, what is required is a representation that exploits *prior knowledge of faces in general* in order to mediate generalisation across pose [239, 240]. The shared

3D structure which causes difficulty for the object-based approach can be exploited in the form of prior knowledge of faces.

9.2   The Role of Prior Knowledge

Structural and statistical prior knowledge of faces enables new faces to be efficiently represented and subsequently identified by comparison to their encoded representation. Statistical knowledge can only be effectively exploited *if* structural constraints are sufficiently satisfied through establishing correspondence. In other words, statistical knowledge about faces is best represented based on *2D shape* and *shape-free texture* [76]. We should try to determine the extent to which prior knowledge of shape and texture can be exploited for identification at multiple views.

Structural Knowledge: Although far from trivial, it is nevertheless possible to establish a certain amount of correspondence between different face images at the same or similar pose. However, given two images of faces at significantly different poses, even partial correspondences become much harder to establish. This implies that it is harder to extract shape-free texture and it is therefore more difficult to accurately estimate statistical knowledge about face images.

Statistical Knowledge: A face undergoing rotation in depth results in a significantly nonlinear transformation in image space. Therefore, linear models are far from sufficient for modelling face space across large pose variation.

In order to cope with nonlinear variations in both shape and texture, *learning* any prior knowledge about the texture of faces becomes more important. It is also true that the goodness of any statistical knowledge of faces is now more crucially dependent on the accuracy of the correspondence established between shapes at different poses.

9.3   View Correspondence in Identification

Let us now re-address the problem of learning structural knowledge in the form of nonlinear, 2D shape models across different views. Instead of trying

Figure 9.1 A 2D shape of a face across pose can be defined by a set of facial landmark feature points and their corresponding local grey-level structures.

to establish correspondences between individual facial feature points across views, one can learn a form of holistic shape based on a set of feature points. This gives more consistent and robust constraints for correspondence. In other words, if one is able to model the nonlinear shape variations of faces between different views, one implicitly solves the problem of establishing correspondences for a set of facial landmark points across these views.

At a fixed or restricted view, the 2D shape of a non-rigid object such as a human face can in general be modelled using a linear *active shape model* (ASM) based on a set of facial landmark feature points and their local grey-levels [67, 68, 200]. While this approach can be used to model and recover some changes in the shape of an object, it can only cope with linear variations at a fixed view. It is difficult for a linear ASM to cope with nonlinear shape variations across views and the inconsistency introduced in the landmarks as a result. We illustrate the problem through the example given in Figure 9.1. One could attempt to fit a 2D shape model to such images of faces rotating in depth from the left to the right profile view. However, the local grey-levels around the landmarks vary widely in this case. This is highlighted for one of the landmark points, marked '$\mathcal{A}$', which clearly cannot be established across views solely based on local grey-levels. Due to self-occlusion, local 2D image structures correspond to different parts of the 3D structure. To overcome this problem, we describe a multi-view, nonlinear active shape model that learns to capture all possible 2D shape variations in a training set and performs a nonlinear shape transformation during matching [292, 294]. First, let us introduce the concept of a linear ASM.

9.3.1   Learning Linear Shape Models

Active Shape Models (ASM) are flexible models that have been used for the modelling and representation of a range of objects [67, 200]. An ASM consists of two parts:

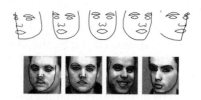

Figure 9.2 The top row shows the first principal mode of shape variation learned by the PDM from the training data. The lower row shows examples of matching $2D$ shape to face images using a linear PDM covering a restricted range of views ($\pm 20°$).

(1) A Point Distribution Model (PDM) is used to model the shape of an object and its variations using a set of landmark points.

(2) A set of Local Grey-Level (LGL) models are used to capture the local grey-level variations observed at each landmark point of the shape PDM.

A PDM can be used to represent the shape of a face as a set of N labelled landmark points in a vector $\mathbf{x} = (x_1, y_1, \ldots, x_N, y_N)$. In order to generate a flexible model that captures the intrinsic variations of a face, M aligned (translated, rotated and scaled) example face images are acquired as the training data set. The modes of variation of the face shape are captured by applying PCA on the deviations of the M example faces from the mean face shape, $\boldsymbol{\mu}$. An example is shown in Figure 9.2. Using PCA, valid shapes can be represented by a small set of principal components as:

$$\boldsymbol{\alpha} = \mathbf{U}^{\mathrm{T}}(\mathbf{x} - \boldsymbol{\mu}) \qquad (9.1)$$

where the kth column of $\mathbf{U}$ is the kth eigenvector of the covariance matrix whose eigenvalue is λ_k. The compactness of the model is achieved by retaining only the modes of variations (principal components) which account for most of the variance (largest eigenvalues). Any shape projected to the PCA space can be approximated and projected back into the input space using:

$$\mathbf{x} = \boldsymbol{\mu} + \mathbf{U}\,\boldsymbol{\alpha} \qquad (9.2)$$

PCA is also used to model the Local Grey-Level (LGL) at the location of each landmark point of the PDM. An LGL model is learned for each landmark and together with the PDM these are used to construct an Active Shape Model (ASM). An iterative search process is used to match an ASM to a novel face image. Each iteration consists of two steps:

(1) Given a starting position for the 2D shape of a face, one aims to move all the individual landmark points *independently* towards their local 'ideal' positions, known as the *local target points*. This is based on the LGL models learned from the training examples.

(2) Once plausible movements have been estimated for each of the landmarks, the positions of the other landmarks are taken into account using the PDM. This ensures that the overall shape remains valid within the modes of variation learned by the PDM from the training examples.

In general, the local target points only give an initial estimate for the shape of a face. This initial shape may not be a valid one according to the PDM. Therefore the shape is projected into the PCA space of the PDM, the shape space, for comparison using Equation (9.1). In this shape space, there exists a continuous region known as the Valid Shape Region (VSR). This VSR defines the following limits for all valid shape variations in the directions of the principal components:

$$-3\sqrt{\lambda_k} \leq \alpha_k \leq +3\sqrt{\lambda_k} \qquad (9.3)$$

If the projected initial shape given by the local target points is outside the VSR of the PDM, the nearest valid shape is projected back to the landmark feature space using Equation (9.2). This gives a new starting position for the shape of the face in the image and Step (1) is repeated. This iterative process is continued until the changes in the shape become negligible [149].

Unfortunately, linear ASMs of faces can only cope with very limited pose variations [292]. An implicit but important assumption is that correspondences between landmark points of different views can be established solely based on the grey-level information. This is clearly not true, as illustrated by the example given in Figure 9.1. Large, nonlinear shape variations are introduced due to changes in pose and the grey-level values around the landmarks are view-dependent. Figure 9.3 shows examples of failing to establish landmark correspondences when fitting a linear ASM of faces across views. In general, 2D image structures do change according to 3D pose. In order to find correspondences between landmarks across large variations in pose, nonlinear ASMs are required.

Figure 9.3 Examples of failing to establish facial landmark correspondences when fitting shapes to images using linear ASMs across views.

9.3.2 Nonlinear Shape Models

A multi-view, nonlinear, active face shape model can overcome many of the limitations of a single-view, linear ASM [292, 294]. Such a multi-view model is learned from a set of labelled face images and their corresponding 2D shapes across the view sphere [134, 251]. In particular, the model is required to perform a nonlinear transformation between significantly different views in order to extract shape-free textures for learning statistical knowledge of facial identities. This nonlinear model transformation is achieved using a type of nonlinear PCA, the Kernel PCA (KPCA) introduced in Chapter 3. It is important to point out that in order to constrain model search in KPCA space so as to both speed up and avoid local minima in model transformation across views, one aims to utilise any form of contextual knowledge. The use of labelled pose information on all the training images and their corresponding shapes is one obvious strategy to adopt. This is realised by explicitly encoding 3D pose information in a 2D active face shape model representation. In other words, both the shape PDM and the corresponding LGL models for the landmarks are trained by concatenations of feature vectors and their corresponding known pose angles. Figure 9.4 (a) shows examples of training face shapes across views from profile to profile. They were used to train a nonlinear active face shape model consisting of a PDM using 80 landmark feature points [292, 294].

Now, given an initial position of a novel face in an image, one can apply this pose-indexed and KPCA-based, nonlinear, active face shape model to match faces at different poses. The process of matching the nonlinear face ASM to a novel image finds both the 2D shape and the corresponding 3D pose of the face. Such a multi-view, active face model can be used to establish nonlinear shape correspondence with both known and unknown (novel) faces across views from profile to profile (see Figure 9.5).

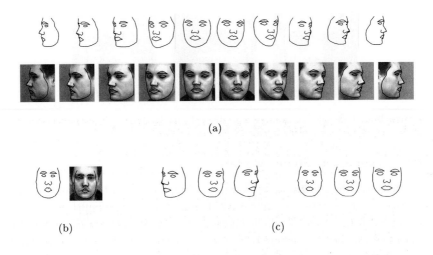

(a)

(b)   (c)

Figure 9.4 (a) Examples of training shapes across views and their super-impositions onto face images are indexed by 3D pose in yaw spanning ±90°. A PDM shape model is defined by 80 landmark feature points. (b) The average shape at the frontal-view for a given training database. (c) First two modes of shape variation.

The ability to establish shape correspondences can be extended to encompass both shape and texture at either a fixed view [66] or across poses [293]. Such models effectively approximate dense correspondence for every pixel based on sparse shape information alone. This is computationally more attractive than conventional methods such as computing optic flow [20, 21]. Figure 9.6 shows examples of establishing correspondences for both facial texture and shape between different poses. Each row in the figure shows an example of texture and shape fitting using either a person-specific or a generic model. In these examples, the leftmost images are the target face images. The second column shows bootstrapped initial fitting. Then images obtained at successive iterations are shown. The penultimate column shows the result of fitting after convergence. Finally, the rightmost column shows the recovered shape overlaid on the original image. Such models give some indication as to how structural and statistical knowledge can be learned and utilised for establishing correspondences between different poses and can thus provide approximately shape-free texture across views. Let us now turn to the possibilities of learning statistical models of facial identities at different poses.

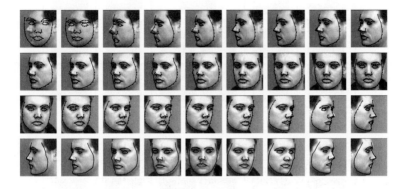

(a)

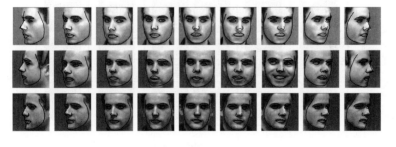

(b)

Figure 9.5 Examples of using a multi-view, active face shape model to establish non-linear correspondence between facial landmark feature points across views from profile to profile. (a) Shape correspondence on a known face across yaw. (b) Shape correspondence on unknown (novel) faces at different poses.

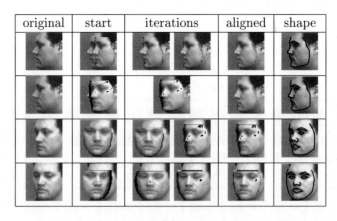

(a)

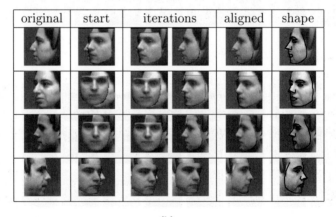

(b)

Figure 9.6 Aligning both texture and shape of multiple faces to novel images. (a) Fitting a person-specific model. The first example was initialised with a pose offset of 20° and a x-translational offset of 5 pixels. The second, third and fourth had pose offsets of 40°, 50° and 40° respectively. The faces are 30 pixels wide. (b) Fitting a generic model. The first example was initialised with a pose offset of 40°. The second example had a pose offset of 50° and x-offset of −4 pixels and y-offset of −3 pixels. The third and fourth examples had pose offsets of 90° and 40° respectively and they both had an x-offset of −6 pixels.

9.4   Generalisation from a Single View

Given sufficiently accurate correspondence between views, face images normalised in both scale and shape are obtained and can be used for the
purpose of identification. A face can be represented by concatenating representations of $2D$ shape and shape-free texture to form a vector, $\mathbf{x}$. We
shall now consider the problem of identifying faces across views in such a
representation space.

Let us consider a difficult multi-view identification problem: A face has
previously been observed only at a single, static pose $\boldsymbol{\gamma} = [\theta \; \phi]$. Its identity
has been modelled in some way based upon this one image. At some later
point in time, the face is again observed but at a significantly different pose.
The task is to identify the face despite the fact that it has only previously
been observed at a single, significantly different pose. Later we will address
a more realistic scenario in which sequences containing pose change are
available for learning and identification rather than single, isolated images.

9.4.1   Identity by Linear Combination

Let $\mathbf{x}_i^\gamma$ denote a previously observed face at pose $\boldsymbol{\gamma}$, possibly in the form of
concatenated $2D$ shape and shape-free texture vectors. One approach is to
then represent this face using a linear combination of K other faces at the
same pose [22]. We will call these K faces *prototypes*. The representation
is obtained by solving for coefficients α_k in:

$$\mathbf{x}_i^\gamma = \sum_{k=1}^{K} \alpha_k \, \mathbf{x}_k^\gamma \qquad (9.4)$$

The vector $\boldsymbol{\alpha}_i = [\alpha_1 \alpha_2 \ldots \alpha_K]$ is then used to represent the face. The
coefficients can be found using Singular Value Decomposition (SVD). The
underlying assumption behind such a representation is that faces at some
fixed pose form a linear (vector) space. This is not true in general although
it is a good approximation if an appropriate degree of correspondence has
been established between the different face images. In that case, $\mathbf{x}$ would
denote both 2D shape and shape-free texture obtained by setting faces in
correspondence. A similar approach was described in Chapter 8 for fixed-
view identification in which case the face space was approximated as a linear
subspace using PCA.

One can use this concept of representation by linear combination to represent a face in terms of other faces at the same pose. Subsequently, given a novel face $\mathbf{x}_j^\xi$ at pose $\boldsymbol{\xi}$, identification is performed by first obtaining a representation vector $\boldsymbol{\alpha}_j$ in terms of the K prototype faces:

$$\mathbf{x}_j^\xi = \sum_{k=1}^{K} \alpha_k \mathbf{x}_k^\xi \tag{9.5}$$

Identification is then based on *the similarity of $\boldsymbol{\alpha}_j$ to the stored face representations*. In particular, if $\boldsymbol{\alpha}_j$ is sufficiently similar to $\boldsymbol{\alpha}_i$ then the face can be identified as i. This method makes the following two assumptions:

(1) A face at a given pose can be represented as a linear combination of faces at that pose.
(2) The same linear combination is also valid at other poses.

It is helpful to ask under what theoretical circumstances these assumptions will hold exactly. It was noted that the first of these two assumptions is only accurate when different faces are set in dense correspondence so that 2D shape and texture are separated. Let us first consider the shape. In this case, $\mathbf{x}$ denotes the $2N$-dimensional vector of 2D shape (image coordinates). The linear classes theorem [354, 356] then states that the second assumption is accurate if the *3D shape* of the face i can be expressed as a linear combination of the 3D shapes of the K prototype faces. In other words, if $\mathbf{x}^{3D}$ denotes a $3N$-dimensional vector of 3D coordinates:

$$\mathbf{x}^{3D} = \sum_{k=1}^{K} \alpha_k \mathbf{x}_k^{3D} \tag{9.6}$$

Secondly, in the case of shape-free texture, $\mathbf{x}$ denotes a vector of intensity values. These intensity values are sampled from the *same points* on the face at different poses. Under Lambertian shading and with unchanging illumination, the texture remains unchanged and the assumption is therefore valid. In practice, however, the assumption is inaccurate due to occlusions, non-Lambertian shading and changing illumination.

It seems clear that the above model is only approximate. One way to assess whether it is a reasonable approximation is to use it to synthesise new images of faces at novel poses. In particular, once $\mathbf{x}_i^\gamma$ has been represented as $\boldsymbol{\alpha}_i$ using Equation (9.4), an image of the same face can be synthesised at a new pose by combining the K prototype faces at the new pose using exactly the same coefficients α_i. In fact, when synthesis is performed in this manner, the resulting images are quite convincing suggesting that the approximation to a linear class is reasonable provided that pixel-wise correspondence is established so that 2D shape and texture are treated separately [354, 356]. It is important to note that correspondence between images at *different poses* is not needed. However, correspondence between different faces at the same pose is required for the model to be accurate and we have seen that this cannot always be accurately established. Loss of correspondence will imply that the assumptions made by the linear combinations method become less accurate.

It is worth pointing out that when a face is represented as a linear combination of K prototype views the coefficients are found by minimising the reconstruction error in a least-squares sense using SVD. This is similar in essence to representations using PCA but without the further approximation implied by retaining only the first few principal components. The objective implicit in this approach is to allow a *faithful reconstruction* of the original view from the coefficients and the K prototype face views. However, for our purpose of multi-view identification, we need a representation scheme that can effectively mediate generalisation of identification across pose and such a scheme need not facilitate accurate reconstruction.

9.4.2   Identity by Similarity to Prototype Views

Instead of the linear coefficients resulting from Equation (9.4), a face image can be represented in terms of prototype views by measuring its *similarity* to each of the prototypes [101]. Let us consider a representation based on a measure of similarity $h(\mathbf{x}_i, \mathbf{x}_k)$ between two face image representations $\mathbf{x}_i$ and $\mathbf{x}_k$. In particular, consider a vector $\boldsymbol{\alpha}_i = [\alpha_1 \alpha_2 \ldots \alpha_K]$ of similarity measures obtained by comparing a face view $\mathbf{x}_i^\gamma$ at pose γ to a set of K prototype faces at the same pose:

$$\alpha_k^\gamma = h(\mathbf{x}_i^\gamma, \mathbf{x}_k^\gamma), \qquad k = 1 \ldots K \tag{9.7}$$

A novel face is thus represented by a vector of *similarities to prototypes*. This concept is illustrated in Figure 9.7.

If K is greater than the dimensionality, N, of each view, $\mathbf{x}$, then this representation amounts to an expansion in which the K example faces are used to determine basis functions. If $K < N$ then the representation $\boldsymbol{\alpha}_i$ will not be unique to $\mathbf{x}_i$ but can nevertheless be a useful representation.

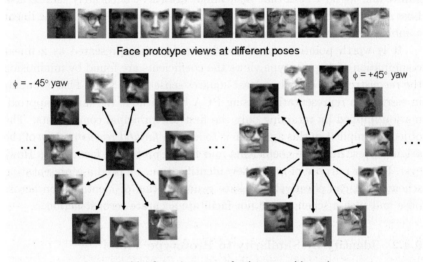

$$\alpha_i(\phi) = [\alpha_1, \ldots \alpha_k, \ldots \alpha_K] \quad \text{where } \alpha_k = h(\mathbf{x}_i, \mathbf{x}_k)$$

Figure 9.7 Illustration of representation using similarity to prototype views. A database contains example faces (top) of K different people at different pose angles. For a given pose, a new face image $\mathbf{x}_i$ (centre of circle) is compared with each face prototype view at that pose (perimeter of circle) using a similarity function $h(\cdot)$. The similarity measures α_k are concatenated into a similarity vector α_i. In the example shown, $K = 11$ prototypes are used to represent a face. The similarity vector at any pose therefore has 11 dimensions.

As with the linear space method, this similarity vector can be used to perform identification across pose under the assumption that it provides a pose invariant representation, i.e. $\boldsymbol{\alpha}_i^\gamma$ does not vary with $\boldsymbol{\gamma}$. Some relatively simple similarity measures suited to different representations, $\mathbf{x}$, are Pearson's correlation coefficient, a modified inverse Euclidean distance and a radial Gaussian function. In fact, the similarity function, $h(\cdot)$, can have many forms and could even be the result of a complex matching process. Also note that $h(\cdot)$ need not return a single scalar value but could in fact return a vector of values which together constitute a measure of similarity. Also, recall that $\mathbf{x}$ can denote a template-based representation or alternatively the 2D shape and shape-free texture after correspondence has been established.

9.5 Generalisation from Multiple Views

Solving the problem of generalisation from a single view is necessary when a face must be identified based solely on a single image. In practice, however, it is reasonable to expect that more than one familiar view will be available. For example, when a face is observed live or from a recorded video sequence, a range of views are observed. How can generalisation best be performed from these observed views? The problem then is how to interpret novel views between familiar views. Let us now consider the problem of generalising from a limited set of views to other views at previously unseen poses.

Given a single *training* view $\mathbf{x}_i^\gamma$, a vector $\boldsymbol{\alpha}_i^\gamma$ of linear coefficients or *similarities to prototypes* was used to encode the face from the available view and identification was performed by assuming that $\boldsymbol{\alpha}_i$ was pose invariant. If we believe this assumption then we should attribute any observed variation in $\boldsymbol{\alpha}_i$ with pose to noise. Given several views it would then be useful to estimate $\boldsymbol{\alpha}_i$ by averaging the corresponding vectors obtained from each available view.

In fact, $\boldsymbol{\alpha}_i$ is not pose invariant and this is especially true when exact correspondence is not established. Instead of imposing the invariance assumption, we can attempt to learn from examples how $\boldsymbol{\alpha}_i$ varies across views. Weaker assumptions than invariance such as smooth or linear variation with pose can be used [134]. Ignoring temporal variation for now, we can treat different views as temporally uncorrelated. Variation in $\boldsymbol{\alpha}_i$ with pose change can be modelled in terms of a generic mean transformation together with a superimposed person-specific transformation.

Consider the problem of learning a mapping from a face at pose γ to the coefficient vector $\boldsymbol{\alpha}^\gamma = [\alpha_1 \alpha_2 \ldots \alpha_K]$ expected at that pose. Given a training set of K prototype faces at pose γ, the expected or mean vector of similarities can be computed:

$$\overline{\boldsymbol{\alpha}}^\gamma = E(\boldsymbol{\alpha}^\gamma) = \frac{1}{K(K-1)} \sum_{j=1}^{K} \sum_{k=1, k \neq j}^{K} h(\mathbf{x}_j^\gamma, \mathbf{x}_k^\gamma) \qquad (9.8)$$

Identification can then be based on the assumption that $\boldsymbol{\alpha}_i^\gamma - \overline{\boldsymbol{\alpha}}^\gamma$ is invariant with respect to pose.

The above computations require many examples to be available at *discrete* poses across the view-sphere. In reality, however, the view-sphere is continuous and the face representation vectors, $\boldsymbol{\alpha}$, should therefore vary continuously with pose. Let us consider a more general problem of continuously correlating the face coefficients with changes in pose.

Ideally, face coefficients should be interpolated and extrapolated at least as well as would be achieved by assuming them pose invariant. To compensate the inaccuracy of such an assumption, one subtracts $\overline{\boldsymbol{\alpha}}$ from all local, pose specific coefficient vectors and aims to learn an offset function $f_{off} : \Re^2 \to \Re^K$ which adjusts a pose γ by expected offsets $\Delta \boldsymbol{\alpha} = [\Delta \alpha_1 \Delta \alpha_2 \ldots \Delta \alpha_K]$ from the global mean ($\overline{\boldsymbol{\alpha}}$). As a result,

$$\boldsymbol{\alpha} = f_{av}(\boldsymbol{\gamma}) = f_{off}(\boldsymbol{\gamma}) + \overline{\boldsymbol{\alpha}} \qquad (9.9)$$

The offset function $f_{off}(\cdot)$ can be learned using, for example, a Radial Basis Function (RBF) network or Support Vector Machines (SVM). This approach models both *pose variant* face coefficients across the view-sphere where sufficient training samples are available, and *pose invariant* coefficients in between. The above function aims to approximate the constancy assumption in poorly sampled areas of the view-sphere. In well sampled areas of the view-sphere on the other hand, the predicted average coefficients are improved by learned local offsets from training samples. The effect is populating the view-sphere with multiple discrete familiar views.

If there is more than one training view available for a particular face, the way in which coefficients vary with pose specifically for that face ought to be modelled using contiguous function approximation. For example, given a frontal and profile view, linear interpolation can be employed to predict values for intermediate views. Consider a simple case when view changes are caused by variations in tilt angle, θ. If similarity measures of known faces at two views, θ_1 and θ_2, are available, identification at novel views θ between θ_1 and θ_2 can then be performed by linear interpolation such as:

$$f_{per}(\theta) = \alpha^{\theta_1} + \frac{\theta - \min(\theta_1, \theta_2)}{|\theta_1 - \theta_2|}\left(\alpha^{\theta_2} - \alpha^{\theta_1}\right), \quad \theta_1 \le \theta \le \theta_2 \quad (9.10)$$

One would like to extend this simple interpolation to extrapolation over the view-sphere. In general, consider learning from examples a function $f_{per} : \mathcal{R}^2 \to \mathcal{R}^K$ which takes pose $\gamma = (\theta, \phi)$ to offsets from the coefficients predicted by the above average model (Equation 9.9). This requires first subtracting the global mean $\overline{\alpha}$ and the local offset transformation $f_{off}(\gamma)$ from the examples. One can then learn a person-specific function $f_{per}(\gamma)$ with localised basis functions such as RBF or SVM. Overall then,

$$\alpha = f_{per}(\gamma) + f_{off}(\gamma) + \overline{\alpha} \quad (9.11)$$

This ensures reasonable extrapolation and should further improve identity discrimination near training examples. There are a number of desirable features from this approach to modelling variations in face coefficients:

(1) It should allow extrapolation to be performed *at least as well as* would be achieved by either assuming pose invariance or through generic transformation of the coefficients.
(2) It should tolerate highly non-uniform sampling of the view-sphere, e.g. from typical face sequences of a given scenario.
(3) It should still give acceptable identification from relatively few examples.
(4) The method can provide a measure of confidence.

9.6   Biological Perspectives

In psychophysical experiments investigating the effect of pose upon identification by humans, subjects are typically shown pictures of faces at various poses during a learning phase. They are subsequently shown test pictures of faces at various poses and asked to perform some identification task. The results have not always been consistent due largely to procedural differences. The main findings are outlined as follows.

On Familiar Faces

The effect that pose has on identification depends on the familiarity of the face to be identified. If the face is already familiar then the accuracy of episodic memory is largely unaffected by pose change [37]. Similarly, when the face is seen at the whole range of poses during a learning phase, there is then no viewpoint preference in identification tests [153, 308]. This may suggest that there is no canonical view for face identification. Once we have been exposed to many views of a face, we can recognise it approximately equally well from any reasonable viewing angle. Computational models such as those introduced in Section 9.1 can be broadly regarded as reflecting such findings. On the other hand, our ability to learn from inverted (upside-down) faces is poorer and identification of inverted faces is pose-dependent. When shown an inverted face at a range of poses during learning, recognition is subsequently best near the frontal view [153]. This suggests that some form of prior knowledge of upright faces is used to encode and recognise upright faces.

On Unfamiliar Faces

If a face is unfamiliar and is only seen at a single pose during learning then subsequent identification of that face is pose-dependent. Our ability to generalise from a single learned pose to novel poses is limited [37, 45, 152, 153, 337]. Again, there do not seem to be canonical views (i.e. preferred test poses) for identification. However, identification performance is dependent upon the *learning* view. The best single view for learning is found at a y-axis rotation (yaw) of between 22.5° and 67.5° from the frontal view. This is known as the *three-quarters (3/4) view advantage*. While this advantage is significant for shaded faces, it has less effect when the faces are textured [337]. The 3/4 view advantage is probably due to the approximate bilateral symmetry of faces and in particular the symmetry of shape [337]. Generalisation from a frontal face deteriorates with increasing rotation in depth, while the 3/4 view shows a peak in generalisation performance for the opposite symmetric view. However, this effect is not strong for profile views [153]. Generalisation to an artificially generated mirror symmetric (flipped) 3/4 view image of a face is even better than to the true symmetric view [338]. Even without texture and hair, we are still very sensitive to the remaining asymmetries in the shape of a face. Identification performance drops if the symmetry is disturbed by asymmetric illumination [338]. The use of symmetry for identification has also been proposed from a computational standpoint [211, 275, 355, 357, 358].

While humans can generalise reasonably well to novel poses of upright faces, the ability to generalise to novel poses of inverted faces is significantly worse [239]. This suggests that the mechanism used to generalise across pose is class-based where upright faces form a distinct class [239].

The effects of changes in pose and expression [37, 84, 193, 201, 255] and in illumination [239] all have direct relevance to the *robustness* of the face recognition processes. Experiments have shown that when people are asked to identify unfamiliar faces they are good at identifying faces they have seen at the same pose. However, they are worse at identifying faces whose pose has changed and worse again if both pose and expression have changed [37]. More dramatic deterioration occurs when the faces are disguised through changes in hair style or the addition of spectacles [255].

In addition to psychophysical studies on human vision, there have also been neurobiological findings on the effect of pose on face identification in other biological vision systems. For example, it was noted in the previous chapter that about 10% of face-selective cells found in monkey temporal lobe show sensitivity to identity [263]. This sensitivity to identity has been found in cells responsive to the range of different head poses studied. There are cells which prefer person A at frontal view, person B at profile view etc. As well as pose-specific cells there are cells that exhibit pose-invariance, responding to many different views of the head. About 10% of these pose-invariant cells also exhibit sensitivity to identity.

9.7 Discussion

In this chapter, we have focused on the problem of identifying faces across significantly different views due to changes in pose. The problem is of both computational and practical importance. Computationally, appearances of the same face vary considerably across different poses, more so than those of different faces at a single-view. Such variations are intrinsically nonlinear. This nonlinearity makes establishing accurate correspondence difficult. Furthermore, it substantially increases the complexity of the statistical distributions of face identities in face space making them less separable. Identification therefore becomes more difficult. Not surprisingly, the central computational issue of concern here is how knowledge of the identity of a face at a single or a set of familiar view(s) can be generalised to novel views for identification. Equally importantly, we considered how structural knowledge about shape can be learned and used to provide the necessary correspondence for obtaining approximately shape-free texture information.

Effective solutions to such computational problems are also important for practical applications. Human subjects are almost always in motion and as a result, their facial appearances are undergoing constant change, largely due to changes in pose. It is extremely unrealistic to assume that one can always acquire face images of a potential subject of interest under very similar if not identical fixed-view conditions to those in which the statistical knowledge of facial identities was learned. The ability to effectively generalise (transform) existing knowledge about identities from familiar views to novel views is therefore crucial.

So far, different views of faces have been treated as a collection of snapshots in isolation. The problem of learning transformation functions of face identities between views may be made unnecessarily hard as a result. Realistically, however, faces are observed continuously in space and over time. Consequently, the changes in 2D facial appearance across views ought to be spatio-temporally continuous and progressive. An intuitive but also intriguing question to ask is to what extent the temporal continuity and *ordering of different views* can be exploited in the modelling of knowledge about face identities over time. In other words, *how can we identify faces in motion?*

10 Identifying Moving Faces

He does smile his face into more lines than are in the
new map with the augmentation of the Indies.

— William Shakespeare, Twelfth Night

In the real world, faces appear to be almost always in motion. A face is usually viewed over an extended period of time during which different views of varying appearance are observed. Temporal continuity means that these views can be naturally associated with the same face. It is perhaps clear that facial motion provides an observer with multiple, different views and this in itself facilitates learning and identification. However, a moving face provides more than just many *static views* with their variations in viewpoint (rigid motion) and expression (non-rigid motion): it also provides dynamic, *temporal* information. Perception of non-rigid facial motion caused by muscle movements is obviously useful for understanding facial expressions but is it also useful for identification? Let us try to address the problems of learning and identification of moving faces in a temporal setting. In particular, we can ask what role temporal information extracted from rigid and non-rigid motion plays in identification.

There has been relatively little research on identification of moving faces. We feel that this is due to a commonly held belief that computation on image sequences is necessarily more complex and expensive than computation on static images. It is quite widely perceived that temporal knowledge such as motion contained in moving faces may not provide more useful information for identification than multiple static images. To examine such misconceptions, we begin this discussion by reviewing psychophysical evidence for the role of motion in identification. We then describe a few machine-based methods.

10.1   Biological Perspectives

Many psychophysical face recognition studies have focused on examining static *picture recognition* rather than realistic face recognition [38]. However, there have been several studies, particularly in recent years, which provide intriguing evidence for the role of temporal information in face identification.

10.1.1   Learning and Identity Constancy

Faces are viewed over extended periods of time during which the identity of the observed face remains constant. This provides an obvious cue as to how to associate the many images of a face. An unidentified view following an identified view is almost certainly of the same face. There is psychophysical evidence that the process of learning a representation of a face for identification purposes is affected by this temporal regularity. In one experiment [362], subjects were presented with *sequences* of unfamiliar faces, each consisting of five images from left to right profile views. These sequences were constructed by interleaving images of different faces so that the identity changed as the head appeared to turn from profile to profile. When subsequently presented with pairs of images and asked whether they were of the same face, subjects confused faces more often if these faces had appeared within the same sequence during learning. This suggests that *temporal ordering* and an *identity constancy assumption* are used to constrain the association of different views during learning [362].

10.1.2   The Effect of Temporal Order of Pose on Learning

We have seen that different views of a face appearing in sequence seem to be more readily associated during learning. This is at least in part due to temporal proximity of views. However, further psychophysical experiments suggest that temporal information has a greater role to play in learning to represent individual faces.

Hill *et al.* [153] presented subjects with views of shaded 3D models of unfamiliar faces. Each face was seen at the same five poses: left profile, left three-quarters, frontal, right three-quarters and right profile views. One group of subjects was shown these views in sequence so that the head appeared to rotate. Another group was shown exactly the same views but in random order. When subsequently tested on static views, identification was significantly better if a face had been learned from an ordered sequence. This experiment suggests that temporal ordering of face rotation in depth facilitates learning of previously unfamiliar faces. However, the use of just five views at poses separated by 45° meant that the sequences were not of continuous motion. Indeed, in a similar experiment by Christie and Bruce [61] which used even fewer views (2-3) to construct sequences of head 'nodding' and 'shaking', no advantage was found for ordered sequences. In another experiment, Pike *et al.* [270] compared learning from continuous motion sequences captured at video frame rate with learning from five static views of heads rotating through 360°. They found a significant advantage for the continuous motion sequences although it was not clear to what extent identification was improved simply by virtue of the increased number of views contained in the continuous sequences. These experiments, particularly that of Hill *et al.* [153], suggest that *temporal information facilitates learning.*

10.1.3   The Effect of Motion on Familiar Face Identification

The above experiments were all concerned with the effects of using sequences for learning previously unfamiliar faces. We can also ask whether already learned, *familiar* faces are more easily identified when viewed in image sequences. A significant problem with designing psychophysical experiments to investigate this question is that we can nearly always identify a familiar face from a single, static image, at least under good viewing conditions. It is often difficult to demonstrate an advantage for sequences due to this ceiling effect. However, this does not mean that temporal information plays no role in identification, even under ideal viewing conditions. It is often the case that *we observe moving faces under less than ideal conditions so that identification from any single snapshot becomes difficult.* Consider, for example, identifying faces captured on video tapes obtained from CCTV security cameras at petrol stations.

Sequences in which spatial information is degraded in various ways have been used to investigate the role of temporal information. In a classic experiment, Johansson [173] attached small illuminated markers to a human actor's body and recorded the actor in motion. The video contrast was adjusted so that when played back, only the illuminated markers were visible. These moving light displays removed nearly all spatial, structural visual information while retaining temporal information in the form of the markers' trajectories. Johansson's method has been used to study faces by covering actors' faces with black make-up and scattering numerous visible white spots over the surface of the face [13]. When shown sequences in which only the white spots were visible, non-rigid facial motion helped observers in recognising that they were seeing a face and in interpreting facial expression [13, 44]. However, while identification performance was significantly better when the white spots were in motion, it was still highly inaccurate and provided somewhat limited evidence for the use of temporal information [44].

A limitation with moving light displays is that temporal information is severely degraded since it is only available at sparse points on the face. As an alternative, similar experiments have been performed using face images in photographic negative [187, 197]. It was argued that whilst sequences of negative images retained all their temporal information, cues to structure from shading and texture were severely disrupted. Knight and Johnston [187] used short head-and-shoulders sequences of famous people talking to camera. Identification accuracy from these sequences was compared to that of a single "typical" image from each sequence. Accuracy was significantly better from sequences. Lander *et al.* [197] found that this motion advantage was also present when these negatives were presented inverted (upside-down), contradicting an earlier study [187]. Similar results were obtained with binary images obtained by thresholding face images [187]. It is not clear though from these experiments whether the advantage gained using sequences is due to temporal information or simply to the increased number of views in the sequences. However, in a further experiment, identification from sequences was compared to identification from the same number of static images displayed simultaneously. There was still a consistent advantage for sequences. Finally, it was found that altering the dynamics of motion, by either slowing down the frame rate or by disrupting the rhythm of the sequence (by repeating some frames more than others), also reduced identification rates significantly [197].

Together, these findings suggest that motion provides additional cues for identifying familiar faces. Furthermore, motion demonstrably increases accuracy under a variety of degraded viewing conditions.

10.2 Computational Theories of Temporal Identification

Let us now consider plausible computational theories for the role of motion in identification. The face representation schemes described in previous chapters have all been static or *atemporal*. The concern has been to represent the static structure of faces in a way which is temporally invariant. In light of the psychophysical findings reviewed so far, spatio-temporal representation schemes intrinsically incorporating temporal information would seem to be more attractive. While temporal change is clearly a useful cue for gauging atemporal structure, an efficient perceiver should also use it as a cue to recognition in its own right [329]. Here we explore both of these possibilities.

10.2.1 Atemporal Representation

It has been suggested that motion aids face identification primarily because it enables recovery of 3D shape. Given a predominantly rigid motion, such as a face rotating in depth, structure-from-motion, for example, could recover atemporal 3D shape information [342]. However, we have discussed in preceding chapters the converging psychophysical, neurobiological and computational evidence for 2D view-based representation of faces. In particular, human ability to generalise to novel images beyond the range of familiar views is very limited [40]. This seems to be at conflict with the assumption that moving faces provide cues for recovering 3D structure since any 3D facial structure would not be restricted to familiar views.

Alternatively, it is more likely that structural information is extracted from moving faces in a face-specific manner rather than using a generic structure-from-motion approach. The knowledge that the object being viewed is a face imposes constraints and the knowledge that the object is likely to be a *particular* face imposes even stronger constraints. Let us assume for the moment an atemporal, view-based scheme and explore how motion can be used to assist learning and identification.

Temporal proximity of images provides temporal binding of perceptually salient properties. Temporally proximal face images have similar pose, illumination and expression and are almost certainly of the same person. These temporal constraints provide information useful for learning a view-based representation and for accessing such a representation during recognition. It was shown, for example, that temporal constraints can be exploited to improve both 3D face pose estimation and tracking (Section 7.9). The use of temporal filtering and prediction largely overcame problems of noise and ambiguity encountered in static pose estimation. Accurate pose estimation can improve identification by facilitating appropriate indexing of a view-based representation. Temporal constraints can also be used to track the face in a representational parameter space. For example, the identity constancy constraint in a face sequence can be exploited in decoupling the identity from pose, lighting and expression variations during tracking and discriminating between faces in a database [105]. In such an approach, the sources of variation in each image are approximately isolated. For example, the parameters of a face are partitioned into those that affect identity and those that describe the residual effects of pose, lighting and expression. Discriminant functions provide an initial estimate of the face identity. The accuracy of this estimate is improved by modeling the dynamics of the residual variations and tracking the face in a sequence of images. Using a sequence of images a corrected estimate of the true identity is recovered.

Alternatively, a moving face could provide temporally correlated information that facilitates effective view transformation to a nearby familiar view. Temporal information should allow generalisation over larger pose intervals than is achievable using only static matching.

10.2.2   Spatio-temporal Signatures

Rather than using temporal information simply to mediate an atemporal representation, the temporal information may be used for recognition in its own right. Stored representation need not be atemporal but can be spatio-temporal. Most existing object recognition theories, including view-based schemes, are concerned with static objects. Extensions are needed to account for temporal representation.

There is evidence from psychophysical experiments with moving light displays that biological motion is represented as viewer-centered, spatio-temporal traces [50]. Further evidence for object representation in terms of spatio-temporal signatures was provided by Stone [328, 329]. For example, when an unfamiliar object was learned from a sequence of it rotating in depth, that object was subsequently identified more reliably if seen rotating in the same direction than observed rotating in the opposite direction. This suggests a representation using an object-specific, spatio-temporal signature, although the exact nature of this signature remains obscure.

The psychophysical experiments described in Section 10.1.3 used sequences in which the motion was largely due to facial expression changes during speech, suggesting that such motion is predictive of identity. Intuitively, we might expect idiosyncratic, person-specific, temporal information to be contained in such facial movements. However, this possibility has not been properly explored in computer vision. Preliminary experiments were performed by Luettin *et al.* [213]. They modelled lip motion during speech using hidden Markov models and results indicated that these spatio-temporal models were useful for speaker identification.

Faces observed while undergoing rotation in depth also provide temporal information including constrained configural changes of facial appearance over time. Intuitively, this implies that the spatio-temporal knowledge of how individual faces change and move in space provides a means for predicting how a face will appear across all possible views. Such spatio-temporal face signatures can potentially play a significant role in identification [280]. In the following sections, we describe computational methods that can be used to exploit models for temporal prediction of holistic facial trajectories and temporal correlation in view transformation for the identification of moving faces.

10.3   Identification using Holistic Temporal Trajectories

In order to exploit the observation that moving faces embed additional temporal information which is used by human vision for face identification, one must first choose a form of representation that can be used to extract temporal information which is person-dependent. An obvious means for extracting temporal information is to compute the temporal trajectories of all the pixels in the images of a moving face by establishing dense correspondence between images. However, this process essentially requires the recovery of optic flow which is both computationally under-constrained and prohibitive in cost. In addition, temporal information derived from optic flow is pixel-based which may not provide the necessary holistic, correlated descriptions among different parts of a face. If temporal structures of a holistic representation of face appearance can be computed, the task of identification would be to find the underlying spatio-temporal signature that can describe the temporal characteristics of these holistic facial temporal structures in feature space.

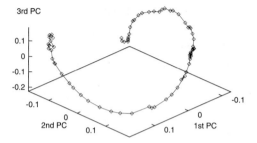

Figure 10.1   A trajectory in the face space of a moving face rotating in depth.

It has been shown that a set of example holistic temporal trajectories of moving faces form temporal structures (manifolds) in feature space [133, 247] (see also Sections 6.2 and 6.3). If person-specific temporal information can be used to predict novel trajectories of a moving face, the task of identification is implicitly achieved [135, 280]. This implicit measure of change in temporal structure can be regarded as a temporal signature of a face. In order to extract and visualise holistic facial trajectories, one can first reduce the dimensionality of the representation using, for example, PCA. Similarly to the manifolds formed by continuous pose change shown earlier (Figure 10.1), the trajectories of projected images of a moving face form a non-linear manifold in face space.

Given the trajectories of normalised coefficient vectors as a representation of holistic facial dynamics, one approach to prediction is to use recurrent neural networks. Such models have both feed-forward and feedback connections. For computational efficiency and simplicity in learning, here we consider a type of partially recurrent network for such a task in which the majority of connections are feed-forward and adaptable with a few selected fixed feedback connections to a set of *context units*. Several architectures have been suggested [110, 178,

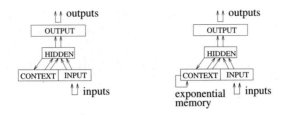

Figure 10.2 Left: An Elman network. Right: Inclusion of exponential memory.

241] which have in common this use of a set of context units to receive the feedback signals and act as memory for the recent past required in dynamic tasks.

Elman [110] suggested the network architecture suitable for prediction and recognition of temporal structures (Figure 10.2). The network consists of (1) four sets of units: the input, hidden, output and context units, (2) a set of feed-forward connections and (3) a set of fixed feedback connections from the hidden to the context units. The context units hold a copy of the activations of the hidden units from the previous time step and thus help to remember the past internal state. At the same time, the hidden units encode input patterns so that the layer interconnections build an internal representation of the relationship between successive inputs in a time series.

The extra connections in recurrent networks develop internal representations that are sensitive to temporal context, i.e. they provide a temporal memory. However, due to the increased number of weights and more complex dynamics, there is generally a problem with the stability of networks of this kind. For complex temporal structures where the next input depends not only on the previous time step but also on ones earlier in the series, an augmented context layer can be used. This may explicitly use an exponential memory decay where each context unit has an exponential memory of the internal state (right in Figure 10.2). The exponential encoding of the hidden unit activation is formulated according to:

$$\mathbf{c}_t = (1 - \kappa)\, \mathbf{h}_t + \kappa\, \mathbf{c}_{t-1} \tag{10.1}$$

where the decay constant κ lies in the interval $[0, 1]$, $\mathbf{h}_t$ represents the vector of the hidden unit activation values at time t and $\mathbf{c}_t$ represents the context vector at time t. Thus, in the expansion of $\mathbf{c}_t$, the main term is from the previous time, $t - 1$, but a secondary term is due to $t - 2$, a third to $t - 3$ and so on until the effect becomes negligible.

In order to extract the temporal signature of a face we track and segment a set of face sequences with a fixed number of frames taken from the
head movement of a person. We use PCA to reduce the dimensionality
of the face sequence and project every image frame to its face subspace.
An Elman network is then used to learn possible temporal signatures of
one face class where the input and output patterns of the network are
the face vectors in the eigenspace. The temporal change in these vectors
over successive frames can then be measured by their temporal Euclidean
distance. This information is considered to be relevant to the temporal
signature of a face class in a given spatio-temporal context. Such recurrent networks are able to learn to some extent facial spatio-temporal
characteristics from examples and cope well with temporal scaling [135,
280]. However, a significant limitation of this approach is its lack of scalability. Multiple networks may be required to allow for multiple hypotheses
to be examined simultaneously. These networks are also sensitive to temporal segmentation and in this regard, determining the starting point of a
temporal structure can be problematic.

An alternative way to recognise and predict temporal structures is to
use the Condensation algorithm [29, 136, 170, 171, 363]. This algorithm
can predict and track multiple hypotheses in feature space over time. Unlike Kalman Filters, the Condensation algorithm could be exploited for
tracking and recognising multiple spatio-temporal face signatures as temporal structures simultaneously. It propagates multiple matches and applies
computational resources to more fully explore the most likely ones. Due to
the algorithm's ability to propagate multiple hypotheses over time, it can
potentially predict the likelihood of each face at a given time.

10.4   Identification by Continuous View Transformation

Instead of modelling the variations between holistic, temporal facial trajectories for identity prediction, one may consider that the temporal information from moving faces is more likely to be used for view transformations.
Such transformations enable identification of novel views of moving faces
based only on a small set of familiar prototypical, learned views. Following
this interpretation, temporal information from moving faces can be used
to provide the necessary temporal correlation for both view transformation
and identification [134]. Such an approach utilises a database of example

views given by a small set of prototype faces and employs representation in terms of similarity measures to prototypes (see Chapter 9).

Earlier we described a method for tracking pose using similarity to prototypes (Section 7.9.2). A term which penalised changes in the similarity vector over time was used to constrain the search for pose. In the previous chapter we adopted the assumption that while different faces had different similarity vectors, these vectors were approximately invariant to pose change. The pose tracking method which penalises change in the similarity vector is thus essentially imposing an *identity constancy* assumption.

In addition to tracking 3D pose and therefore performing implicit view transformation between familiar views, temporal correlation can facilitate recognising and tracking identities of moving faces. For a chosen set of K prototypes at a given view γ, let the similarity vectors $\boldsymbol{\alpha}_m^\gamma$ of M different people to the prototypes be their identity measures at view γ. Recognition of a novel face image $\mathbf{x}_i$ at time t can then be performed by maximising:

$$H(m) = h(\boldsymbol{\alpha}_i^\gamma, \boldsymbol{\alpha}_m^\gamma) + \kappa \, h(\boldsymbol{\alpha}_m^\gamma, \boldsymbol{\alpha}_{t-1}) \qquad (10.2)$$

where $m = 1 \ldots M$ and $h(\boldsymbol{\alpha}_i^\gamma, \boldsymbol{\alpha}_m^\gamma)$ is the similarity measure between the similarity vectors of image $\mathbf{x}_i$ and a known face m at view γ. Function $h(\boldsymbol{\alpha}_m^\gamma, \boldsymbol{\alpha}_{t-1})$ is the similarity measure between similarity vectors of the previous (at $t-1$) and the current (at pose γ) recognised faces. In other words, whilst the first term finds the best match to a known face, the second term imposes an identity constancy assumption over time. The constant κ controls a trade-off between the two terms and its value will also depend on the degree of change in a face's similarity measures across views.

10.5 An Experimental System

Face pose and identity can be recognised and tracked surprisingly well using the above model based on similarity-to-prototypes over time, even when faces undergo large view transformations. Figure 10.3 shows a screen-dump of an experimental, multi-view, face tracking and recognition system implemented on a PC platform. Its task is to identify detected and tracked face images across the view-sphere in live video input against a pool of subjects of interest. A face is represented by its measures of similarity to eight prototypes across the view-sphere. The screen is divided into four parts displaying useful information about system performance.

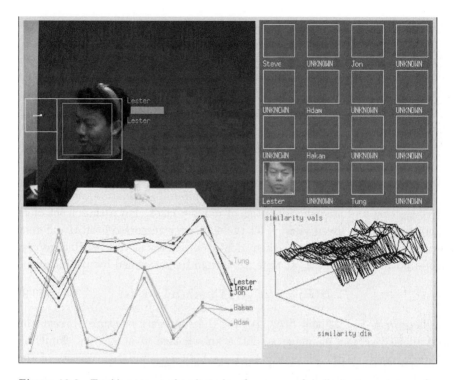

Figure 10.3 Tracking temporal trajectories of measures of similarity-to-prototypes for identification and 3D pose estimation across views over time.

At the top left of the screen, the current image frame is shown with the following information superimposed: an outer box surrounding a face defines the current region of interest; an inner box defines the maximal bound for a multi-scale face correspondence and alignment process required before identification; the current estimate of the 3D pose of the face is shown by a dial box to the left of the face; the *temporal belief* in the identity of the face is shown at the top of an overall confidence bar to the right of the face. The identity determined using the current frame only is shown below this bar. The subject wears a six degrees-of-freedom Polhemus electro-magnetic sensor that provides ground-truth values for 3D head pose. This enables the accuracy of the system's pose estimates to be quantitatively evaluated as described in Section 7.9.2.

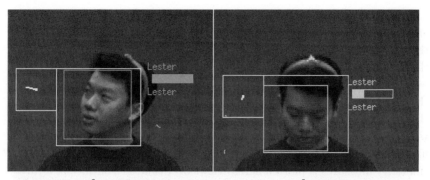

frame t_1 frame t_4

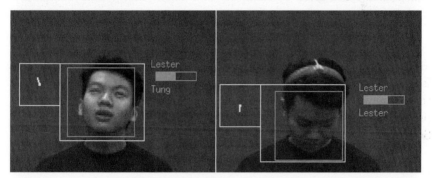

frame t_2 frame t_5

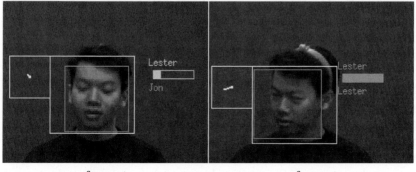

frame t_3 frame t_6

Figure 10.4 Tracking and recognising identity and pose across views over time.

At the top right of the screen, a collection of 16 frontal view image icons are used to indicate 16 different faces (six of which are known identities in this case). The visible icon displays the overall belief in the identity of the face tracked across views over time, i.e. the identity on top of the overall confidence bar on the right of the face image. Its brightness shows the overall confidence in this identity. At the bottom left of the screen, the eight similarity measures for the current face image are shown along with those of the six known faces at the same pose. The closest match is highlighted. At the bottom right of the screen, the temporal trajectory of similarity measures is plotted across views over time as a surface in a three-dimensional space given by similarity dimension (one to eight), similarity values and time.

It is worth pointing out that there is no requirement for a face to be exposed to the system at frontal or near frontal views in order to perform identification. In fact, these experiments indicate it is usually the case that frontal views of faces are more ambiguous to identification and more likely to be subject to error. This can be interpreted as being consistent with the psychophysical notion of *three-quarters (3/4) view advantage* introduced in Section 9.6. The following two examples illustrate such a phenomenon.

Figure 10.4 shows six frames of tracking and recognising the identity and pose of a face over time. It can be seen that the identity of the face was established, at approximately three-quarters view in frame t_1, with full confidence. The tracked temporal belief in the identity was consistent with the current frame recognition. However, in frames t_2 and t_3 when the face was undergoing exposure to near frontal views, the frame-wise recognition became erroneous and as a result, the confidence in the tracked temporal belief in the true identity weakened although it remained correct. Correct identification finally recovered when alternative views of the subject became available over time in frames t_4, t_5 and eventually, in t_6 when belief confidence recovered fullly. This example illustrates how recognition of moving faces can be made fault tolerant to frame-wise mis-identifications. Figure 10.5 shows the frame-wise measures of similarity-to-prototypes for the example sequence of Figure 10.4. Figure 10.6 gives the tracked temporal trajectory of the similarity measures for the face captured in that sequence.

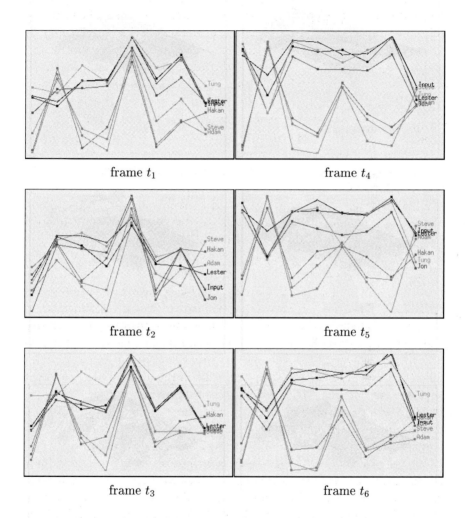

Figure 10.5 Frame-wise measures of similarity-to-prototypes for the face recognised and tracked in Figure 10.4.

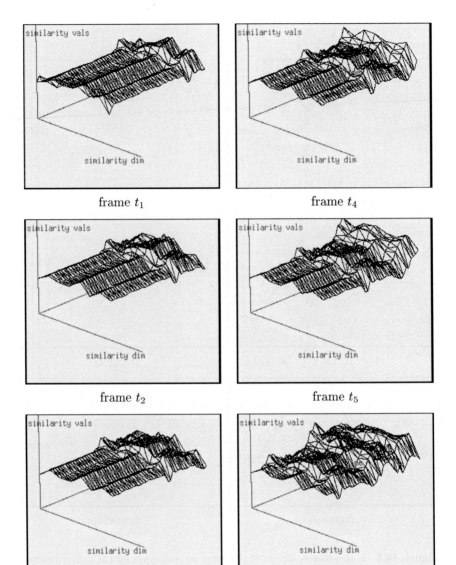

Figure 10.6 Tracked trajectories of similarity measures for the face in Figure 10.4.

10.6   Discussion

In comparison to the many established theories and algorithms for face identification based on static views, research on utilising temporal information in the process of identifying faces in motion remains in its infancy. However, computational and psychophysical evidence suggests that the recovery of motion information is useful not only for object recognition in general, but also for face identification in particular.

Naturally, the additional static structural information provided by observing many images from a sequence is useful. Beyond that, there is the more important question over the extent to which temporal information can aid recognition by enhancing and determining our knowledge of the object in question. Although the psychophysical experiments do not yet provide firm conclusions about the nature of the information provided by motion, they nonetheless point firmly towards the use of temporal information in the human perceptual system and its importance in object recognition. To this end, we have examined the computational plausibility of using temporal information to model the appearance of moving faces and have suggested a number of ways in which spatio-temporal signatures of faces may be utilised for identifying moving faces.

In Part III of this book, different models of facial identity have been introduced under different assumptions about viewing conditions, ranging from single and multiple static views to continuously changing views caused by motion. Given these models, an immediate and important question one may ask is under what conditions such models of identity can be effectively and robustly employed for face recognition in a natural and dynamic scene. This in fact raises the question of perceptual integration initially introduced in Part I.

Object recognition is a perceptual process which involves deriving effective representations of objects matched to known categories or labels such as individual objects (e.g. the face of a specific person) or types of object (e.g. all human faces). In general, this process can be regarded as *meaningful perception* [94]. However, it should have become clear that the perceptual process of recognising dynamic objects such as faces involves a great deal more than merely matching and assigning labels. Computations are required to provide information about the motion, colour, location, viewpoint, size, surface textures and even 3D configurations of objects of interest. Some of this computation can be regarded as *sense perception*, which may appear to have little to do with modelling identity unless one asks the following questions:

(1) How are sense and meaningful perception related?

(2) Are computations carried out by different perceptual processes simply 'pipelined' sequentially from sense to meaningful perception in a bottom-up, data-driven fashion or are they processed in a more complex, closed-loop manner?

(3) Do high-level knowledge and top-down, model-based inference play any part in sense perception?

In the next Part of this book, we will examine these questions in more detail and suggest plausible solutions for perceptual integration in the context of dynamic perception of human faces.

PART IV

PERCEPTION IN CONTEXT

11 Perceptual Integration

Apprehension of external objects must always be an act of our power of realisation, and must therefore be accompanied by consciousness, for it is a mental function. The meaning we assign to our sensations depends upon experiment, and not upon mere observation of what takes place around us.

— Hermann von Helmholtz [360]

Initially proposed as a general model to explain the functions of human vision and consequently subjected to serious criticism, the *Gestalt Theory* [138] has nevertheless directly or indirectly influenced the workings of many computer vision models for object perception. For instance, in the context of segmentation, Gestalt theory suggests that perceptual organisation is in essence based upon constructing simple and regular forms. This can be expressed by the following four principles: *similarity* (e.g. common colour and texture), *continuity* (e.g. smooth surface and lines), *good form* (e.g. symmetrical shape) and *common fate* (e.g. moving together). Such principles have been widely applied in computer vision to object representation by symmetry [33, 309] and similarity [100], visual motion estimation by continuity [128, 151, 274] and motion grouping by common fate [223, 324]. At this point, one may come to the conclusion that the perception of objects is simply a matter of summing the output parts from various sensory-based visual processes. However, this is far from sufficient, not least because of the ambiguities and noise in the image data.

11.1   Sensory and Model-based Vision

Let us start with Helmholtz's notion that visual perception is in fact *unconscious inference* [360] and similarly, Gregory's notion that perception is *problem solving* in the sense that given the slenderest clues to the nature of surrounding objects, a vision system identifies them and acts not so much according to what is directly sensed, but to what is believed. One not only believes what one sees: to some extent one sees what one believes [142]. One then considers that perception is really an opinion on the state of affairs in the surrounding environment rather than passive response to sensory stimuli. This leads to the notion of *model-based vision*, implying that recognition is applied to an unsegmented representation of a scene without boundaries of objects and that it essentially involves an iterative process of search-and-match. When a sufficiently good match is found between an object model and a part of an image, an instance of the known model is said to be recognised. Once an object is recognised, the known properties of this type of object are applied to perform both spatial grouping and temporal correspondence [210, 343, 344, 345].

Studies in cognition and psychophysics generally support the plausibility of model-based grouping. In particular, the human visual system enables objects to be recognised before the scene has been divided into units, i.e. segmented [265]. However, the model-based approach provides no account of the development of object perception in young children and our ability to occasionally perceive the existence of a *thing* without perceiving what that thing *is* [326]. One can conceivably draw the conclusion that model-based recognition can only be computationally tractable if it is perceptually integrated with a process of learning that can be used to both bootstrap and adapt the models based on direct sensory information. In other words, meaningful perception (recognition) can only be performed based on both a set of bottom-up, general, sensory-based processes and a body of top-down, specific, knowledge-based models which are *learned* from sparse and noisy sensory data. Learned models must be used to perform perceptual control on the sensory processes in order to overcome ambiguity and uncertainty. In the context of dynamic vision, there are a number of questions that together constitute a general problem which we refer to as the problem of *perceptual integration*:

(1) What are the entities upon which segmentation is based? Are they decomposed parts of a physical scene or object-oriented, conceptual entities? In other words, should segmentation be sensory-based or model-based?

(2) At what stage in the perceptual process is object-specific knowledge used?

(3) What is the connection between grouping object boundaries in space and matching the identity of an object over time?

(4) What is the relationship between the ability to perceive objects in real-time from limited sensory information and the ability to form judgements about the unity and identity of objects by maximising perceptual resources?

(5) Is the mechanism for object perception specific to each kind of object or generic?

More specifically, the problem of perceptual integration resides in the following questions:

(1) How can knowledge be represented at a level that is readily accessible? In other words, on what representation should integration be performed in order to access knowledge? Possible answers are:

   (a) Input representational space: hybrid feature subspaces can be fused to give a single correlated representation, although large differences in subspace variance can be a problem.

   (b) Parameter space: fusion of intermediate representations.

   (c) Semantic level: using semantic constraints or heuristics.

(2) What mechanism is used to distribute and invoke such knowledge?

Figure 11.1 illustrates different aspects of perceptual integration in a closed-loop framework of sensory and meaningful perception.

11.2   Perceptual Fusion

A straightforward approach to perceptual integration can be taken from a *data fusion* point of view. Data fusion is traditionally used to increase the accuracy of a set of measurements obtained independently and to overcome poor sensor reliability or uncertainty in individual sensor outputs. In particular, different sources of visual information undergoing fusion are usually

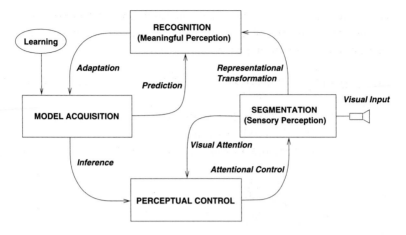

Figure 11.1 Perceptual integration of bottom-up, sensory-based processes with top-down, model-based vision.

based on different assumptions, some of which may be invalid at any given time. By performing data fusion, the assumptions are in effect "factored out" [64]. Hence fusion can reduce the dependence of a system upon invalid *a priori* assumptions and make the overall performance robust.

Suppose that an object model can be quantified by a set of measurable values, *a parameter set.* If this set is readily accessible to sensory processes, then integration implies a degree of *perceptual fusion.* In other words, perceptual integration is the computation required to compensate predicted model parameter values with actual available visual measurements so as to provide a coherent and *most probable explanation* of the sensory data.

Let us now illustrate perceptual fusion by describing a working system that performs robust face tracking by fusing different, largely independent estimates of the 3D pose, image position and scale of a face [313, 314]. One approach to perceptual fusion is through the estimation of covariance matrices from different observations. The covariance matrices of 2D image positions and 3D pose can be learned from training examples. This has the advantage that the constraints are derived (learned) from practical measurement rather than heuristics. Computationally, the problem of tracking moving faces implicitly requires pose-invariant face detection. We previously introduced a generic, identity-independent face model for pose estimation based on similarities to prototypes across the viewsphere (Sections 6.5 and 7.9). Under suitable conditions, a temporal trajectory of tilt and yaw angles can be computed from live video input [134, 251]. However, measures of similarity to prototypes can provide poor estimates in a number of circumstances:

(1) local optima distract the search toward the wrong position, scale and pose,
(2) the input face may be poorly aligned with the prototypes,
(3) the illumination conditions may vary, and
(4) training images may be poorly aligned both in position and pose.

Acquiring accurate estimates of face image position is crucial for robust pose estimation using similarity-based representation. The noise in similarity measures can be compensated by incorporating different visual cues over time. For instance, skin colour is an inexpensive and effective visual cue that can be computed in real-time at each frame to estimate the head position in the image frame (Chapter 4). A face's position can also be detected using models based on support vector machines (Sections 5.4.4 and 6.6). The head bounding box is expected to be larger than the face box and the displacement between the positions of the two bounding boxes is strongly correlated with the head pose. Figure 11.2 shows an example. The outer-most box is obtained by spatially clustering skin-coloured pixels. An SVM-based face model is then used to search within this box to find the face. The system performs a localised search around the face box to obtain the head box [203, 313, 314].

In order to track the face's image position in correlation to its 3D head pose, a temporal state can be defined for all correlated observations including the position of the face (x, y) *relative* to the head, the scale (s) of the face box, and the head yaw (ϕ) and tilt (θ):

$$\mathbf{q} = [x \, y \, s \, \phi \, \theta] \tag{11.1}$$

The scale (s) is the ratio of the face box size to the prototype image size in a similarity database.

The general problem of modelling multi-variate observations as correlated temporal states over time was discussed in Chapter 7. In particular, we described the use of Kalman filters and the Condensation algorithm. The Kalman filter estimates the state by propagating a Gaussian density function over time. Condensation is more generic and flexible due to its propagation of a multi-modal density function [29, 136,

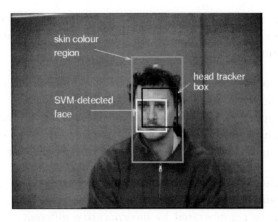

skin colour
region

head tracker
box

SVM-detected
face

Figure 11.2   Different sources of information can be fused to initialise the process of
both tracking the image positions of a face and estimating its 3D head pose over time.

170]. The multiple modes can be thought of as multiple state hypotheses
and by propagating these, Condensation is often able to recover from distractions. To track states over time using Condensation, a state transition
distribution $p(\mathbf{q}_t|\mathbf{q}_{t-1})$ and a state-conditional measurement distribution
$p(\mathbf{x}_t|\mathbf{q}_t)$ must be modelled. For the state transition distribution $p(\mathbf{q}_t|\mathbf{q}_{t-1})$,
a straightforward approach to Condensation can use a heuristic function,
and then arbitrarily add independent Gaussian noise to each element of the
state [29]. This approach has two obvious problems. Firstly, the noise parameters are not estimated from measurement, and could cause the tracker
to lose lock. Secondly, the assumption of independence of state elements
under-constrains the search space. Consequently, the model is computationally inefficient and the propagation process is likely to expend a lot
of samples exploring irrelevant local optima. To address these problems,
state covariance can be modelled and used to augment the Condensation
algorithm.

Let us return to our example. When a person turns their head, there
is a correlated change in the image position of the face. A state transition
covariance matrix, $\mathbf{\Sigma}_{\Delta\mathbf{q}}$, can be systematically estimated from examples of
people varying their head pose freely. Experiments have shown that there
is a strong correlation between change in relative face x-position and yaw
and a strong correlation between change in relative face y-position and tilt.
Changes in x and ϕ have a larger magnitude than changes in y and θ [313,

314]. Assuming that these correlations are independent of *absolute* pose and position, the state transition distribution can be modelled as a fully-covariant Gaussian:

$$p(\mathbf{q}_t|\mathbf{q}_{t-1}) = \frac{1}{\sqrt{2\pi}|\Sigma_{\Delta\mathbf{q}}|^{\frac{1}{2}}} \exp\left(-\frac{1}{2}\left(\Delta\mathbf{q}_t - \boldsymbol{\mu}_{\Delta\mathbf{q}_t}\right)^{\mathsf{T}} \Sigma_{\Delta\mathbf{q}}^{-1}\left(\Delta\mathbf{q}_t - \boldsymbol{\mu}_{\Delta\mathbf{q}_t}\right)\right)$$
(11.2)

where $\Delta\mathbf{q}_t = (\mathbf{q}_t - \mathbf{q}_{t-1})$ denotes state change in two successive time frames.

The measurement distribution $p(\mathbf{x}_t|\mathbf{q}_t)$ models the displacement between the face and head position. Let the signed x-difference between the centres of the face and head boxes be δx. The state-conditional measurement distribution can then be:

$$p(\mathbf{x}_t|\mathbf{q}_t) = p(H_t|\mathbf{q}_t)\,p(\delta x|\phi)$$
(11.3)

where H_t is the similarity measure at time t defined by Equation (7.23), $p(H_t|\mathbf{q}_t)$ is a similarity-based weighting function given the hypothesised state, and $p(\delta x|\phi)$ is a modelled density function expressing the dependence of face box x-displacements on yaw angle. The latter function incorporates observed correlations between face position and pose. It is interesting to note that similar use of displacements in the y-direction generally seems to be unreliable. This is largely due to varying neck lines, hair colour and illumination conditions. The two components of Equation (11.3) work together in order to constrain the process of simultaneously tracking head pose and face image position and scale. The two constituent densities are as follows:

(1) A compounded similarity weighting function over a set of training sequences $\mathcal{X}$ defines a state conditional density function:

$$p(H_t|\mathbf{q}_t) = \frac{1}{\kappa}\exp\left(-\frac{\|H_{max} - H_t\|}{2\,\sigma_H^2}\right)$$
(11.4)

where κ is a normalisation constant, H_{max} the maximum and σ_H the standard deviation of H-values observed over the training set $\mathcal{X}$ respectively.

(2) The displacement density function is based on the observation that facial position displacements are correlated with pose. For example, as a subject turns his head to the left, the box surrounding the face moves left-of-center of the body, while the box surrounding the

head tends to stay central. This function also constrains the face
position to lie close to the independently tracked head position so
that tracking is not distracted by non-faces.

Figure 11.3 shows an example of continuous visual tracking of 3D head pose
and 2D face image position and scale, utilising multiple sources of information including skin-colour, expected head region, SVM face detection and
3D pose tracking in parameter space over time. The tracked face image
(upper-left) and head pose are shown in each frame. In this example, the
tracking process accurately follows the face and head pose until time t_{11}
when the tracker momentarily loses lock on face position and starts to move
away from the face. It regains lock at t_{13}. At t_{12} the system is starting to
lose pose but recovers gradually over time. Tracking was performed using
Condensation with five hundred states sampled at each time frame [313,
314]. The ability of the tracking process to recover from momentary loss of
lock demonstrates the importance of fusing the face position and pose. Lack
of this fusion would have made the tracking process unstable and prone to
wandering off to incorrect poses or non-faces in the image frames.

11.3   Perceptual Inference

A primary role of *perceptual inference* is to control visual attention based
upon prior knowledge, the recognition of objects and the environment in
which these objects appear [4, 10, 56, 129, 131, 132, 340]. For instance,
identification of an object in a known scene can be utilised to predict its
future movement based on knowledge of the behaviour patterns of that object (or similar objects) within that environment (or similar environments).
Such predictions are useful, for example, in controlling visual attention and
directing visual grouping based on motion and colour cues.

   A vision system interprets a given scene according to its internal beliefs.
Based on these beliefs, it draws its attention for purposive collection of expected visual evidence. Such acts may be performed either consciously or
subconsciously (Figure 11.4). Objects such as human faces moving within
a particular environment appear as moving patterns with perhaps iden-
tifiable spatio-temporal characteristics (Figure 11.5 (a)-(d)). The ability
to effectively track and identify a face moving in a scene can be greatly
enhanced if it is perceived as contextually dependent. This is illustrated

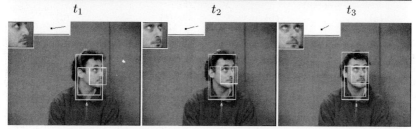

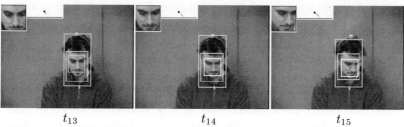

Figure 11.3 Perceptual fusion of 2D face position alignment and 3D pose tracking.

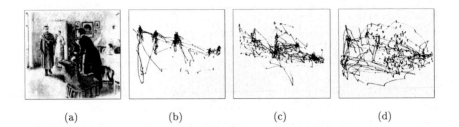

(a)   (b)   (c)   (d)

Figure 11.4 After Yarbus [374]: Reproduction of (a) Repin's picture of "An Unexpected Visitor" along with records of an observer's eye movements when asked (b) the ages of the members of the family in the room, (c) what the family had been doing before the arrival of the unexpected visitor and (d) the locations of the people and objects in the room.

by the example shown in Figure 11.5 (e). When observing a person walking into a room, the observer has expectations regarding his next possible move. These expectations have associated uncertainties so he is watched with, possibly subconscious, anticipation. As observation continues, the observer's expectations of his activity (behaviour) and identity are likely to become more certain.

Inference is based on causal dependencies between visual observation and the scene context. Correlations between object interpretation and *a priori* knowledge about the object can be modelled using probabilistic Bayesian belief networks (see Appendix C for details). This is because inference is largely about imposing expectations upon observations. Computationally, this can be regarded as the problem of selectively collecting uncertain and incomplete image information according to predictions of known models. Belief networks provide an attractive solution for addressing such a problem [257]. There are a number of examples in which inference has been modelled as a graph network of causal correlations over a parameter set [11, 56, 64, 132, 257]. Similarly, hidden Markov models (HMMs) are probabilistic models of causal dependencies between different states in sequential patterns and constitute a special case of Bayesian belief networks [257]. Let us now examine more closely how inference and attentional control can be performed using HMMs.

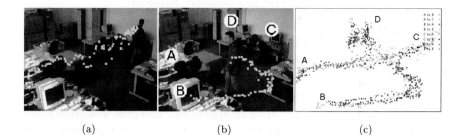

(a)   (b)   (c)

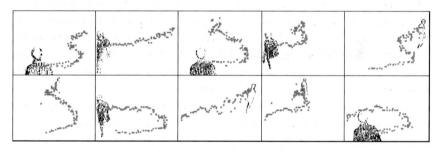

(d)

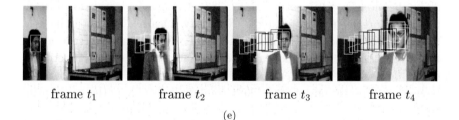

frame t_1 frame t_2 frame t_3 frame t_4

(e)

Figure 11.5 A known environment imposes context-dependent, spatio-temporal constraints on an object's appearance, activity and identity. (a) An example face trajectory in a known office environment. (b) Four contextually significant landmarks in this scene: a coffee machine **A**, a computer terminal **B**, a photocopier **C** and a door **D**. (c) The typical spatio-temporal patterns of face appearance in this office scene are intrinsically constrained by the landmarks. (d) The most typical behaviours in this environment. (e) In a given scene, visual inference must be based on both image data and knowledge about the scene. When tracking and identifying a subject moving through space and over time, such knowledge may include, for example, the identity of the subject and the scene layout under which the subject's movements are constrained.

11.3.1   Inference using Hidden Markov Models

Context-dependent, spatio-temporal characteristics of a moving object can be regarded as a set of conditional dependencies in space and over time. For example, whilst the 2D appearance and 3D pose of a moving face can only change continuously and smoothly, the identity of a detected face remains constant. Such spatio-temporal dependencies are also likely to be qualitative and probabilistic. If facial appearance and pose in a given scene are considered as observations, the regions of interest in the image space where such observations can be best collected are effectively constrained by salient locations (landmarks) in the scene. Such landmarks can be regarded as probabilistic states. To this end, HMMs provide a framework for performing both attentional control in the detection and tracking of facial appearance in the image space, and for perceptual inference of both 3D pose and identity in the parameter space.

The parameters of an HMM are first learned from a set of example training sequences. Learning an HMM can be characterised as a process of establishing the impact of data from each image (observation vectors over time) of each learning sequence on the model's partial, conditional beliefs (i.e. its probability distributions) by forward and backward propagations along the model's graph network [282, 283]. Details of a learning algorithm for HMMs are given in Appendix C. Naturally, a learned HMM can be used to classify an unknown temporal sequence of observation vectors. More interestingly, however, a model can also generate sequences that inherit the causal dependencies between successive time frames. These can therefore be used as expectations of most likely combinations of hypotheses. In principle, an HMM can be employed to perform computations for a number of tasks given example sequences of image observation vectors such as face images that appear in a particular temporal order in a given scene. These computations are as follows.

(1) *Learning*: Given an observation sequence $\mathcal{X}=\{\mathbf{x}_1, \mathbf{x}_2 \ldots \mathbf{x}_T\}$ and an HMM, the model parameters λ are adjusted to maximise $P(\mathcal{X}|\lambda)$.

(2) *Classification*: Given an unknown observation sequence $\mathcal{X}$ and a set of trained models λ_i, the sequence can be classified by $\max_i P(\mathcal{X}|\lambda_i)$.

(3) *Inference*: An HMM can generate maximum-likelihood state and observation sequences reflecting the intrinsic statistical characteristics of the training set.

(4) *Attentional control:* Given an observation $\mathcal{X}$, an HMM can give a single most likely state sequence $\mathcal{Q} = \{q_1, q_2 \ldots q_T\}$.

Whilst prediction models such as Kalman filters and the Condensation algorithm are typically only able to predict the next frame, i.e. the next time step, due to the lack of any representation of *a priori* knowledge about the underlying structure of a temporal sequence in a given scene, an HMM is able to predict the further ahead since *a priori* knowledge about the scene is explicitly represented in a model. Essentially, an HMM represents the probabilistic spatio-temporal characteristics of a visual observation vector at two levels: At the hidden level, a sequence of state vectors represent a sequential combination of *hidden* hypotheses, i.e. scene-dependent contextual constraints which are not explicitly visible in the image data. At the visual level, a sequence of observation vectors model the combination of image data over time most likely to have given rise to the state sequence.

11.3.2   Closed-loop Perceptual Control

For inference, an HMM can be employed to generate the most probable observation sequence using maximum likelihood evaluation on the model probabilities of state transition and state-dependent observation vectors at each time frame [131]. However, maximum likelihood sequences generated by an HMM trained with past observations only reflect the statistical knowledge about the object and the scene captured from past experience. This is perhaps over-committing, not least because the dynamics of a specific instance of an object can often be quite different from the past "norm" depending on the current scene. To address this problem, current image information can be used to adapt or *augment* the model statistics learned from past observation thereby tuning the model for more accurate prediction depending on the specific scene. This brings us back to the notion of *closed-loop* perceptual inference and control.

Recall from Figure 11.1 that perceptual control is regarded as a closed-loop process that on one hand, adjusts the underlying expectations of object appearance in the image space (attentional control) and on the other hand, simultaneously overcomes the ambiguities and noise in the image data (visual attention). This notion of closed-loop sensing and control can be implemented using HMMs with instantaneous visual augmentation.

One way to adapt a hidden Markov model is to introduce a degree of randomness into the process of sequence generation, i.e. instead of generating the maximum likelihood sequence, the state transition and observation output at each time frame are based on a unified random selection in the appropriate probability distribution of the model. However, it is often the case that although such random generation is desirable for generating observation vectors, it is too sensitive and unstable in state transitions as any randomly triggered early transition will cause the sequence to wander away without reflecting any intrinsic statistical nature of the object in motion. To overcome this problem, a mixed random output with a durationally-controlled state transition can be adopted [129, 131, 289]. This is known as a *semi-hidden* Markov model [283].

11.4   Vision as Cooperating Processes

A simplistic approach to perceptual integration is to view visual processes such as attention, segmentation, face detection, correspondence, alignment and recognition as independent steps in a sequential, feed-forward system. However, this approach will often fail in dynamic scenes when image data become noisy and when conflicting information is computed by different processes. Different from the notion of perceptual fusion, let us now consider at the system level how these vision processes can co-operate in a closed-loop fashion, combining *where* tasks (sensory perception) with *what* tasks (recognition as meaningful perception). For example, knowledge of face pose and identity can be used to constrain subsequent localisation and tracking. Furthermore, face detection can help to confirm the spatial context. Vision as cooperating processes for dynamic face recognition is illustrated in Figure 11.6.

11.4.1   Visual Attention and Grouping

In order to detect and track people and their faces sufficiently quickly, efficient methods for focusing attention are necessary. Two visual cues that can be computed with the required efficiency are based upon motion and colour, which are complementary as attentional cues under different circumstances if perceptual integration is performed. A focus of attention process based on motion and colour is illustrated in Figure 11.7 (a). Colour models

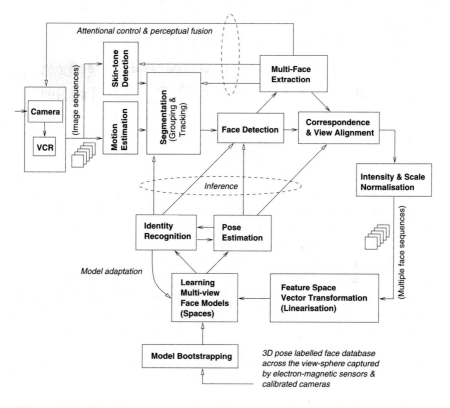

Figure 11.6 Closed-loop, cooperating vision processes for dynamic face recognition.

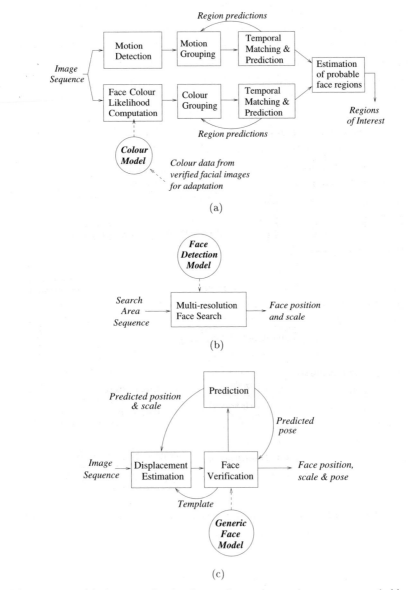

Figure 11.7 (a) An example visual attention and grouping process: probable face regions are estimated using motion and colour-based tracking. (b) An example face detection process. (c) An example face tracking process.

are not robust under significant changes in illumination conditions and so robust colour-based face tracking might therefore seem to require a solution to colour constancy. This may not be necessary when other visual cues such as motion and facial appearance are also used. For instance, once a face is being reliably tracked and verified using a face model, its apparent colour can be used to update a scene-specific, adaptive colour model. Perceptual integration would enable the attentional process to learn about variations in apparent face colour and can even correlate these changes with different times of day and regions of the scene. An adaptive colour model can be built for object tracking under variations in illumination and camera parameters (Section 7.5).

A common source of ambiguity in grouping is that the number of people in a scene is not usually known *a priori*. In general, people can enter or leave the scene or become fully occluded and then reappear at any time. Robust and consistent tracking requires dynamic initialisation, maintenance and termination of multiple regions of interest. If separate non-overlapping regions of interest are located first using grouping processes, prediction of the tracking parameters must be used to perform attentional control in grouping. As a result, for instance, a region cannot extend outside a bounding window determined from its predicted mean and covariance matrix. Furthermore, if regions merge while each has an associated face being tracked, the grouping process can be forced to keep them separate. A tracked region is only used as a focus of attention for higher-level processing once confidence can be accumulated that the region is both persistent and consistent. A simple measure of such confidence is the ability to reliably track the region for several consecutive frames. Attentional control can be performed using hidden Markov models in which causal constraints can be learned to capture the minimum and maximum possible scale of people, their orientation (heads uppermost) and approximate aspect ratio.

11.4.2   Face Detection, Tracking and Identification

Searching for a face in a given image is initialised in probable face regions where no face is currently being tracked. Such a face detection process is illustrated in Figure 11.7 (b) (also see Chapter 5). Once a face is detected, it is tracked over time and the tracking process is illustrated in Figure 11.7 (c). In general, the tracking process provides estimates of face position (or displacement), scale and pose. Estimates of affine and pose parameters as

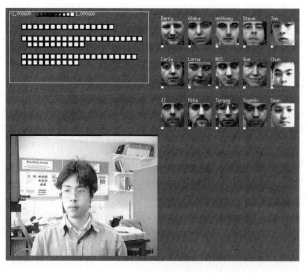

(a)

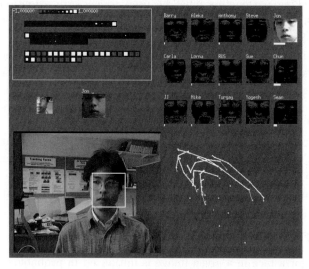

(b)

Figure 11.8 Screen-dumps of an on-line face recognition system running on a PC. (a) Initialising all faces equally likely. (b) The face has been identified and highlighted.

well as knowledge regarding identity can all be used to improve efficiency and robustness. The tracking process also provides a measure of confidence in each resulting face image. Several low confidence frames indicate that the tracking process has probably failed and if a probable face region still exists, face detection is performed again to re-initialise tracking.

Face search in an image frame can be extremely expensive, especially during detection, and is subject to large errors. This is mainly due to the fact that the process of finding a face-like sub-image region in a given image frame is subject to a number of parameters that cannot be effectively determined in the current image alone. As a result, heuristics are often applied in order to limit the search space and therefore the computation if real-time performance is required. To overcome these problems, perceptual integration can be performed using a belief network to control a set of parameters over time including:

(1) the scale of a face image
(2) the centres of face regions in the image space
(3) the probability of the existence of a face in the image space given its history
(4) the predicted displacement of a face over time in the image space
(5) the estimated pose of a face
(6) the identity of a face if known

Figure 11.8 shows an example of an integrated face detection, tracking and identification system implemented on a PC platform. The task is to classify the subject as one of the 15 people shown. Hinton diagrams are shown at the top-left of each screen-dump. A plot of the trajectory of the tracked face in a 2D principal component subspace is shown at the bottom-right.

11.5 Biological Perspectives

The theories and principles of object perception constitute perhaps one of the most active areas of study of human vision. A key aspect of object perception that largely remains a mystery is the form of visual integration. Here we give an account of some psychophysical and neurobiological findings either directly or indirectly related to the perceptual process of visual integration in humans.

Psychophysics

Psychophysical experiments on sense perception and the task of parsing (segmentation) provide evidence that at the age of four and a half months, when infants begin to reach for objects, they reach for object boundaries without any knowledge about the objects themselves. More interestingly, infants' perception (representation) of object boundaries appears to persist in the absence of visual information: they even try to reach for the borders of the objects when the lights are turned off and the reaching takes place in the dark [326]. An infant's ability to segment foreground from background relies more on motion and depth than on uniformity of texture and colour. The latter are likely to be more knowledge-based than sensory-based [5]. These studies might seem to support the Gestalt theory of a general, sensory-based segmentation. However, they do not suggest use of principles of maximising uniformity in colour and texture or regularity and smoothness of shape. Infants are also sensitive to colour and surface patterns but knowledge of objects is involved here. This is also the case for infants' perception of partially occluded objects which emerges at the age of about two months.

Let us now consider selective attention and object-based visual representation. Experiments have shown that visual representations support memory for shape and colour associations only when the features are perceived to belong to the same object. This implies that representations are object-based [361] and goes beyond previous suggestions regarding visual attention [15, 97, 183, 334]. Object-based visual processing extends beyond selective attention to memory representation of stimuli presented for more extended periods [361]. Such observations relate to an early study known as Kahneman and Treisman's "object file" [180]. Such a file is regarded as a token representation of an object for which its spatio-temporal location mediates the association of local visual features of the object. More importantly, it was suggested that attending to an object on the basis of its spatio-temporal location serves to establish a file in which information about the object's visual features is organised. Initially and when the object remains in the field of view, the object's spatio-temporal position gives both the basis for collecting information as an "object token" and the means for accessing such a token.

Finally, regarding knowledge and learning, it seems that infants undergo a developmental change in their perceptual ability during their first four months. Although the nature of this change is not entirely clear, it has been suggested that the change depends on the maturation of the neural systems underlying the perception of coherent motion and the control of attention to spatially separated parts of the visual field [174]. Such change may reflect the emergence through a learning process of a neural system for specific object perception [319]. Infants appear to share some aspects of adults' abilities to perceive object identities over successive encounters. In particular, infants perceive object identity by first analysing the spatial locations and motions of the objects concerned. Unlike adults, on the other hand, infants do not appear to perceive object identities by analysing the uniformity of object shape, colour and texture. These limitations appear to be overcome during a process of developing abilities to recognise objects of known kinds [326].

Neurobiology

The neocortex is highly organised into six distinct cortical layers. These layers exhibit multiple scales of computation and include neural circuits linking neurons both within and between layers. Cortical interactions occur both bottom-up and top-down. In fact, there are massive top-down pathways throughout the cortex although traditionally it has been largely rejected that top-down attention plays an important role in visual perception due to the consideration that top-down feedback cannot operate quickly enough to influence cortical information processing. Neurobiological studies suggest otherwise [143]. In fact perceptual, attentional and learning processes carried out by visual cortex correlate strongly in the cortical organisation. Consider, for example, the processes of perceptual grouping and attentional control. Perceptual grouping is the process whereby the brain organises images into separate regions corresponding to objects and background and such a process has been traditionally regarded as largely *preattentive* without conscious attention. Attentional control, on the other hand, enables the brain to selectively process only information of interest and aims to prime our vision system to expect an object with particular properties to appear at a given location [97]. One might therefore expect that perceptual grouping and attentional control are not performed at the same time within the same cortical areas. In fact, the opposite is true: visual cortex generates perceptual grouping and focus of attention upon objects of interest at the same time within the same cortical areas: V1 and V2. What is not clear though is how such integration is performed. Furthermore, recent neurobiological experiments have shown that attentional processing occurs throughout the entire visual cortex including cortical areas which were previously considered to perform only preattentive processing. One plausible explanation of these findings hinges on the association between attentional control and learning.

A human brain can rapidly learn huge amounts of information throughout its lifespan. What is remarkable is that it does this without just as quickly forgetting what has already been learned! In other words, the brain solves the *stability-plasticity dilemma*. It has enough plasticity to learn from new experiences without losing the stability that prevents rapid forgetting [143]. Top-down attentional control is considered to play a key role here. Following *adaptive resonance theory*, attentional control helps solve the stability-plasticity dilemma in learning by selecting, synchronising and amplifying the activities of neurons within the regions of attentional focus and as a result, suppressing the activities of irrelevant neurons which would otherwise destabilise learned memories. Those attentionally focused cells would then activate bottom-up pathways and generate a kind of feedback resonance. Such resonances provide the basis for adaptive learning to associate information across different levels of processing into context-specific models of objects and events [144].

11.6   Discussion

It is clear that perception of objects and in particular moving faces benefits enormously from effective perceptual integration. Among other limitations, a purely sensory-based approach cannot deal with the incompleteness often induced by visual occlusion, for example. Other sources of non-sensory information and above all, *a priori* knowledge, are not just convenient but necessary if effective perception is to be achieved. Meaningful perception invokes object-specific knowledge about the properties and permissible transformations of perceived objects. Such a model-based approach can help to resolve potential ambiguities in sensory-level computation as in segmentation under occlusion. Effective visual perception must imply that sensory and meaningful perception are closely integrated. The key to a successful integration must be that high-level knowledge needs to be represented in such a way that it is accessible at the right level of computation.

The ambiguity of sensory data is the main motivation for perceptual fusion. Sensory ambiguity can be caused, for example, by occlusions from the projection of a 3D object into 2D images or by noise in the imaging process. Apparent visual motion in the image can easily and plausibly be interpreted as resulting from many alternative stimuli rather than the physical movement of an object in the 3D scene. Clearly, such ambiguity can be greatly reduced if any knowledge about the object being perceived is readily accessible to the sensory processes that perform such tasks as correspondence, grouping and tracking.

When the assumptions made by a perceptual process are violated, the output of that process becomes unreliable or simply unavailable. In a vision system, this is likely to occur on an intermittent basis. For example, when a subject stops moving, motion-based visual cues can no longer be relied upon. Reliability may also be linked with the imaging process, which may be affected by noise intermittently. To overcome the problem, a measure of the reliability of each perceptual process can be taken into account at a given instant, allowing an unreliable computation to be phased out so that it does not degrade the overall result. Estimates of uncertainty in the outputs of multiple cooperating visual processes enable data fusion to be performed and lead to increased efficiency and robustness. This can be regarded as a data fusion approach to perceptual integration.

The notion of perceptual control implies that the process of recognition and prediction is used to explain away ambiguities in visual input. Furthermore, if vision is to be computationally effective, visual attention and information processing need to be highly selective and purposive [4, 10, 12, 56, 321]. Probabilistic belief networks provide a framework for perceptual integration and control. Such a framework provides a means of performing both bottom-up, data driven processing and top-down, expectation driven processing in the on-line computations. For example, Bayesian belief networks can be exploited to give most probable explanations of uncertain and incomplete image data by utilising probabilistic expectations of the observed objects in a given scene. Hidden Markov models can be employed to model attentional control. For example, visual adaptation of a pre-learned HMM on-line can be exploited to produce dynamically updated prediction of how a moving face will appear in the immediate future and where in the field of view. These models are used essentially to encode high-level knowledge by modelling dynamic dependencies and contextual constraints amongst the observation parameters in a known environment.

Beyond that, a vision system utilising a collection of processing modules can be regarded as cooperating processes. To that end, belief networks can also be employed to provide a generic framework for coordinating vision processes at such a system level.

12 Beyond Faces

*I have long considered it one of God's greatest mercies
that the future is hidden from us. If it were not, life would
surely be unbearable.*

— Eugene Forsey

We have hoped from the outset to interest the reader in the problems and
plausible solutions, the possibilities and the improbabilities involved in finding a path toward our goal of implementing artificial seeing machines able
to recognise moving objects such as human faces in dynamic environments.
Beyond this, we might hope to have instilled in some, a greater desire to
realise and utilise machines able to understand images of dynamic scenes:
machines that possess a sense of dynamic vision. Development of such
machines is of course a far broader problem than we could hope to have
addressed here. Vision is much more than recognition. Dynamic vision as
a completely general problem without context is computationally under-
constrained, ambiguous and often conceptually uncertain. Semantic constraints must be imposed if effective and meaningful visual interpretation
and perceptual understanding are required. Vision as part of a perceptual
system can be enhanced greatly by utilising both high-level semantic knowledge and other forms of non-visual information. Visual perception ought
to be used to actively aid interaction and decision making within the context it serves. This notion of *perception in context* extends far beyond face
recognition. In the following, we highlight a few recent trends for setting
perception in context.

12.1   Multi-modal Identification

An individual's facial appearance and gait provide two of the most natural cues for our biological vision system to perform effective and effortless *human recognition*. By natural we imply passive and non-intrusive. It also seems that such visual cues do not necessarily require any awareness or cooperation on a subject's behalf. However, almost by their virtues, these more natural modalities are also computationally more challenging. Research and development of machine-based gait recognition systems is still in its infancy [78, 196] while automatic face recognition systems remain sensitive to changes in lighting conditions and pose. Alternative modalities that can provide more accurate automatic identification in certain contextual settings include iris, hand, fingerprint, and voice recognition [156, 172]. Iris patterns contain very strong discriminatory information and in scenarios where good images of a person's iris can be obtained, provide a powerful means of automatic identification [82]. In many circumstances, however, acquiring iris images can be involved, obtrusive and therefore far from natural.

Overall, a robust identification system may require the fusion of several modalities. Ambiguity and computational cost can be reduced if visual information is combined from several visual and non-visual forms of measurement. In many cases, each modality is recorded separately and pre-processed independently [137, 352]. A notable exception to this is the synchronised video recording of face, voice and lip motion in the M2VTS database that includes the recordings of subjects rotating in depth and counting from "0" to "9" [269]. In general, multi-modality requires perceptual fusion at different levels including:

High-level or **decision-level fusion**: Each modality is analysed separately and the results are combined using simple averaging, voting or joint probability and likelihood [93, 95, 185, 352].

Mid-level or **module-level fusion**: Analysis of the combination of different modalities is performed at various intermediate levels of processing [179].

Low-level or **signal-level fusion**: Modalities are combined at the acquisition level [73, 137, 313].

Multi-modal identification systems usually perform better than their single modality counterparts, particularly in noisy environments [47]. However, issues arise concerning the adjustment of the weighting of each modality and the normalisation of independent variables when used in a combined representation.

12.2 Visually Mediated Interaction

Computer-based modelling of human activities and behaviour is becoming an increasingly important area of research with the massive increase of accessibility to both digital video cameras and the computing power required to process acquired video streams. Such vision models and algorithms will not only greatly improve existing machine vision applications such as visual surveillance in law enforcement and traffic control, they will also make many previously unenvisaged but potentially very useful applications possible. These include intelligent human-computer interfaces in virtual reality and for disabled people.

The notion of *visually mediated interaction* (VMI) in which the computer acts as an intelligent mediator between two remotely-communicating parties, perhaps intrinsically requires a rather extensive understanding of human cognitive behaviour. Is that possible for computer vision-based systems? Given currently available telecommunications bandwidths, only a limited amount of visual information can be transmitted between the parties. An intelligent computer system should behave similarly to that of a human vision system by panning and zooming the cameras at either end to actively respond to the needs of the communicating parties and thereby explicitly sample and send only the relevant information in the context of communication. This kind of system effectively helps create the communicative experience for both parties in a similar way to a cameraman or film director. Such capabilities intrinsically require machine understanding of the context based on captured images of the scene [225, 312, 315]. Fast and robust computer vision-based VMI will inevitably play an essential role in the booming telecommunications and broadcasting industries where video conferencing and unmanned television studios are becoming increasingly more desirable.

A striking example of VMI is that of video conferencing using an intelligent camera system. Suppose that several people in the same room are taking part in a video conference with another party at a remote site. Rather than the camera taking a static view of the communicants the whole time, it interprets the subjects' behaviours and responds by panning, zooming and focusing in on areas of interest in the scene not unlike a professional cameraman. An example of such a system is shown in Figure 12.1. The subjects are able to control the pan and zoom of the camera by using emphatic gestures. A more practical scheme would use two cameras: one static camera to obtain a wide-angle view of the scene and a second, movable camera to focus on the currently attended area. In order to make the system totally transparent during the video conference, it would have to be as intelligent in some ways as a human observer: it would listen to the conversation for contextual information, focus on the current speaker, and move to new regions of interest.

An extension to VMI is the notion of a *personal agent* for an advanced computer operating system, enabling users to create and communicate with a customised personality that could perform increasingly numerous and complex tasks and assess the reactions of the user. This intelligent agent would use speech recognition, possibly supplemented with lip reading, and nonverbal facial cues and identity to interpret the user. The agent's face would be created synthetically and would respond with synthesized speech and artificial expressive movements [127].

As an important part of a robust, real-time VMI system, the computation required to recognise and interpret human gestures would involve the detection and subsequent classification of a typical gesture. Such interpretations require not only semantics to be attached to the recognised gesture but also to be used as cues for responding to the recognised gestures accordingly. Both tasks can only be served effectively if contextual information is exploited [312, 315].

It should come as no surprise that human gaze and head pose are strongly correlated with behaviour and often indicate our intentions. Identity and head pose can play an important role in intelligent vision systems capable of mediating interaction [251, 312, 315]. Analysis of facial information is valuable not only for the interpretation of user intention and emotions but also in order to synthesise such behaviours and thus create computers with anthropomorphic appearance. For example, machines that monitor the face could become part of digital video conferencing and video telephone systems of low bandwidth, tracking both the location and signals of the face. Combined with synthesis of the face and speech recognition

| frame t_1 | frame t_2 | frame t_3 |

| frame t_4 | frame t_5 | frame t_6 |

| frame t_7 | frame t_8 | frame t_9 |

Figure 12.1 Computer vision-driven visually mediated interaction in which a machine vision system recognises and interprets human faces and gestures for actively controlling a camera to select (pan, tilt and zoom to) the most relevant view in the changing visual context of a dynamic scene.

and translation, these systems could become universal translators where a foreign language and the correct lip movements and facial expressions are imposed on audio and video sequences of a speaker.

General interpretation of behaviour is an unrealistic goal at present since cognitive studies still cannot adequately explain why we associate certain meanings with certain behaviours. A more modest approach is to associate semantics with a sub-set of behaviours that are appropriate for a given application. Interpretation is not, however, a simple mapping from recognised behaviour to semantics. Even in a restricted setting, the same behaviour may have several different meanings depending upon the context in which it is performed. This ambiguity is exacerbated when several people are present: is the behaviour part of a communication, and if so, with whom? For example, a person waving on a beach could be greeting somebody, deterring an insect or, if up to his neck in water, calling for help! Although a movement may be performed slightly differently according to the intended meaning, the question arises as to whether these differences can be accurately measured. Contextual information is a more realistic tool for the interpretation of behaviour and intention.

12.3   Visual Surveillance and Monitoring

Another area in which computing facial information can be of great importance is *automated visual surveillance*. This primarily involves the interpretation of dynamic scenes captured on image sequences. Computer vision-based surveillance systems aim to automate not only the detection but also the prediction of defined alarm events in a given visual context [56]. However, most existing commercial surveillance systems suffer from high levels of false alarm events because they are largely based on simple motion-sensing detectors [234]. As a result, current systems cannot be automated, in the sense that meaningful decisions cannot simply be made based on the detection of motion presence alone. Instead a system requires manual intervention. For example, a human operator is likely to be required to identify possible fraudulent behaviour in the video footage before relevant image frames can be selected for face identification.

In contrast, dynamic vision based surveillance systems capable of detecting, tracking and recognising faces in the context of known and abnormal behaviours can be used to greatly assist crime detection and prevention.

In addition, the ability to detect and identify moving faces in a dynamic scene can provide important additional knowledge for profiling fraudulent and abnormal behaviours. The definition, interpretation and computability of normal and fraudulent behaviours are largely context and identity dependent. Automated learning of *a priori* knowledge for associating normal behaviours with human identities in a given context is both challenging and can be extremely useful. Such contextual knowledge can clearly facilitate bootstrapping of learning and consequently recognition and prediction of abnormal behaviours. It can help to investigate the scalability of behaviour models learned from pre-recorded examples in a database.

Human activities captured on video footage are characterised by the spatio-temporal structure of their motion pattern. These structures are intrinsically probabilistic and often ambiguous. Similarly to the problem of interpreting and identifying facial appearances in a dynamic setting (Chapter 10), behavioural structures can be treated as temporal trajectories in a high-dimensional feature space of correlated visual measurements. Human behaviour understanding can benefit greatly if knowledge of the presence and identity of faces in a given context can be utilised effectively. For example, the spatio-temporal structure of a simple behaviour such as a person walking towards a telephone box in a public place can be represented by the trajectory of a multivariate observation vector given by the position, speed and identity of a human subject. Temporal structures of human behaviour and activities are often modelled either as stochastic processes or graph-based belief networks under which salient states or nodes of a structure are closely associated with landmarks or causal semantics in the given scene context [56, 131, 132, 175].

Given such computer vision capabilities, it is most likely that automated visual surveillance systems will be created that, perhaps without our awareness, look for known criminals and check for criminal or simply unauthorised activities. In particular, face recognition systems will be used to control access to restricted areas such as bank vaults, ATMs, offices and laboratories or to screen large populations for immigration control, shop security, and welfare and benefits claims (see Appendix B for an overview of some of the existing commercial face recognition systems). Since multi-modality can provide more robust and consistent recognition, face recognition systems are also likely to be designed to interface with other forms of access control devices utilising biometrics such as iris, fingerprint and hand geometry.

Similar to the notion of a personal agent introduced in the context of
visually mediated interaction, another example of utilising facial information is automated visual monitoring. A mechanism for assessing boredom
or inattention could be of considerable value in workplace situations where
attention to a crucial, but perhaps tedious task is essential. These scenarios include air traffic control, space flight operations, or watching a display
monitor for rare events. Systems being developed for the motor industry
aim to monitor the alertness and awareness of drivers based on cues such
as eyelid separation and could take appropriate action if drivers lose their
concentration. In such monitoring systems, one's own agent could provide
helpful prompts for better performance [127]. We can imagine "supportive home environments" that visually monitor and analyse the behaviour
of their occupants and detect unusual or dangerous events. Such systems
could prove especially useful for elderly residents living alone. A special
advantage of machine monitoring in these situations is that other people
need not be watching (in contrast to Orwell's "Big Brother" scenario). Instead, a personal supportive environment helps to ensure our health and
safety whilst providing additional benefits such as entertainment and communications.

12.4   Immersive Virtual Reality

On a rather different though highly relevant note, immersive virtual reality requires one essential element of computation: effective interpretation
of viewer behaviour and intention, typically head pose, walking, bending
and reaching gestures, in order to acquire in real-time the changing virtual
viewpoint and interactions of the viewer. Intrinsically, *immersive virtual
reality* implies that viewer behaviour is constantly incorporated in scene
reconstruction. There are two substantial advantages associated with a
model that captures and allows predictions of viewer behaviour and intention. The first is concerned with the quality of *visual service*, and the
second with *interaction* [320]. The quality of visual service can be largely
provided by a high, constant frame-rate rendering that is independent of
the complexity of the current field of view. A lag is allowed between viewer
actions and rendering updates if that is not below the threshold of perception, usually at 15 Hz. In order to maintain the frame rate, especially
for a complex scene, a *level of detail* algorithm is usually adopted which

attempts to provide on-line representations of graphical objects as a cost function of the current viewing parameters and object motions. However, this conventional method does not support any form of interaction since it only considers the relationship between the viewpoint and the scenario and does not take into account the likely future behaviour of the viewer, nor the relationship between events in the scenario and the intention of the viewer.

In order that the viewer's behaviour can directly drive the visual presentation of a dynamic scene, one requires a computer-based perceptual behaviour model that can automatically interpret the viewer's reaction to the present scene. An important aspect of this user-machine interface is the machine's ability to construct a *predict-ahead viewer behaviour model* based on visual tracking of identity, body posture and intention. To this end, computer vision-based, dynamic face models can be applied to the development of a viewer-centered behaviour model as a function of scene activity through learning. Such models will be able to provide a viewer-centered, intentionally-driven scene representation in immersive virtual reality. This is not that dissimilar to the models and some aspects of the computation required in visually mediated interaction introduced earlier.

12.5   Visual Database Screening

Object recognition in general and face recognition in particular have recently been applied to the problem of searching image and video databases. This is referred to as *content-based indexing* since it enables automatic visual indexing and screening of the content of a visual database without the need for skilled, manual indexing based on carefully selected keywords or verbal descriptions [3, 202, 281, 298, 364]. Application of face recognition in content-based search of visual databases is currently limited to the segmentation of broadcasting videos. In most cases, the sections where the news-reader appears are identified and extracted. In such cases the news-reader is usually facing the camera at a constant distance from it.

Future applications will involve the use of face recognition algorithms to identify and extract known faces from old film footage under less constrained conditions. For example, a politician could be automatically located in old newsreels even if the politician was not in the centre of the shot or was perhaps relatively unknown so that his presence was not even mentioned in any of the captions or news reports. Alternatively, you might be watching a recording of a football game and ask the computer to find and play back sequences of your favourite player scoring a goal.

◇

TO CONCLUDE, in the course of this book we have described algorithms and methodologies capable of representing, learning and identifying the visual appearances of dynamic objects such as moving faces. Although these have been illustrated using the specific problems associated with understanding faces, they certainly can also be exploited as a basis for modelling and learning the appearance and behaviour of both human activities and other objects. We hope that in the not too distant future, these algorithms will be generalised and further developed to give birth to a host of computer vision-based applications which, at the end of the twentieth century, exist only in our imaginations.

And if you find her poor, Ithaka won't have fooled you.
Wise as you will have become, so full of experience,
you'll have understood by then what these Ithakas mean.

— C.P. Cavafy, Ithaka

PART V

APPENDICES

A Databases

The development of any face recognition system requires the formation of a database of face images or sequences. The content of such databases depends largely on the purpose and functionality of the face recognition system. Broadly speaking, any face database can be used either for (a) the development and evaluation of face recognition algorithms or (b) the enrollment of face images for an application-driven operation.

An algorithm for learning and recognising faces requires a database that is representative of the appearance variations that are expected to be learned and recognised. As we have discussed, it is very difficult to develop algorithms for recognising faces under all possible appearance variations robustly and consistently. Therefore, variations need to be carefully controlled and where possible quantified. In addition, the database used for the evaluation of any face recognition system must be formed so that it includes face variations similar to the ones used in the developmental stage of the system. Naturally, care must be taken that images used during evaluation come from a disjoint set and can be used to quantify the interpolation and extrapolation abilities of a system.

A.1 Database Acquisition and Design

Acquisition of a database requires careful consideration of how to control a number of experimental variables that in effect define the possible appearance variations in face images. The extent to which each of these variables is controlled systematically will ultimately depend on the aims of the study to be performed using the database. As suggested in the introduction of this book (Chapter 1), the sources of variability in facial appearance can be either *intrinsic* or *extrinsic*. Intrinsic variation arises from the physical nature of people and their faces. Other sources of variation are extrinsic in that they also depend on the observer and the context. The way in which the subjects are selected will depend on the nature of the study. They might be chosen at random from a larger population. Alternatively, it is often helpful to select subjects according to the intrinsic characteristics of their faces.

A.1.1 Intrinsic Experimental Variables

When assembling a face database, the nature of the population can be considered in terms of the following intrinsic variables: Age, Ethnicity, Sex. A database should be representative of the population targeted by the application rather than representative of the human population at large. For example, a system for access control to a Tokyo bank should not be developed with a database containing many Caucasians or young children. In order to develop face recognition systems to cope with ageing, subjects may be required to return for several acquisition sessions at intervals of months or even years.

Once the number and nature of the subjects have been decided, the subjects must be prepared prior to acquisition. When acquiring a particular face, the following intrinsic variables can be controlled

Facial Expression: What variation in facial expression is desired and how is it to be controlled? How are the subjects instructed?

Clothing: Are there any restrictions on clothing? For example, are hats and scarves to be worn?

Facial Occlusion: To what extent are subjects' faces occluded by spectacles, jewellery and make-up?

Hair: Should the hair be covered, e.g. with a bathing cap?

A.1.2 Extrinsic Experimental Variables

During the acquisition of face images we can decide upon the environment and control the acquisition device to be used in forming our database. The number of images and sequences per subject will also vary from study to study. The following sources of extrinsic variation should be considered:

Alignment: Face images can be aligned at acquisition time by aligning facial features such as the eyes. Alignment is dealt with in greater detail in Section A.2.

Background: A homogeneous background can be useful. A carefully prepared background can allow automatic segmentation by chroma-keying.

Camera adjustment: The lens used and the distance from the subject will affect image quality and the degree to which perspective effects are present. Camera focus is also important.

Illumination: The number of light sources, their positions and type could be controlled.

Imaging device: Most commonly used are monocular CCD cameras that capture 2D images or image sequences. Alternatively, 3D face representations can be captured using binocular systems or laser-range finding devices.

Pose: The precision and mechanisms with which head pose relative to the image-plane is controlled. This is addressed in greater detail in Section A.2.

Scale: The width and height of a face in pixels.

Face images could be aligned after data acquisition in order to form data suitable for learning algorithms. However, this alignment process cannot be fully automated. Therefore, it is preferable to avoid, or at least to ease, this normalisation process by ensuring that face images are properly aligned at acquisition time.

A.2   Acquisition of a Pose-labelled Database

While many databases of frontal views are available, there is currently a distinct lack of image data available for views ranging continuously over the view-sphere. Here, we describe the acquisition of a database of views labelled with 3D pose angles and we show how the experimental variables listed above are controlled [134, 251].

A.2.1   Using Artificial Markers

In order to measure the effects of pose change, other degrees of freedom such as image-plane translations and scale changes can be carefully removed by manually cropping the images. An important point to note is that rotation of a head results in a horizontal translation of the face in the image-plane. This makes the alignment of images of different poses rather difficult. A

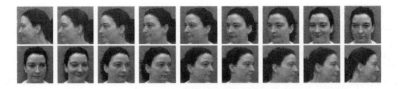

Figure A.1 A set of 18 example face images captured using artificial markers.

simple approach based on alignment of facial features results in sequences in which the *centroid* of the head translates horizontally as the head rotates in depth. Alternatively, images are aligned approximately around the visual centroid of the head, either automatically using visual tracking or manually.

A simple way to acquire pose-labelled face images is to use artificial markers. Whilst the subject is seated on a swivel chair in the middle of a semi-circle, markers are placed around the semi-circle at intervals of $10°$. A camera is placed at $0°$ to the subject at the same height as the markers. Before we start the acquisition of images the height of the swivel chair is adjusted such that the centre of the subject's frontal view image is aligned with the centre of the camera. Then acquisition of the images is performed by asking the subjects to look at the markers on the wall positioned from $-90°$ (left profile view) to $+90°$ (right profile view) in $10°$ increments. An example set of face images captured using this system is shown in Figure A.1. Alternatively, images varying only from $0°$ (frontal view) to $90°$ can be captured and profile-to-profile sequences can be generated by mirroring.

Aligned face templates suitable for pose understanding can be obtained, for example, by using the eyes as anchor points. These templates are of fixed size and exclude most of the background and hair. Firstly, a frontal view $(\theta = \phi = 0°)$ is captured interactively by specifying with a mouse the points on each eye nearest to the side of the head: (x_{leye}, y_{leye}) and (x_{reye}, y_{reye}). The width of all templates is set to $W = x_{reye} - x_{leye}$ and the height to $H = 1.2W$. A rectangular face template is captured with upper-left vertex at $\left(x_{leye}, \frac{y_{reye} - y_{leye}}{2} + 0.2H\right)$. Subsequent templates are captured by specifying with a mouse the most extreme point on the eye nearest to occlusion by the head, (x_{occ}, y_{occ}), and then capturing a template with an upper vertex at $(x_{occ}, y_{occ} + 0.2H)$.

A disadvantage of this method using artificial markers is that pose labelling is noisy as the subjects do not necessarily look straight at the locations of the markers. Some subjects, for example, have a tendency to move their eyes towards the markers rather than turn their head. It is also very difficult to control and measure head tilt using this method. Nevertheless, it has the advantages of low cost and relative ease of set-up. Face images acquired can be used for initial experiments and enrollment in commercial applications. However, for more extensive system analysis and evaluation of face recognition algorithms, one requires a much more systematic and precise methodology for acquiring and labelling example images.

A.2.2 Using Sensors and a Calibrated Camera

An acquisition system that uses an electro-magnetic sensor and a calibrated camera was built to obtain carefully aligned and normalised face images labelled with pose angles. The resulting alignment is consistent across subjects and smooth across pose [134, 251]. An electro-magnetic, six degrees-of-freedom Polhemus tracker with a sensor and a transmitter is used. It provides the 3D coordinates and orientation of the sensor relative to the transmitter. The sensor is rigidly attached to a head-band worn by the subject so that it follows the head's movements and changes in orientation. A monocular image acquisition system is calibrated to the magnetic sensor's 3D coordinate system. This allows the 3D position of the face relative to the sensor to be obtained. The location of the head in the image can then be determined using back-projection of this 3D position onto the image-plane. Thus, well cropped images are acquired. The sensor orientations are used to label each image with head pose angles in both yaw and tilt. Fig. A.2 shows the acquisition system.

Camera calibration: In order to locate and align the 2D head images, the camera is calibrated with respect to the sensor. This involves determining camera parameters using a set of 3D positions of the sensor and their corresponding 2D projections on the image-plane. Both intrinsic and extrinsic camera parameters were estimated. The intrinsic parameters are focal length and radial distortion. The extrinsic parameters are the position and orientation of the camera relative to the sensor's coordinate system. We adopted a camera model initially proposed by Tsai [339]. The calibration process requires a set of calibration points. Each calibration point

Camera   **Sensor on head-band**

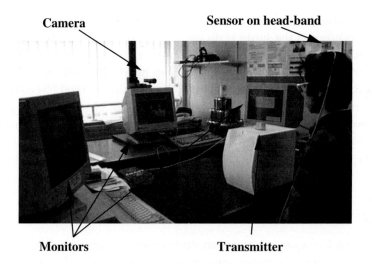

Monitors   **Transmitter**

Figure A.2 An automated, multi-sensor acquisition system for capturing a face database across the view-sphere.

consists of a 3D sensor position and its 2D image. The origin and axis of the 3D space is set by the magnetic transmitter.

Head alignment and labelling: The position of the sensor relative to the head can be somewhat arbitrary. However, the position and scale of the heads in the images acquired needs to be consistent for different people. Therefore, a few facial features were manually located for each subject in order to bootstrap the acquisition process by determining a scaling factor and a 3D point inside the head. In other words, the facial features' 3D coordinates were used to determine the coordinates of a 3D point inside the head relative to the sensor's 3D coordinates. This point was rigidly 'attached' to the facial features (eyes and upper lip) and its projection was used as the centre of the acquired head images. The image was then cropped as determined by the scale factor and re-sampled to a fixed number of pixels.

The first step is to obtain the relative 3D coordinates of various facial feature points relative to the sensor. This is achieved as follows. The subject's eyes and the middle of the upper lip are located in the frontal view. These features are fairly rigid with respect to the head. Two horizontally aligned boxes and a vertical line across the middle of the line joining the boxes are overlaid on the screen to help the operator to find the frontal view by assessing bilateral facial symmetry. The centre of each box is aligned with the centre of an eye. The line between the centres of the two *eye boxes* is the inter-ocular line and is made to be always horizontal, thus minimising the amount of rotation of the head in the image plane. The distance between the upper lip and the midpoint of the inter-ocular line segment is used to determine the size of an image crop box. We now have the 2D projections of facial feature points on the image plane.

An estimation of the 3D coordinates (x, y, z) of a feature point was made by recovering its depth which was initially set to the sensor's depth, z_s, from the image plane. The feature point was then aligned with its corresponding feature at profile view. The change in depth, z_{offset}, of the feature point was recovered using the change in its coordinates due to alignment and applying an inverse perspective projection to them. The depth of the feature point was set as $z = z_s + z_{offset}$. With this new depth and its 2D position recovered at frontal view, x and y were found using inverse perspective projection to recover their corresponding values in camera coordinates and translation to make them relative to the sensor's position. Three 3D feature points were located on the face: right and left eye (eye_r, eye_l), and the middle of the upper lip $(ulip)$.

The centre of the crop box was set as the projection of the midpoint of the line, s_{line}, from $ulip$ to the midpoint of the inter-ocular line between eye_r and eye_l. Finally, the size of the crop box was determined by inverse rotating s_{line} such that it was vertically aligned and parallel with the image plane. The projection of s_{line} was obtained and used as the scale factor. Figure A.3 (a) illustrates the details of the cropping process and (b) shows image data acquired for one subject across the view-sphere.

A.3   Benchmarking

Benchmarking and quantitative comparison of different face recognition methods require the use of shared, standard databases. Several publicly available databases have been used in recent years for evaluation by different research groups allowing a certain level of comparison on the sub-problem represented by the databases used. Particularly noteworthy in this respect is the FERET (Face Recognition Technology) program sponsored by the United States Department of Defence's Counter-

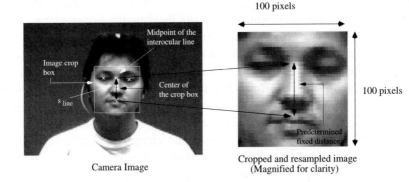

(a)

(b)

Figure A.3 (a) The projections of the feature points ($eye_r, eye_l, ulip$) are shown as × marks. The centre of the image is seen as the projection of the midpoint of the line between the midpoint of the inter-ocular line segment and the upper lip point. The scale factor for the image crop is determined by scaling the projection of s_{line} to a predetermined distance in the cropped and re-sampled image on the right. (b) Face images of a person from example views across the view-sphere. There are 133 images per person with y-axis rotation in the range $\pm90°$ and x-axis rotation in the range $\pm30°$ at intervals of $10°$.

drug Technology Transfer Program. Within this program, large face databases were acquired and released in a controlled manner to selected development sites in the USA for development and evaluation [266, 268]. As with any database, FERET has been designed with particular applications in mind and results should be considered within the context of these applications. Any specific database design will tend to favour one algorithm over another, while altering the database and thus the problem will often favour a different algorithm. There is a danger that programmes such as FERET are seen as defining face recognition and that rather than encouraging research on a whole range of issues pertaining to face recognition, they polarise research effort on a narrower problem of engineering, with the "best" methods gaining commercial advantage. Benchmarking is a laudable aim but test results must always be placed in context. We echo a previous call for *"less emphasis on the 'headline' recognition result, and more discussion of the testing methodology and the chosen variability in the data"* [291]. A list of public domain databases is given in Section A.5.

A.4 Commercial Databases

Once a face recognition system has been developed and is being applied, a database is formed by enrolling the people the system is aimed to identify. Environmental conditions in commercial applications are more difficult to control than those found in research laboratories and care should be taken that the conditions during enrollment reflect the variability of the conditions under which the system will be operated.

In order to restrict the variability in facial appearance, many of the commercial face recognition systems currently available enroll subjects in purpose-built cubicles where the lighting conditions, the face pose and distance of the subjects to the camera, are as much as possible, held constant. During recognition, the acquisition of the images is performed with the cooperation of the user, who usually has to go to a similar cubicle and look towards a camera from some specified distance. As a result, most of the systems currently available are only able to recognise subjects from frontal or near frontal views.

Most of the face recognition systems to date are built either for experimental purposes or to address the needs of an organisation with a limited number of people enrolled. However, if these techniques were to be used in systems capable of recognising people from a larger population, there are a number of issues that need to be addressed. Systems dealing with a large number of identities should be able to operate effectively as the number of subjects increases to its operational capacity and should only gracefully degrade as the system accommodates more subjects than envisaged at the time of its design [30]. In operating such a face recognition system, one needs to consider enrollment, updating and retrieval of information.

Database enrollment: A requirement for most large commercial face recognition applications is that there is a constant throughput of people and a very small turnaround time. This requires an image acquisition system that is able to identify people in real-time without intervening with their activities. An additional complication facing applications is that during enrollment a check must be made to confirm that a person has not been enrolled before under another identity. This task requires the identification of a person against all the information already in the database. This implies that a system only capable of verification cannot enroll subjects autonomously.

Updating: In most commercial systems, failure to identify a person who has already been enrolled is resolved by the manual intervention of an operator and the addition of the new, unrecognised image to the database. Such cases highlight the need for a mechanism to be put in place that updates the database as subjects age or alter in appearance. In addition, it is also desirable for the database to be updated by adding new subjects and deleting ex-subjects.

Distributed databases: Information on peoples' identities will often be held in distributed databases that are networked. This imposes the extra requirement that any facial appearance information is coded in a format that is fast to transfer though the network so that on-line, real-time identification is possible. Identity information for verification purposes could be held on smart cards carried by users.

The performance of a system is measured against its false acceptance and false rejection rates. Developers of commercial systems need to take this into account and not allow their rates to deteriorate as the scale of the database grows. However, it should be noted that all the systems developed are based on statistical information and thus by definition there is an element of error and inaccuracy. What all the systems hope to achieve is to perform better and faster than a human identifier carrying out a similar task. However, they cannot and will not by definition always be able to derive the absolute truth.

A.5   Public Domain Face Databases

Several face image databases have been made publically available by researchers around the world. Links to most of these databases can be found on the World Wide Web at the *Face Recognition Home Page* maintained by Peter Kruizinga (http://www.cs.rug.nl/~peterkr/FACE/face.html). Here, we give what we hope is a reasonably comprehensive list. We briefly describe the content of each database and the extent to which various experimental variables have been controlled during acquisition.

The Olivetti and Oracle Research Laboratory (ORL)
(http://www.cam-orl.co.uk/facedatabase.html)

- 92×112, 256 grey levels, PGM format, 40 subjects, 10 per subject. Approximately upright frontal views. Variation in lighting, facial expression (open/closed eyes, smiling/not smiling) and glasses. Dark homogeneous background [301].

The Turing Institute, Glasgow (http://www.turing.gla.ac.uk/)

- VRML models, 65 subjects, C3D 2020 capture system.

Carnegie Mellon University
(http://www.ius.cs.cmu.edu/IUS/har1/har/usr0/har/faces/test/)

- A database for testing frontal view face detection algorithms. Image co-ordinates of facial features are provided for the faces to be detected. GIF format, grey-scale [297].

University of Stirling (http://pics.psych.stir.ac.uk/)

- The PICS database contains several sets of face images:
  - 313 images, approximately 35 subjects, each at 3 poses (frontal, 3/4 and profile) and with 3 expressions at each pose.

- 493 images, approximately 70 subjects, each with 4 expressions at frontal view, 2 expressions at side view, and one frontal view with a bathing cap over hair.
- Provided by Ian Craw of the University of Aberdeen: 689 images, variation in pose (14), facial expression (4) and illumination, colour, several images per subject at different times.

MIT Media Lab. (ftp://whitechapel.media.mit.edu/pub/images/)

- 128×120, 8-bits grey-scale, RAW byte format, 16 subjects, 27 per subject, variation in illumination scale and pose. A larger database may also be available [341].

Weizmann Institute of Science, Israel
(ftp://eris.wisdom.weizmann.ac.il/pub/FaceBase/)

- 512×352 (pixel aspect ratio of 12:11), grey-scale, 28 subjects, three different facial expressions, y-axis pose change, horizontal illumination change [2].

Yale University
(http://giskard.eng.yale.edu/yalefaces/yalefaces.html)

- GIF format, grey-scale, 15 subjects, 11 per subject with different facial expressions and lighting: centre-light, w/glasses, happy, left-light, w/no glasses, normal, right-light, sad, sleepy, surprised, and wink. Illumination changes are quite extreme [17].

M2VTS ACTS Project (Multi-modal Biometric Person Authentication)
(http://www.tele.ucl.ac.be/M2VTS/)

- An audio-visual database intended for speech verification and speech/lips correlation studies as well as face recognition. It consists of 286×350 pixels, 37 subjects, 5 sequences per subject taken at one week intervals. In each sequence, the subject counts from "0" to "9" and then performs y-axis rotation from frontal to left profile, to right profile and back to frontal view. Those with glasses repeated the head rotation without glasses. Head pose was not controlled with much precision and the speed of rotation varies. A distribution fee is charged for this database. An extended database with more than 1000 GB of sequences is planned for release [269].

University of Michigan (`http://www.engin.umich.edu/faces/`)

- More than 2000 subjects, one image per subject, Colour JPEG, approximately frontal views, mostly head and shoulders. Background and illumination vary.

USENIX (`ftp://ftp.uu.net/published/usenix/faces`)

- Images of more than 5000 faces, one image per subject, mostly frontal views with variable viewing conditions [223].

University of Bern
(`ftp://iamftp.unibe.ch/pub/Images/FaceImages/`)

- Sun rasterfile format, 8-bits grey-scale, 512×342, 30 subjects, 15 images per subject, varying pose and contrast, carefully controlled illumination [1].

PEIPA (Pilot European Image Processing Archive)
(`http://peipa.essex.ac.uk/`)

- This archive contains data provided by groups at the University of Essex and the University of Manchester.
  - **Essex**: Colour GIF, 180×200 and 192×144, approx. 150 subjects.
  - **Manchester**: 512×512 PGM format.

Purdue University
(`http://rvl1.ecn.purdue.edu/~aleix/aleix_face_DB.html`)

- More than 4000 frontal view images of 126 people. Facial expression, illumination and occlusions were varied in a controlled manner. Each person took part in two sessions separated by 14 days [219].

A.6 Discussion

In order to learn view-based models that account for large rotations away from the frontal view, a database of face images over a range of the viewsphere and labelled with 3D pose angles can be used. We have described the acquisition of such a database using either artificial markers or a magnetic sensing device and a calibrated camera.

Acquisition of a face database requires careful design and will inevitably depend upon the nature of the proposed study. Large databases have been made available in the public domain, enabling direct comparisons to be made between different algorithms. A list of currently available databases was given. It should be borne in mind, however, that any given database is not truly representative. The lowest error rate on a particular database under a particular evaluation regime indicates a good solution to a constrained subproblem and does not imply that the algorithm is somehow the best face recognition algorithm. It is therefore desirable that databases used for benchmarking purposes also include imperfect images with face variations that divert from the expected case. Such cases are more likely to appear in real-life scenarios when implementing a practical face recognition scheme [269].

Whilst benchmarking might help to identify how the various experimental face recognition systems perform under varying conditions, the real challenge is the use of the systems in natural environments with poor conditions. Transfer of face recognition systems to commercial applications is by no means trivial and in many cases it depends on fundamental assumptions made during the conception of the original experimental systems.

B   Commercial Systems

Real-time machine vision systems are commonly regarded as user unfriendly, temperamental and expensive due to the requirements of specialised image acquisition systems and high-powered workstations. However, the need for such specialised hardware is fast disappearing in recent years judging both by performance and cost. Enormous progress in real-time imaging hardware aimed at the mass PC market has made video capture, storage and processing readily accessible using standard off-the-shelf PC-based imaging systems at very low cost.

The trend for the commercialisation of low cost machine vision systems is perhaps most visible in the field of biometrics using face and iris recognition. This is largely due to the enormous application potential offered by these systems. Some of the methods described in this book and elsewhere are indeed reflected commercially. However, most current face recognition systems can only operate under very constrained conditions. For instance, one of the most common features of the current systems is to impose very stringent constraints on viewing angle and lighting conditions. In fact, almost all systems only work with snapshots of frontal or near-frontal face images. It is also true that the definition for what constitutes "face recognition" is often ambiguous. In view of the difficulties highlighted throughout this book, perhaps it comes as no surprise that most of the current commercial systems largely perform a very similar task, i.e. one-to-one verification, under restricted conditions. However, different considerations have been taken into account in identifying applications that aim to maximise the potential of a given method. In addition, face recognition is increasingly combined with other form of biometrics such as voice or fingerprint recognition in order to provide a more robust and accurate person identification system.

In the following, we draw up a list of considerations for the characterisation of commercial systems before describing a number of typical commercial products to reflect the methods adopted for applications targeted. It is worth pointing out that such a list is by no means an exhaustive review of the industry. Rather, this exercise has two main purposes. Firstly, it highlights the importance of defining application constraints in the process of adopting existing methods from research laboratories for commercial systems. Secondly, it identifies remaining research issues.

B.1   System Characterisation

Commercial face recognition systems seem to cover a large range of applications from electronic banking (e.g. ATM machines), video-conferencing, access control in prisons, immigration and internet logins to off-line database search and indexing. Most systems essentially perform the one-to-one identity verification task described in Section 1.3 although different systems have different operational conditions and requirements. A small number of systems are also aimed at performing the classification task against a small population. Finally, a few systems are used for screening a database in order to discard the poorest matches, leaving a much smaller number of candidate matches for human assessment.

Overall, there is a lack of criteria for system characterisation and evaluation. Here we list criteria we consider to be useful for characterising a commercial face recognition system.

Product

(1) `Users`: The targeted end-users and market sectors.
(2) `Recognition task`: The type of recognition task, i.e. verification, classification, known/unknown or full identification.
(3) `Platform`: The hardware platforms and software packages used as well as details of any integrated solutions.
(4) `Imaging medium`: The type of images used e.g. image sequences captured directly from a video camera or from videotape, or static images captured directly from a camera or from photographs.
(5) `Database`: The size and nature of the database of known people.
(6) `Speed`: The rate at which identification needs to be performed. Real-time image acquisition and recognition may be essential in many applications.
(7) `Accuracy`: The recognition accuracy required. Accuracy should be assessed in terms of *false-negative* and *false-positive* error rates. The

risks associated with each type of error are application dependent. It is important to consider whether the system is to be used as a primary stand-alone or secondary device when assessing these risks.

Approach

(1) `Algorithm`: The type of algorithm adopted, e.g. view-based or 3D model-based, static or dynamic.
(2) `Face image acquisition`: Whether manual or automatic face detection and tracking are used during enrollment and recognition processes.
(3) `Adaptability`: Automatic, on-line learning to progressively optimise performance for specific applications (adaptation of database).
(4) `System tuning`: The various control parameters that can be tuned for a particular operational environment. These typically include the operating point which determines the trade-off between false-positive and false-negative errors.
(5) `'Phoney' detection`: The mechanisms adopted for dealing with photographs, artificial masks or other physical models of faces.

Constraints

(1) `Extrinsic`: The ability to deal with extrinsic variables such as viewpoint, distance to the camera, lighting conditions and background motion.
(2) `Intrinsic`: The ability to deal with intrinsic variables such as facial hair, hair-style, glasses and facial expression.

B.2   A View on the Industry

Most face recognition systems currently on the market have been developed by joint-ventures between university research laboratories and capital investors seeking commercial exploitation of increasingly active research in face recognition over the past decade. In more recent years, large corporations in the main-stream IT industry have also started to either acquire or fund development work utilising face recognition technology for applications such as video-conferencing and internet access. However, most commercial systems are based on just a few underlying recognition engines. Here, we aim to characterise some of the main-stream commercial face recognition systems according to the criteria described above.

B.2.1   Visionics Corporation

Visionics has developed the **FaceIt** series of software packages which have been licensed to various third parties for a wide range of applications. The packages can be characterised as follows.

Product

(1) `Users:` There are several packages aimed at different end users. These range from a low cost package (**FaceIt PC** and **FaceIt NT**) for data access control and network security to a large scale database application for national ID and to a more expensive system that aims to detect and track a frontal view face before performing identification (**FaceIt Surveillance**). Targeted applications include on-line one-to-one verification tasks such as electronic banking using ATM machines and immigration border control, as well as one-to-many tasks such as CCTV control room applications.

(2) `Recognition task:` One-to-one verification and one-to-many identification.

(3) `Platform:` Windows 9x, NT and Unix/Linux.

(4) `Imaging medium:` On-line image sequences captured by a video camera or off-line image databases.

(5) `Database:` An application-dependent database is acquired through enrollment sessions. Several snapshots may be acquired for each individual in order to represent some of the variation of their facial appearance in the database.

(6) `Speed:` Given a good frontal view, the face is typically found in less than a second.

(7) `Accuracy:` It is proposed that **FaceIt** systems can be used as primary stand-alone devices for targeted applications.

Approach

(1) `Algorithm:` The algorithm is based on the *local feature analysis* method developed at Rockefeller University [259]. It involves the extraction of localised image features using multi-scale filters and

the encoding of such feature images using PCA. The method is based on images from a single pose. The system also allows for the manipulation of several video streams and can schedule them based upon returned confidence levels.

(2) `Face image acquisition`: Unlike most other commercial systems, **FaceIt** aims to automatically find a moving frontal face view within a given distance from the video camera without requiring the users to be actively cooperative. However, the mechanism can be very sensitive to lighting changes. This is because the detection of a face is performed by direct temporal differencing over two successive image frames of the video sequence. It is claimed that the system can simultaneously detect and track multiple faces in constrained environments.

(3) `Adaptability`: Recent developments include on-line, application dependent adaptation of a given database.

(4) `System tuning`: An operator can trade-off false-positive and false-negative error rates and tune the system to the lighting and background conditions.

(5) `'Phoney' detection`: A live-face test option requires the user to smile or blink, enabling the system to verify the presence of a real face. However, this slows down the identification process.

Constraints

(1) `Extrinsic`: The face detection process is reported to be able to capture face images in varying size and the recognition mechanism is able to cope with a certain amount of affine transformation and up to $\pm 35°$ tilt and yaw. **FaceIt** works best with a static background. It is also claimed that it works reasonably well with cluttered and moving background.

(2) `Intrinsic`: Recent reports state that the algorithm can cope with changes in skin tone, eyeglasses, facial expressions and hair style, although there is neither qualitative nor quantitative description of the extent of change allowed and robustness under such change.

B.2.2   Miros Inc.

Miros Inc. is the provider of the **TrueFace** software. It acquires images, automatically locates faces and normalizes for variations in size, view, rotation, translation, and lighting. **TrueFace** uses multiple neural networks to match normalized facial features with those stored in a database.

Product

(1) Users: Applications include electronic banking using ATM machines, surveillance, internet access, login control and physical access control. Software range from a low-cost system for one-to-one verification (**TrueFace PC, TrueFace Network, TrueFace Web**) to more expensive one-to-many identification systems (**TrueFace ID**) and an integrated one-to-one physical access control system that includes both software and hardware (**TrueFace Access**).

(2) Recognition task: One-to-one verification and one-to-many identification. For verification applications, a PIN or password is supplied by the user or some other device.

(3) Platform: Windows 9x and NT.

(4) Imaging medium: Some products use static images captured interactively and other products use image sequences captured from a video camera or videotape.

(5) Database: The system captures one or two images of each individual per enrollment or verification attempt. Multiple enrollment sessions allow multiple images per person to be stored in the database.

(6) Speed: It is claimed that typical throughput is 1-2 seconds on a 266 MHz Pentium II machine with 64 MB of RAM. This includes the time to find the face and verify it.

Approach

(1) Algorithm: A hybrid of neural networks and proprietary image processing algorithms are used.

(2) Face image acquisition: Acquisition is interactive and involves one or two video cameras. For physical access control, a key pad or magnetic card reader is optional. For most applications, the user must cooperate actively. For surveillance applications, images are captured by an operator when the person looks at a hidden camera.

(3) `System tuning`: An adjustable threshold trades off false-positive and false-negative errors. There are also several parameters that control the face-finding algorithm which can be tuned to improve the performance for a particular application.

(4) `'Phoney' detection`: A stereo view of the user can be used to prevent any attempt to defraud the system using 2D pictures of an authorised user. For applications with only one camera, the person is required to move their head during the capture of an image sequence so that an approximate stereo view can be generated and analyzed.

Constraints

(1) `Extrinsic`: It is claimed that several normalizing stages compensate for different viewpoints, camera distances and reasonable lighting conditions. Recognition accuracy degrades as more extreme conditions prevail, such as the person looking further away from the camera, or harsh shadows across the face.

(2) `Intrinsic`: Large changes in hair-style or facial hair require re-enrollment. Normal changes in skin tone do not affect recognition accuracy. It is claimed that eyeglasses do not reduce accuracy unless there is a large reflection from them which masks the eyes. Since typical applications involve cooperative users, the software is designed to handle only normal facial expressions. A description of the degree of changes allowed was not available.

B.2.3   VisionSpheres Technologies

UnMask and **UnMask+** are the two commercially available face recognition programs from *VisionSpheres Technologies* based on research done at McGill University. These systems have the following features:

Product

(1) `Users`: Potential applications are likely to be in government agencies where well controlled conditions can be enforced and the input can just be a still image. For example, the Division of Motor Vehicles in West Virginia has tried to apply **UnMask** to verify identities of drivers when they require a renewal or duplicate driver's license.

(2) `Recognition task:` **UnMask** performs one-to-one verification. **UnMask+** is primarily designed to cope with classification tasks based on the same algorithms.

(3) `Platform:` Windows-based software.

(4) `Imaging medium:` Single images taken from a static digital camera or sequences captured using a CCD video camera.

(5) `Database:` Feature-based templates extracted from face snapshots are stored.

(6) `Speed:` It is claimed that the software can perform all preprocessing, feature extraction and face matching within half a second on a 200 MHz Pentium-based PC. However, the need for manual acquisition provides the performance bottleneck.

(7) `Accuracy:` The system is designed as a secondary verification device and for use with other biometrics such as fingerprints.

Approach

(1) `Algorithm:` Spatial, geometric relationships between key facial features such as eyes, nose and mouth are extracted and stored in a template. Matching is performed based on overall facial appearance.

(2) `Face image acquisition:` In one mode the process requires a manually activated digital or video camera which takes a single face image against a plain background. Pre-defined facial features are located manually by an operator only when the system fails to automatically locate them. The systems thus have semi-automatic face detection but no tracking functions at present.

Constraints

In general, recognition systems based on explicit measurement of image features will have difficulty with extrinsic or intrinsic changes that make establishing feature correspondence difficult or impossible. Changes in viewpoint will likely fail both systems here.

(1) `Extrinsic:` Despite intensity normalisation both systems are still likely to be sensitive to lighting changes when image-based facial features are inconsistent. Other variations such as in scale, image orientation and face location can be addressed since the acquisition process is manually operated.

(2) Intrinsic: The feature-based method can cope with facial expression to some extent. On the other hand, spectacles and changes in facial hair style could cause the systems to fail.

B.2.4 Eigenface-based Systems: Viisage Technologies, Intelligent Verification Systems and Facia Reco

Viisage Technologies has developed the **Face ID** software series to perform one-to-one verification tasks based on an eigenface approach [260, 341]. The main features of the systems are as follows.

Product

(1) Users: Likely end-users are government agencies involved in criminal investigation and prevention. *Viisage* distributes DLLs for end-users to build application-specific systems.

(2) Recognition task: Off-line database screening or one-to-one verification. The systems rely on PIN numbers to initialise a verification.

(3) Platform: Windows 95 or NT.

(4) Imaging medium: **Face ID** works with static face images captured by a digital camera or photo-realistic face composite sketches. It is proposed that such a composite sketch of a person can also be compared against a database of digital mug-shots for possible matches. It is not clear what degree of detail in texture is required. Since the systems are based on eigenfaces, holistic facial texture and shading are the primary information encoded.

(5) Database: In order to obtain statistically meaningful eigenfaces, the choice of the training database is fundamental in the sense that it has to be statistically representative. One effective solution is to update the database by selecting face images which are near misses in the recognition phase to adapt and tune the database for a specific population.

(6) Speed: It is claimed that enrollment and identification are performed within 3 seconds. However, speed is limited by the fact that the entire acquisition process is manually driven.

Approach

(1) `Algorithm`: The systems are based on the eigenface approach. As described earlier in this book, the main feature of eigenfaces is that they capture holistic, linear statistical variations in the database. Good face image segmentation and tracking are essential. **Face ID** partially addresses these issues by employing manual face detection and segmentation by a human operator.

(2) `Face image acquisition`: The system utilises a static digital camera. The user needs to present himself or herself to the "point of use" before a digital image is captured. An attempt has also been made to utilise images captured by a video camera. For instance, a digital drivers' license-ID card system was proposed which utilised *Viisage*'s **SensorMast** device. The latter uses both a motorised color video camera and automatic control of lighting in order to capture a portrait image of a user. It is not clear how applicable such a complex and controlled operation is in practice. Users are required to be actively co-operative.

(3) `System tuning`: Operators can set threshold values for tuning the recognition error rate for different applications. However, the setting of these threshold values is somewhat arbitrary. For instance, they can be set to different values for each image stored in the database!

Constraints

(1) `Extrinsic`: Eigenface algorithms suffer poor performance under changes not represented in the training database. They are typically sensitive to lighting and can only cope with small pose changes.

(2) `Intrinsic`: Provided that face image segmentation and alignment can be achieved consistently, eigenface-based algorithms are less sensitive to local image feature change. They can cope reasonably well with spectacles and limited changes of facial hair.

Other eigenface based systems include **FaceKey** marketed by *Intelligent Verification Systems*, **Real-time Sherlock** marketed by *Facia Reco* and *Viisage Technologies*. The main difference between **Face ID** and **Real-time Sherlock** is that the latter also utilises an on-line face detection program which aims to automate the data acquisition process in both database enrollment and verification.

B.2.5 Systems based on Facial Feature Matching: Plettac Electronic Security GmbH, ZN Bochum GmbH and Eyematic Interfaces Inc.

Plettac Electronic Security GmbH has recently taken over the face identification system **FaceVACS** (Visual Access Control Systems) developed by *Siemens Nixdorf.* **FaceVACS** is one of the few systems that was developed mainly for Unix based platforms. The main features of the system are:

Product

(1) Users: **FaceVACS** targets applications such as access control, safe deposit box access, time and attendance control. Potential end-users include financial institutions. Currently **FaceVACS** is under test by German banks that aim to provide customers with unattended, 24 hour access to their safety deposit box. The system functions based on PIN numbers.

(2) Recognition task: One-to-one verification.

(3) Platform: **FaceVACS** and its associated **Synapse 2** accelerator board provide a hybrid software-hardware solution which aims to enable developers to use parallel correlation of images from multiple views in order to speed up the recognition process.

(4) Imaging medium: A few image frames of a person are captured on-line for verification.

(5) Database: A set of feature vectors are computed from one or a few face images of each person and stored.

(6) Speed: It is claimed that face detection, alignment, feature extraction and identification can be performed in 0.5 second on a 233MHz Pentium system.

Approach

(1) Algorithm: Given a normalised face image, a pre-defined set of image grid positions are superimposed onto the face image which is also aligned according to the positions of the eyes. At every grid point, person-specific features are extracted and compressed into

a characteristic feature set. This feature extraction is based on a set of multi-order Gaussian derivative filters. In order to cope with lighting changes, during enrollment, several images of a face are captured and a common set of features are extracted for this face. The task of identity verification is performed by measuring the similarity between a set of stored feature vectors of different known people and the feature vector computed from the current test image. Thresholding is used to give the best match.

(2) `Face image acquisition`: For both enrollment and verification, snapshots are captured by fixed view, static digital cameras. A neural network-based face detection program is run over the captured image in order to locate the face in the image. Furthermore, an eye detector based on a similar neural network is applied to the face region detected in the image. In order to cope with image scale change, the detected face image is normalised in scale according to the distance between the detected eye positions.

Constraints

(1) `Extrinsic`: Like **UnMask** of *VisionSpheres*, **FaceVACS** suffers from similar problems under changes in lighting and viewpoint. However, **FaceVACS** does perform appropriate alignment and scale normalisation.

(2) `Intrinsic`: Similar to **UnMask**, the system can better cope with expression than facial hair although the computation is necessarily expensive. Wearing glasses can, however, impose difficulties in eye detection, and thus in alignment and feature extraction.

ZN Bochum GmbH and *Eyematic Interfaces Inc.* are two companies established to exploit and develop face verification systems using feature-based matching, based on research carried out at the University of Southern California and the University of Bochum [189, 195] which used Gabor wavelet representation and flexible graph matching. ZN offers two products, **ZN Face II** for applications in access control, and **PHANTOMAS** for face database search in forensic applications [188]. The **ZN-Face II** application has the following characteristics:

Product

(1) Users: The main target application for **ZN-Face II** is physical access control.

(2) Recognition task: One-to-one verification.

(3) Platform: Pentium PC based.

(4) Imaging medium: The video stream is analyzed by the face detection step and an image frame of a person is captured on-line for verification. The video stream is also evaluated for the detection of intrinsic face motion.

(5) Database: A set of feature vectors based on Gabor functions is computed from a single face image. Each set of feature vectors represents a known person.

(6) Speed: It is claimed that face detection, feature extraction and verification are performed in 0.5 seconds on a Pentium II-400 system.

Approach

(1) Algorithm: The feature-based matching algorithm adopted by **ZN-Face** is based on Gabor wavelet representation of a given image. This is essentially a flexible 2D graph with a finite number of predefined image grids computed for each image. By matching graphs of different facial images, identity verification can be performed [195]. The method is similar in principle to **FaceVACS** except that the feature vectors here are given by a fixed number of grids at which a set of multi-scale Gabor wavelet responses, known as Gabor jets, are computed by convolving an image with Gabor wavelets. The grid positions are usually assigned to typical locations of facial features.

(2) Face image acquisition: A user needs to step in front of a system console and glance at the tinted, slanted glass. A snapshot of the face is automatically taken when the distance and image alignment between the face and the screen (camera) is as required.

(3) Adaptability: No automated learning but the administrator may add additional images to the person's record at any time.

(4) System tuning: **ZN-Face II** allows the system operator to change a threshold value for acceptable performance error rate depending on the quality of the images available.

(5) 'Phoney' detection: **ZN-Face** uses an IR-filter glass and IR-illumination since photos and real people have different reflectance

characteristics in near-infrared. Furthermore, **ZN-Face II** incorporates a live check module to avoid fraud by using photos of known persons. The system compensates the global motion of the face and checks for intrinsic motion in the face, such as eye twinkle and mouth motion. It cannot be misled by moving a photographic print in front of the camera.

Constraints

(1) Extrinsic: Due to a normalisation step in the feature extraction process **ZN Face II** is quite robust to global changes in illumination. Changes in 3D pose, however, do matter.

(2) Intrinsic: It is claimed that due to the integral evaluation of facial features, **ZN Face II** performs well under various changes in facial appearance such as the addition of spectacles or facial hair growth. New sample images need to be added into the database to cope with dramatic changes.

ZN Face II and **PHANTOMAS** employ very similar feature extraction processes but due to different target applications, many system properties differ. For example, **PHANTOMAS** is essentially a tool for forensic science. It is designed to search for similar faces in an image database as well as for similarities between a black and white mug-shot and faces of a database. **PHANTOMAS** sorts the faces in order of similarity to a reference face.

Independently from *ZN Bochum GmbH, Eyematic Interfaces Inc.* also explores the same methods [267, 327] for applications where face detection, tracking, recognition and verification are required. Its **Personspotter** is designed for surveillance in buildings, person counting and person recognition. Derivatives of **Personspotter** are designed for ATM cash machine verification scenarios. Face images are sampled when a person walks through an area observed by the camera. The person is not required to look directly into the camera, although the face should appear in frontal view during the course of the acquisition process. **Personspotter** is sensitive to strong viewpoint variation. Face detection fails if the minimum face rotation angle within the sensitive area is more than $25°$ from the frontal view. Face recognition becomes unreliable if the minimum angle within a sequence is higher than $15°$ from the pose of the enrolled faces. The system allows the operator to change a threshold value for acceptable recognition performance. Additionally the system provides switches for different environmental conditions like wide-open room or doorway scenarios.

B.3 Discussion

Most currently available systems focus on applications which require one-to-one verification (authentication) or database screening. During the last year, a few systems have emerged that consider tasks such as one-to-many identification. However, quantitative results on the success rate and performance rate are yet to be made available.

All currently available systems work only with frontal or near-frontal views and none of them can cope with large variation in lighting. The recognition of a face is based on static images that may match the information in the database. It is common to use a single snapshot and even systems that capture images from a video sequence using simple face finding and tracking algorithms perform identification on isolated static images. Current systems cannot cope with multiple faces in the scene and if such a scenario does occur, manual operator intervention is required in the acquisition process.

Overall, there seems to be enormous potential for many intended applications. However, little systematic and objective benchmarking is available for different categories of applications. Although a few attempts have been made, the majority of current systems do not consider the integration of multi-modal solutions.

C Mathematical Details

C.1 Principal Components Analysis

Principal Components Analysis (PCA) is a classical technique for multivariate analysis. It was introduced by Pearson in 1901 [258] and developed by Hotelling [158]. A detailed account is given by Jolliffe [177]. Here we give a brief description of how to perform PCA in the context of face recognition.

Consider a data set $\mathcal{X} = \{\mathbf{x}_1, \mathbf{x}_2, \ldots, \mathbf{x}_M\}$ of N-dimensional vectors. This data set might for example be a set of M face images. The mean, $\boldsymbol{\mu}$, and the covariance matrix, $\boldsymbol{\Sigma}$, of the data are given by:

$$\boldsymbol{\mu} = \frac{1}{M} \sum_{m=1}^{M} \mathbf{x}_m \tag{C.1}$$

$$\boldsymbol{\Sigma} = \frac{1}{M} \sum_{m=1}^{M} [\mathbf{x}_m - \boldsymbol{\mu}][\mathbf{x}_m - \boldsymbol{\mu}]^{\mathrm{T}} \tag{C.2}$$

where $\boldsymbol{\Sigma}$ is an $N \times N$ symmetric matrix. This matrix characterises the scatter of the data set. A non-zero vector $\mathbf{u}_k$ for which

$$\boldsymbol{\Sigma}\mathbf{u}_k = \lambda_k \mathbf{u}_k \tag{C.3}$$

is an *eigenvector* of the covariance matrix. It has the corresponding *eigenvalue* λ_k. If $\lambda_1, \lambda_2, \ldots, \lambda_K$ are the K largest, distinct eigenvalues then matrix $\mathbf{U} = [\mathbf{u}_1 \mathbf{u}_2 \cdots \mathbf{u}_K]$ represents the K dominant eigenvectors. These eigenvectors are mutually orthogonal and span a K-dimensional subspace called the principal subspace. When the data are face images these eigenvectors are often referred to as *eigenfaces* [341].

If $\mathbf{U}$ is the matrix of dominant eigenvectors, an N-dimensional input $\mathbf{x}$ can be linearly transformed into a K-dimensional vector $\boldsymbol{\alpha}$ by

$$\boldsymbol{\alpha} = \mathbf{U}^{\mathrm{T}}(\mathbf{x} - \boldsymbol{\mu}) \tag{C.4}$$

After applying the linear transformation $\mathbf{U}^{\mathrm{T}}$, the set of transformed vectors $\{\boldsymbol{\alpha}_1, \boldsymbol{\alpha}_2, \ldots, \boldsymbol{\alpha}_M\}$ has scatter $\mathbf{U}^{\mathrm{T}}\boldsymbol{\Sigma}\mathbf{U}$. PCA chooses $\mathbf{U}$ so as to maximise the determinant, $|\mathbf{U}^{\mathrm{T}}\boldsymbol{\Sigma}\mathbf{U}|$, of this scatter matrix. In other words, PCA retains most of the variance.

An original vector $\mathbf{x}$ can be approximately reconstructed from its transformed vector $\boldsymbol{\alpha}$ as:

$$\tilde{\mathbf{x}} = \sum_{k=1}^{K} \alpha_k \mathbf{u}_k + \boldsymbol{\mu} \tag{C.5}$$

In fact, PCA enables the training data to be reconstructed in a way that minimises the squared reconstruction error, $\mathcal{E}$, over the data set, where,

$$\mathcal{E} = \frac{1}{2} \sum_{m=1}^{M} ||\mathbf{x}_m - \tilde{\mathbf{x}}_m||^2 \tag{C.6}$$

In this context it is often called the Karhunen-Loève transform. Geometrically, it consists of projection onto K orthonormal axes. These *principal axes* maximise the retained variance of the data after projection.

In practice, the covariance matrix, $\boldsymbol{\Sigma}$, is often singular, particularly if $M < N$. However, the $K < M$ principal eigenvectors can still be estimated using a technique such as Singular Value Decomposition (SVD) [277].

C.2   Linear Discriminant Analysis

Linear Discriminant Analysis (LDA) or Fisher's Linear Discriminant (FLD) is another classical method for multivariate analysis [114]. Here we describe how it is used in the context of face identification [17]. Suppose a data set $\mathcal{X}$ exists, which might be face images for example, each of which is labelled with an identity. All data points with the same identity form a class. In total there are C classes, so $\mathcal{X} = \{\mathcal{X}_1, \ldots \mathcal{X}_c, \ldots \mathcal{X}_C\}$.

The sample covariance matrix for the entire data set is then a $N \times N$ symmetric matrix $\boldsymbol{\Sigma}$:

$$\boldsymbol{\Sigma} = \frac{1}{M} \sum_{\mathbf{x} \in \mathcal{X}} [\mathbf{x} - \boldsymbol{\mu}][\mathbf{x} - \boldsymbol{\mu}]^{\mathrm{T}} \tag{C.7}$$

This matrix characterises the scatter of the entire data set, irrespective of class-membership. However, we can also estimate a *within-classes scatter matrix*, **W**, and *a between-class scatter matrix*, **B**.

$$\mathbf{W} = \sum_{c=1}^{C} \sum_{\mathbf{x} \in \mathcal{X}_c} [\mathbf{x} - \boldsymbol{\mu}_c][\mathbf{x} - \boldsymbol{\mu}_c]^{\mathrm{T}} \tag{C.8}$$

$$\mathbf{B} = \sum_{c=1}^{C} M_c [\boldsymbol{\mu}_c - \boldsymbol{\mu}][\boldsymbol{\mu}_c - \boldsymbol{\mu}]^{\mathrm{T}} \tag{C.9}$$

where M_c is the number of samples of class c, $\boldsymbol{\mu}_c$ is the sample mean for class c, and $\boldsymbol{\mu}$ is the sample mean for the entire data set $\mathcal{X}$.

One wishes to find a linear transformation **U** which maximises the between-class scatter while minimising the within-class scatter. Such a transformation should retain class separability while reducing the variation due to sources other than identity, for example, illumination and facial expression.

An appropriate transformation is given by the matrix $\mathbf{U} = [\mathbf{u}_1 \mathbf{u}_2 \ldots \mathbf{u}_K]$ whose columns are the eigenvectors of $\mathbf{W}^{-1}\mathbf{B}$, in other words, the generalised eigenvectors corresponding to the K largest eigenvalues:

$$\mathbf{B}\mathbf{u}_k = \lambda_k \mathbf{W}\mathbf{u}_k \tag{C.10}$$

There are at most $C - 1$ non-zero generalised eigenvalues, so $K < C$. The data are transformed as follows:

$$\boldsymbol{\alpha} = \mathbf{U}^{\mathrm{T}}(\mathbf{x} - \boldsymbol{\mu}) \tag{C.11}$$

After this transformation, the data has between-class scatter matrix $\mathbf{U}^{\mathrm{T}}\mathbf{B}\mathbf{U}$ and within-class scatter $\mathbf{U}^{\mathrm{T}}\mathbf{W}\mathbf{U}$. The matrix **U** is such that the determinant of the new between-class scatter is maximised while the determinant of the within-classes scatter is minimised. This implies that the following ratio is to be maximised:

$$\frac{|\mathbf{U}^{\mathrm{T}}\mathbf{B}\mathbf{U}|}{|\mathbf{U}^{\mathrm{T}}\mathbf{W}\mathbf{U}|} \tag{C.12}$$

In practice, the within-class scatter matrix (**W**) is often singular. This is nearly always the case when the data are image vectors with large dimensionality since the size of the data set is usually small in comparison ($M < N$). For this reason, PCA is first applied to the data set to reduce its dimensionality. The discriminant transformation is then applied to further reduce the dimensionality to $C-1$. Equation (C.10) can be solved using simultaneous diagonalisation [120].

C.3   Gaussian Mixture Estimation

A Gaussian mixture model is defined as:

$$p(\mathbf{x}) = \sum_{k=1}^{K} p(\mathbf{x}|k)P(k) \qquad (C.13)$$

where $p(\mathbf{x}|k), k = 1 \ldots K$, are K Gaussian density functions. The parameters in such a model are the means, $\boldsymbol{\mu}_k$, covariance matrices, $\boldsymbol{\Sigma}_k$, and mixing parameters, $P(k)$. These can be estimated from a data set using an Expectation-Maximisation (EM) algorithm [89].

C.3.1   Expectation-maximisation

Given a data set $\mathcal{X} = \{\mathbf{x}_1, \ldots \mathbf{x}_m, \ldots \mathbf{x}_M\}$, EM aims to find parameter values that maximise likelihood or, equivalently, minimise the negative log-likelihood function:

$$\mathcal{E} = -\ln\mathcal{L} = -\sum_{m=1}^{M} \ln p(\mathbf{x}_m) = -\sum_{m=1}^{M} \ln\left(\sum_{k=1}^{K} p(\mathbf{x}_m|k)P(k)\right) \qquad (C.14)$$

The EM algorithm is an iterative method for minimising $\mathcal{E}$ by monotonically reducing its value.

The model parameters need to be initiliased before applying EM. A simple initialisation method is to assign the means to a randomly chosen subset of the data points. An often more effective method is the use of a clustering algorithm such as K-means [96] to divide the data into disjoint subsets. A Gaussian component can then be assigned to each subset. While K-means performs a 'hard' clustering of the data into disjoint subsets, a Gaussian mixture can be thought of as performing 'soft' clustering in which each data point belongs, to a greater or lesser extent, to each of the Gaussian components or 'clusters'.

Let the initial parameter values be labelled as *old* values. EM then performs an iterative approximation in order to try to find parameter values that maximise the likelihood by using the following update rules:

(1) Evaluate the posterior probability for every mixture component k

$$P(k|\mathbf{x}) = \frac{p(\mathbf{x}|k)P(k)}{p(\mathbf{x})} \qquad (C.15)$$

where $p(\mathbf{x}|k)$ is given by Equation (3.21). This posterior is the probability that data point $\mathbf{x}$ could be generated by the kth mixture component.

(2) Update the parameters to their *new* values $\boldsymbol{\mu}_k^{new}$, $\boldsymbol{\Sigma}_k^{new}$ and $P^{new}(k)$ where

$$\boldsymbol{\mu}_k^{new} = \frac{\sum_{m=1}^{M} P^{old}(k|\mathbf{x}_m)\,\mathbf{x}_m}{\sum_{m=1}^{M} P^{old}(k|\mathbf{x}_m)} \qquad (C.16)$$

$$\boldsymbol{\Sigma}_k^{new} = \frac{\sum_{m=1}^{M} P^{old}(k|\mathbf{x}_m)\,[\mathbf{x}_m - \boldsymbol{\mu}_k^{new}]\,[\mathbf{x}_m - \boldsymbol{\mu}_k^{new}]^{\mathsf{T}}}{\sum_{m=1}^{M} P^{old}(k|\mathbf{x}_m)} \qquad (C.17)$$

$$P^{new}(k) = \frac{1}{M} \sum_{m=1}^{M} P^{old}(k|\mathbf{x}_m) \qquad (C.18)$$

(3) Repeat steps (1) and (2) for a pre-determined number of iterations or until suitable convergence.

C.3.2 Automatic Model Order Selection

The number of components in a mixture model should be selected to trade-off bias and variance. A constructive algorithm can be used to automatically determine the number of components in a mixture. The available data set is partitioned into disjoint training and validation sets. A mixture model is initialised with a small number of components, typically one. Model order is then adapted by iteratively applying the EM algorithm and splitting components. The likelihood for the validation set is computed after every iteration. The tasks of selecting and splitting components can be performed effectively using the following heuristic scheme. For each component k, define a total responsibility $r(k)$ as

$$r(k) = \sum_{m=1}^{M} P(k|\mathbf{x}_m) = \sum_{m=1}^{M} \frac{p(\mathbf{x}_m|k)P(k)}{\sum_{j=1}^{K} p(\mathbf{x}_m|j)P(j)} \qquad (C.19)$$

Then the component with the lowest total responsibility for the validation set is selected for splitting. This component is split into two new components with covariance matrices equal to Σ_k and means given by:

$$\boldsymbol{\mu} = \boldsymbol{\mu}_k \pm \frac{\sqrt{\lambda_1}}{2}\mathbf{u}_1 \qquad\qquad (\text{C.20})$$

where λ_1 is the largest eigenvalue of Σ_k and $\mathbf{u}_1$ is the corresponding eigenvector. Prior probabilities for the new components are set to $\frac{1}{2}P(k)$.

Let K_i denote the number of components in a model after iteration i and let L_i be the likelihood of the validation set given the model. The initial number of components, K_0, may be set to a low number, e.g. $K_0 = 1$. A constructive algorithm for model order selection is as follows:

```
1.   Apply EM for model with Kᵢ components.
2.   Compute Lᵢ for validation set
3.   IF (Lᵢ ≤ Lᵢ₋₁ + ε) STOP.
4.   Split component k with the lowest total responsibility
5.   Set Kᵢ₊₁ = Kᵢ + 1 and i = i + 1.
6.   Go to 1.
```

C.3.3   Adaptive EM for Non-stationary Distributions

In the context of dynamic vision, data are often sampled from non-stationary distributions. When tracking an object, for example, the colour of the object often changes gradually over time due to changing illumination conditions. When a Gaussian mixture is used to model such a non-stationary distribution, its parameters need to be adapted over time. Here we describe an algorithm for adaptively estimating such a mixture.

At each frame, t, a new set of data, $\mathcal{X}^{(t)}$, is sampled from the object and can be used to update the mixture model*. These data are assumed to sample a slowly varying non-stationary signal. Let $r^{(t)}$ denote the sum of the posterior probabilities (Equation (C.15)) of the data in frame t, $r^{(t)} = \sum_{\mathbf{x}\in\mathcal{X}^{(t)}} P(k|\mathbf{x})$. The parameters are first estimated for each mixture component, k, using only the new data, $\mathcal{X}^{(t)}$, from frame t:

$$\boldsymbol{\mu}^{(t)} = \frac{\sum P(k|\mathbf{x})\mathbf{x}}{r^{(t)}}, \qquad P^{(t)} = \frac{r^{(t)}}{M^{(t)}} \qquad (\text{C.21})$$

---

*Here superscript (t) denotes a quantity based only on data from frame t. Subscripts denote recursive estimates.

$$\mathbf{\Sigma}^{(t)} = \frac{\sum P(k|\mathbf{x})[\mathbf{x} - \boldsymbol{\mu}_{t-1}][(\mathbf{x} - \boldsymbol{\mu}_{t-1})]^{\mathsf{T}}}{r^{(t)}} \qquad (C.22)$$

where $M^{(t)}$ denotes the number of samples in the new data set and all summations are over $\mathbf{x} \in \mathcal{X}^{(t)}$. The mixture model components then have their parameters updated using weighted sums of the previous recursive estimates $\left(\boldsymbol{\mu}_{t-1}, \mathbf{\Sigma}_{t-1}, P_{t-1}\right)$, estimates based on the new data $\left(\boldsymbol{\mu}^{(t)}, \mathbf{\Sigma}^{(t)}, P^{(t)}\right)$ and on the old data $\left(\boldsymbol{\mu}^{(t-T-1)}, \mathbf{\Sigma}^{(t-T-1)}, P^{(t-T-1)}\right)$:

$$\boldsymbol{\mu}_t = \boldsymbol{\mu}_{t-1} + \frac{r^{(t)}}{D_t}\left(\boldsymbol{\mu}^{(t)} - \boldsymbol{\mu}_{t-1}\right) - \frac{r^{(t-T-1)}}{D_t}\left(\boldsymbol{\mu}^{(t-T-1)} - \boldsymbol{\mu}_{t-1}\right) \qquad (C.23)$$

$$\mathbf{\Sigma}_t = \mathbf{\Sigma}_{t-1} + \frac{r^{(t)}}{D_t}\left(\mathbf{\Sigma}^{(t)} - \mathbf{\Sigma}_{t-1}\right) - \frac{r^{(t-T-1)}}{D_t}\left(\mathbf{\Sigma}^{(t-T-1)} - \mathbf{\Sigma}_{t-1}\right) \qquad (C.24)$$

$$P_t = P_{t-1} + \frac{M^{(t)}}{\sum_{\tau=t-T}^{t} M^{(\tau)}}\left(P^{(t)} - P_{t-1}\right) - \frac{M^{(t-T-1)}}{\sum_{\tau=t-T}^{t} M^{(\tau)}}\left(P^{(t-T-1)} - P_{t-1}\right) \qquad (C.25)$$

where $D_t = \sum_{\tau=t-T}^{t} r^{(\tau)}$. The following approximations are used for efficiency:

$$r^{(t-T-1)} \approx \frac{D_{t-1}}{T+1} \qquad (C.26)$$

$$D_t \approx \left(1 - \frac{1}{T+1}\right)D_{t-1} + r^{(t)} \qquad (C.27)$$

Parameter T controls the adaptivity of the model. By setting $T = t$ and ignoring terms at frame $t-T-1$, the model gives a stochastic algorithm for estimating a Gaussian mixture for a stationary signal [27, 336].

C.4   Kalman Filters

A Kalman filter models the state of a system using a Gaussian probability density function which it propagates over time. The Kalman filter provides an estimate of the actual state, $\mathbf{q}(t)$, of a noisy system observed using noisy measurements. Furthermore, it can be used to predict the observations. This is useful for tracking objects, for example, as it constrains temporal matching and can improve efficiency and reliability.

The state estimate is an expected value based on the noisy observation process:

$$\hat{\mathbf{q}}(t) = E\{\mathbf{q}(t) + N(t)\} \tag{C.28}$$

The uncertainty of $\hat{\mathbf{q}}(t)$ is approximated as a covariance matrix $\boldsymbol{\Sigma}_{\mathbf{q}}(t)$:

$$\boldsymbol{\Sigma}_{\mathbf{q}}(t) = E\left\{[\mathbf{q}(t) - \hat{\mathbf{q}}(t)][\mathbf{q}(t) - \hat{\mathbf{q}}(t)]^{\mathsf{T}}\right\} \tag{C.29}$$

Given a new observation vector $\mathbf{x}(t)$, a Kalman filter updates the estimates of the state vector and its associated uncertainty based on predictions $\mathbf{q}^*(t)$, $\mathbf{x}^*(t)$, $\boldsymbol{\Sigma}_{\mathbf{q}}^*(t)$ and $\boldsymbol{\Sigma}_{\mathbf{x}}^*(t)$:

$$\hat{\mathbf{q}}(t) = \mathbf{q}^*(t) + \mathbf{K}(t)[\mathbf{x}(t) - \mathbf{x}^*(t)] \tag{C.30}$$

$$\hat{\boldsymbol{\Sigma}}_{\mathbf{q}}(t) = \boldsymbol{\Sigma}_{\mathbf{q}}^*(t) - \mathbf{K}(t)\mathbf{H}\boldsymbol{\Sigma}_{\mathbf{q}}^*(t) \tag{C.31}$$

where the matrix $\mathbf{K}(t)$ is called the *Kalman gain* and is defined as:

$$\mathbf{K}(t) = \boldsymbol{\Sigma}_{\mathbf{q}}^*(t)\mathbf{H}^{\mathsf{T}}[\boldsymbol{\Sigma}_{\mathbf{x}}^*(t) + \boldsymbol{\Sigma}_{\mathbf{x}}(t)]^{-1} \tag{C.32}$$

and $\mathbf{H}$ transforms a state vector into an observation vector: $\mathbf{x}(t) = \mathbf{H}\mathbf{q}(t)$. The predicted observations and their uncertainty are given by:

$$\mathbf{x}^* = \mathbf{H}\mathbf{q}^* \tag{C.33}$$

$$\boldsymbol{\Sigma}_{\mathbf{x}}^* = \mathbf{H}\boldsymbol{\Sigma}_{\mathbf{q}}^*\mathbf{H}^{\mathsf{T}} \tag{C.34}$$

C.4.1   Zero-order Prediction

In this case, no derivatives need to be estimated and prediction is simply:

$$\mathbf{q}^*(t + \Delta t) = \hat{\mathbf{q}}(t) \tag{C.35}$$

$$\Sigma_{\mathbf{q}}^*(t + \Delta t) = \hat{\Sigma}_{\mathbf{q}}(t) + \hat{\mathbf{G}}_{\mathbf{q}}(t)\Delta t^2 \tag{C.36}$$

where $\hat{\mathbf{G}}_{\mathbf{q}}(t)$ accounts for the unmodelled changes and noise. The longer the time interval since the previous observation, the greater the uncertainty associated with the state prediction.

C.4.2 First-order Prediction

In a first-order predictor the state vector is extended to include the first-order derivatives:

$$\mathbf{q} = [q_1 \; \dot{q}_1 \; q_2 \; \dot{q}_2 \; \cdots \; q_N \; \dot{q}_N]^{\mathsf{T}} \tag{C.37}$$

Prediction is then:

$$\mathbf{q}^*(t + \Delta t) = \mathbf{A}\hat{\mathbf{q}}(t) \tag{C.38}$$

$$\Sigma_{\mathbf{q}}^*(t + \Delta t) = \mathbf{A}\hat{\Sigma}_{\mathbf{q}}(t)\mathbf{A}^{\mathsf{T}} + \hat{\mathbf{G}}_{\mathbf{q}}(t)\Delta t^4 \tag{C.39}$$

where $\mathbf{A}$ is the $2n \times 2n$ block-diagonal matrix:

$$\mathbf{A} = \begin{bmatrix} \mathbf{B} & 0 & \cdots & 0 \\ 0 & \mathbf{B} & \cdots & 0 \\ \vdots & \vdots & \ddots & \vdots \\ 0 & 0 & \cdots & \mathbf{B} \end{bmatrix} \qquad \mathbf{B} = \begin{bmatrix} 1 & \Delta t \\ 0 & 1 \end{bmatrix} \tag{C.40}$$

The matrix $\hat{\mathbf{G}}_{\mathbf{q}}(t)$ accounts for the errors arising from not modelling higher order derivatives as well as from noise. It is block diagonal with blocks of the form:

$$\begin{bmatrix} \sigma_{acc}^2 & 0 \\ 0 & 0 \end{bmatrix} \tag{C.41}$$

Kalman predictions can be extended to the second and higher orders. For a second-order Kalman predictor, $\mathbf{A}$ has block-diagonal sub-matrices such as:

$$\mathbf{B} = \begin{bmatrix} 1 & \Delta t & \Delta t^2/2 \\ 0 & 1 & \Delta t \\ 0 & 0 & 1 \end{bmatrix} \tag{C.42}$$

C.5   Bayesian Belief Networks

Belief networks in general are directed acyclic graphs in which each node represents an uncertain quantity using discrete random variables [257]. The arcs connecting the nodes signify the direct causal influences between the linked variables with the strengths of such influences quantified by associated conditional probabilities.

If we assume a variable in the network is Y_i, and a selection of variables Π_{Y_i} are the direct causes of Y_i, the strengths of these direct influences are quantified by assigning the variable Y_i a link matrix $P(y_i \mid \Pi_{Y_i})$, given any combination of instantiations of the parent set Π_{Y_i}. Here variables are denoted by upper case and specific instantiations of the variables are denoted by lower case. The conjunction of all the local link matrices of variables Y_i in the network (for $1 \leq i \leq N$ where N is the number of variables) specifies a complete and consistent *holistic interpretation* which provides answers to all the probabilistic queries. Such a conjunction is given by the overall joint distribution function over the variables $Y_1, \ldots, Y_N$:

$$P(y_1, y_2, ..., y_N) = \prod_{i=1}^{N} P(y_i | \Pi_{Y_i}) \qquad (C.43)$$

In a belief network, belief commitments are defined as the tentative acceptance of a subset of hypotheses that together constitute the most satisfactory explanation of the observation at hand. Let observations be a set of *measurable variables* denoted by $\mathcal{X}$. If we quantify the degree of coherence between the hypotheses $\mathcal{Y} = \{Y_1, \ldots Y_i, \ldots Y_N\}$ and the observations $\mathcal{X} = \{X_1, \ldots X_i, \ldots X_M\}$ by measures of local belief $BEL(y_i) = P(y_i|\mathcal{X})$, then Bayesian belief revision amounts to the updating of belief commitments by distributed local message passing. Instead of associating a belief with each individual hypothesis locally, belief revision identifies a composite set of hypotheses that best explains the observation. We call such a set the Most-Probable-Explanation (MPE). This implies computing the most probable instantiations of all hypothetical variables given the observation.

Let $\mathcal{Z}$ stand for all the variables including both hypothetical (hidden) and measurable ones, i.e. $\mathcal{Z} \equiv \{\mathcal{Y}, \mathcal{X}\}$. Any particular instantiation of variables $\mathcal{Z}$ that is also consistent with observations $\mathcal{X}$ is regarded as an *extension* or *explanation* of $\mathcal{X}$. The problem then is to find a specific extension $\mathbf{z}^*$ that maximises the conditional probability $P(\mathcal{Z}|\mathcal{X})$ as follows:

If $P(\mathbf{z}^*|\mathcal{X}) = \max_{\mathcal{Z}} P(\mathcal{Z}|\mathcal{X})$, then $\mathbf{z}^*$ is the MPE of the observations and is computed by

(1) Locally evaluating a belief for each variable Y_i as

$$BEL^*(y_i) = \max_{\mathcal{Z}_{Y_i}} P(y_i, \mathcal{Z}_{Y_i}|\mathcal{X}) \qquad \text{(C.44)}$$

where $\mathcal{Z}_{Y_i} = \mathcal{Z} - Y_i$ and
(2) Propagating local messages.

Note $BEL^*(y_i)$ represents the probability of the most probable extension of $\mathcal{X}$ that is also consistent with the hypothetical assignment $Y_i = y_i$. More precisely, local messages are defined as follows.

If a belief node representing a hypothetical variable Y is connected to n parent nodes $U_1, U_2, \ldots, U_n$ and m children $V_1, V_2, \ldots, V_m$, node Y would receive messages $\pi_Y^*(u_i)$ $(i = 1, \ldots, n)$ from its parents and $\lambda_{V_j}^*(y)$ $(j = 1, \ldots, m)$ from its children whereby,

$\pi_Y^*(u_i)$ is the probability of the most probable tail-extension of the hypothetical value $U_i = u_i$ relative to link $U_i \rightarrow Y$. This is known as an *explanation*.
$\lambda_{V_j}^*(y)$ is the conditional probability of the most probable head-extension of the hypothetical value $Y = y$ relative to link $Y \rightarrow V_j$ and known as a *forecast*.

Given local probability $P(y|u_1, \ldots, u_n)$ at each node Y, propagating local messages at Y involves the following computation:

(1) Updating $BEL^*(y)$ and the best value of Y, y^*: For

$$F(y, u_1, \ldots, u_n) = \prod_{j=1}^{m} \lambda_{V_j}^*(y) P(y|u_1, \ldots, u_n) \prod_{i=1}^{n} \pi_Y^*(u_i), \quad \text{(C.45)}$$

$$BEL^*(y) = \beta \max_{u_k} (F(y, u_1, \ldots, u_n)) \qquad \text{(C.46)}$$

where $1 \leq k \leq n$ and β is a scaling constant,

$$y^* = \arg\max (y \, BEL^*(y)) \qquad \text{(C.47)}$$

(2) Parent-bound n messages to $U_1, \ldots, U_n$:

$$\lambda_Y^*(u_i) = \max_{y, u_k : k \neq i} \frac{F(y, u_1, \ldots, u_n)}{\pi_Y^*(u_i)}, \quad i = 1 \ldots n \qquad \text{(C.48)}$$

(3) Child-bound m messages to $V_1, \ldots, V_m$:

$$\pi_{V_j}^*(y) = \beta \frac{BEL^*(y)}{\lambda_{V_j}^*(y)}, \quad j = 1 \ldots m \qquad \text{(C.49)}$$

(4) Boundary conditions: Three types of nodes set up the boundary conditions.

    (a) Anticipatory nodes: uninstantiated variables with no children. For Y, $\lambda_{V_j}^*(y) = \{1, \ldots, 1\}$.

    (b) Observation nodes: directly measurable variables. For a measurable variable $X = x'$, it is regarded as X being connected with a dummy child V' so that $\lambda_{V'}^*(x) = \begin{cases} 1 & \text{if } X = x' \\ 0 & \text{otherwise.} \end{cases}$ Other real children nodes of X, $V_1, V_2, \ldots, V_m$, receive the same message $\pi_{V_j}^* = \lambda_{V'}^*(x)$ from X.

    (c) Root nodes: variables with no parents. Similarly, for each root variable, a dummy parent U' is introduced with permanent 1-value instantiation and $P(y|u) = P(y) = \pi^*(y)$.

Bayesian *belief revision* depicts a computational process that solves the following problems. For each hypothetical variable Y, there exists a best extension of the complementary variables $\mathcal{Z}_Y$, where $\mathcal{Z}_Y = \mathcal{Z} - Y$. The problem of finding the best extension of Y can be decomposed into finding the best complementary extension to each of the neighbouring variables according to the conditional independence between Y and the rest. This information is then used to yield the best instantiation of Y, y^*. The very process of this decomposition resembles the principle of optimality in dynamic programming in that it is applied recursively until it reaches the network's boundary where observational variables are directly measured from the sensory data.

C.6 Hidden Markov Models

A hidden Markov model (HMM) is a probabilistic model of causal dependencies between different states in sequential patterns and a special case of a Bayesian belief network [257]. In discrete form, it can also be regarded as a stochastic finite state network [222]. An HMM $\lambda(\mathbf{A}, \mathbf{b}, \boldsymbol{\pi})$ is defined by the following parameters:

(1) A set of K discrete *hidden* states. The state at time t is $q_t \in \{1, 2, \ldots, K\}$.

(2) A state transition probability distribution matrix $\mathbf{A} = \{a_{jk}\}$, where $a_{jk} = P(q_{t+1} = k \,|\, q_t = j)$, $1 \leq j, k \leq K$.

(3) Probability density functions for each state $\mathbf{b} = \{b_k(\mathbf{x})\}$, where $b_k(\mathbf{x}_t) = p(\mathbf{x}_t \,|\, q_t = k)$, $1 \leq k \leq K$.

(4) An initial state distribution $\boldsymbol{\pi} = \{\pi_k\}$, where $\pi_k = P(q_1 = k)$, $1 \leq k \leq K$.

At any discrete time, t, an HMM, λ, will always be in one hidden state, $q_t = k$, from which it generates an output according to the probability distribution b_k. The parameters $(\mathbf{A}, \mathbf{b}, \boldsymbol{\pi})$ of λ are weighting factors that describe the strength of the dependencies between the states and between the states and observations (outputs). They represent local conditional beliefs and their combined effect gives likely combinations of hypotheses. An HMM can perform a number of tasks based on sequences of observations:

(1) Learning: Given an observation sequence $\mathcal{X} = \{\mathbf{x}_1, \mathbf{x}_2 \ldots \mathbf{x}_T\}$ and a model, λ, the model parameters of λ can be adjusted such that $P(\mathcal{X}|\lambda)$ is maximised.

(2) Prediction: An HMM model, λ, can predict observation sequences and their associated state sequences in which the probabilistic characteristics of the model are inherently reflected.

(3) Sequence classification: For a given observation sequence $\mathcal{X} = \{\mathbf{x}_1, \mathbf{x}_2 \ldots \mathbf{x}_T\}$ by computing $P(\mathcal{X}|\lambda_i)$ for a set of known models λ_i, the sequence can be classified as belonging to class i for which $P(\mathcal{X}|\lambda_i)$ is maximised.

(4) Sequence interpretation: Given $\mathcal{X} = \{\mathbf{x}_1, \mathbf{x}_2 \ldots \mathbf{x}_T\}$ and an HMM, λ, applying the *Viterbi* algorithm [283] gives a single most likely state sequence $\mathcal{Q} = \{q_1, q_2 \ldots q_T\}$.

Let us consider the problem of learning and prediction using HMMs. This involves forward and backward propagations along the model's graph network [257]. More precisely, if $\mathcal{X} = \{\mathbf{x}_1, \mathbf{x}_2 \ldots \mathbf{x}_T\}$, then we can compute for each hidden state k:

(1) the conditional probability, $\alpha_t(k)$, of the model, λ, being in state $q_t = k$ at time t having observed $\mathbf{x}_1, \mathbf{x}_2 \ldots \mathbf{x}_t$:

$$\alpha_t(k) = P\left(\mathbf{x}_1, \mathbf{x}_2, ..., \mathbf{x}_t, q_t = k \mid \lambda\right) = \left(\sum_{j=1}^{K} \alpha_{t-1}(j) a_{jk}\right) b_k(\mathbf{x}_t) \tag{C.50}$$

where $1 \leq k \leq K$, $2 \leq t \leq T-1$ and $\alpha_1(k) = \pi_k b_k(\mathbf{x}_1)$;

(2) the conditional probability, $\beta_t(k)$, of observing $\mathbf{x}_{t+1}, \mathbf{x}_{t+2} \ldots \mathbf{x}_T$, given that the model, λ, had hidden state $q_t = k$ at time t:

$$\beta_t(k) = P(\mathbf{x}_{t+1}, \mathbf{x}_{t+2}, ..., \mathbf{x}_T \mid \lambda, q_t = k) = \sum_{j=1}^{K} a_{kj} b_j(\mathbf{x}_{t+1}) \beta_{t+1}(j) \tag{C.51}$$

where $1 \leq k \leq K$, $t = T-1, T-2, ..., 1$ and $\beta_T(k) = 1$.

The *Baum-Welch* learning algorithm [283] adjusts the parameters of λ given a single observation sequence as follows:

$$\begin{aligned}
\tilde{\pi}_k &= P(q_1 = k \mid \mathcal{X}, \lambda) \\
&= \frac{\sum_{j=1}^{K} P(q_1 = k, q_2 = j, \mathcal{X} \mid \lambda)}{P(\mathcal{X} \mid \lambda)} \\
&= \frac{\alpha_1(k) \beta_1(k)}{\sum_{k=1}^{K} \alpha_1(k) \beta_1(k)}, \qquad 1 \leq j,\ k \leq K
\end{aligned} \tag{C.52}$$

$$\begin{aligned}
\tilde{a}_{jk} &= \frac{\sum_{t=1}^{T-1} P(q_t = j, q_{t+1} = k \mid \mathcal{X}, \lambda)}{\sum_{t=1}^{T-1} P(q_t = j \mid \mathcal{X}, \lambda)} \\
&= \frac{\sum_{t=1}^{T-1} \alpha_t(j) a_{jk} b_k(\mathbf{x}_{t+1}) \beta_{t+1}(k)}{\sum_{t=1}^{T-1} \alpha_t(j) \beta_t(j)}
\end{aligned} \tag{C.53}$$

$$\tilde{b}_k(\mathbf{x}_t) = \frac{\sum_{t=1}^{T} p(\mathbf{x}_t|q_t=k)P(q_t=j|\mathcal{X}, \lambda)}{\sum_{t=1}^{T} P(q_t=j|\mathcal{X}, \lambda)}$$

$$= \frac{\sum_{t=1}^{T} p(\mathbf{x}_t|q_t=k)\alpha_t(j)\beta_t(j)}{\sum_{t=1}^{T} \alpha_t(j)\beta_t(j)}, \qquad 1 \leq k \leq K \quad \text{(C.54)}$$

$$P(q_t=k\,|\,\mathcal{X}, \lambda) = \frac{\sum_{j=1}^{K} P(q_t=k, q_{t+1}=j, \mathcal{X}|\lambda)}{P(\mathcal{X}|\lambda)}$$

$$= \frac{\alpha_t(k)\beta_t(k)}{\sum_{k=1}^{K} \alpha_t(k)\beta_t(k)} \qquad \text{(C.55)}$$

Denominators in Equations (C.52), (C.53), (C.54) and (C.55) are all normalisation constants. The conditional obsevation densities, $p(\mathbf{x}_t|q_t)$ are often modelled as Gaussian or Gaussian mixture density functions. Alternatively, the observations are often modelled approximately by quantising regions of the observation space. This yields a discrete set of observation *symbols* and the observation densities can therefore be represented as a histogram of symbol probabilities.

A reliable estimate of a model λ can only be obtained through multiple learning sequences. Let us denote a set of M example sequences as $\mathcal{X}^{(1)}, \mathcal{X}^{(2)}, \dots \mathcal{X}^{(M)}$, where $\mathcal{X}^{(m)} = \left\{\mathbf{x}_1^{(m)}, \mathbf{x}_2^{(m)}, \dots \mathbf{x}_{T_m}^{(m)}\right\}$ is the mth sequence. If each sequence is independent of all others, we have the following rules for learning the model from multiple sequences:

$$\bar{a}_{jk} = \frac{\sum_{m=1}^{M} \frac{1}{P_m} \sum_{t=1}^{T_m-1} \alpha_t^m(j)\, a_{jk}\, b_k\left(\mathbf{x}_{t+1}^{(m)}\right) \beta_{t+1}^m(k)}{\sum_{m=1}^{M} \frac{1}{P_m} \sum_{t=1}^{T_m-1} \alpha_t^m(j)\beta_t^m(j)},$$

$$\bar{b}_k(\mathbf{x}_t) = \frac{\sum_{m=1}^{M} \frac{1}{P_m} \sum_{t=1}^{T_m-1} p\left(\mathbf{x}_t^{(m)}|q_t\right) \alpha_t^m(k)\beta_t^m(k)}{\sum_{m=1}^{M} \frac{1}{P_m} \sum_{t=1}^{T_m-1} \alpha_t^m(k)\beta_t^m(k)} \qquad \text{(C.56)}$$

where

$$P_m = P\left(\mathcal{X}^{(m)}|\lambda\right) = \sum_{k=1}^{K} \alpha_{T_m}(k) \qquad \text{(C.57)}$$

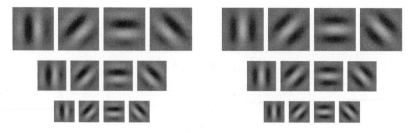

Figure C.1   Gabor wavelet kernels at four orientations and three spatial frequencies. The imaginary (odd) components appear on the left and the real (even) components on the right.

C.7   Gabor Wavelets

Two-dimensional Gabor kernels are sinusoidally modulated Gaussian functions. Gabor wavelets are sets of Gabor kernels with different spatial frequencies and orientations [81]. The Gabor kernels can be defined as follows.

$$\phi_{odd}(x,y) = \kappa \, sin\theta \, \exp\left(-r^2 \left(\frac{k}{\sigma}\right)^2\right) \qquad (C.58)$$

$$\phi_{even}(x,y) = \kappa \left(cos\theta - \exp\left(\frac{-\sigma^2}{2}\right)\right) \exp\left(-r^2 \left(\frac{k}{\sigma}\right)^2\right) \qquad (C.59)$$

where $r^2 = x^2 + y^2$ and, for example,

$$\theta = \{kx, \ k\sqrt{2}(x+y), \ ky, \ k\sqrt{2}(y-x)\} \qquad (C.60)$$

The variance parameter, σ^2, controls the width of the Gaussian envelope and k controls the spatial frequency. The extra Gaussian term in ϕ_{even} makes the kernel admissible (no DC component). A consequence of this is zero response to spatially constant intensity. Figure C.1 shows Gabor wavelet kernels in the spatial domain at three frequencies and four orientations varying by $45°$ from $0°$ to $135°$. These are in fact discrete approximations to Gabor kernels since the Gabor kernels have infinite support.

An approximate Gabor wavelet projection (GWP) of an image is obtained by convolution with a set of Gabor wavelets. The real and imaginary parts of the kernel responses oscillate with their characteristic frequency making them highly sensitive to image-plane translations. However, in a template-based approach, inexact correspondences can be compensated by ignoring the phase and considering only the magnitudes of the responses which tend to vary smoothly over an image [368]. Gabor magnitude and phase images, G_{mag} and G_{pha}, are obtained from the even and odd convolution responses, G_{even} and G_{odd}, as follows.

$$G_{odd}(x,y) = I(x,y) \otimes \phi_{odd} \tag{C.61}$$

$$G_{even}(x,y) = I(x,y) \otimes \phi_{even} \tag{C.62}$$

$$G_{mag}(x,y) = \sqrt{(G_{odd}(x,y))^2 + (G_{even}(x,y))^2} \tag{C.63}$$

$$G_{pha}(x,y) = tan^{-1} \frac{G_{odd}(x,y)}{G_{even}(x,y)} \tag{C.64}$$

A Gabor wavelet projection (GWP) yields images which are locally normalised in intensity and decomposed in terms of spatial frequency and orientation. In a scheme proposed by Würtz [371], a Gabor wavelet transform (GWT) can be performed by convolutions with Gabor kernels in the Fourier domain. A single Gabor function (the mother wavelet) is parameterised by a vector $\mathbf{a}=[a_1 \; a_2]^T$, defining variations in spatial frequency and orientation. Then a GWT in $[-\pi < \boldsymbol{\omega} = [u \; v]^T < \pi]$ is given by:

$$\mathbf{F_a}(\boldsymbol{\omega}) = \exp\left(-\frac{\sigma^2(\boldsymbol{\omega}-\mathbf{a})^2}{2\mathbf{a}^2}\right) - \exp\left(-\frac{\sigma^2(\boldsymbol{\omega}^2+\mathbf{a}^2)}{2\mathbf{a}^2}\right) \tag{C.65}$$

The second term in Equation (C.65) results in admissibility.

Bibliography

[1] B. Achermann and H. Bunke. Combination of face classifiers for person identification. In *International Conference on Pattern Recognition*, volume III, pages 416–420, Vienna, Austria, August 1996.

[2] Y. Adini, Y. Moses, and S. Ullman. Face recognition: The problem of compensating for changes in illumination direction. *IEEE Transactions on Pattern Analysis and Machine Intelligence*, 19(7):721–732, July 1997.

[3] A.V. Aho, S.F. Chang, K.R. McKeown, D.R. Radev, J.R. Smith, and K.A. Zaman. Columbia digital news project: an environment for briefing and search over multimedia information. *International Journal on Digital Libraries*, 1(4):377–385, 1997.

[4] Y. Aloimonos, I. Weiss, and A. Bandopadhay. Active vision. In *IEEE International Conference on Computer Vision*, pages 35–54, London, England, 1987.

[5] M.E. Arterberry, L.G. Craton, and A. Yonas. Infants' sensitivity to motion-carried information for depth and object properties. In C.E. Granrud, editor, *Visual Perception and Cognition in Infancy*, volume 23 of *Carnegie-Mellon Symposia on Cognition*. Erlbaum, Hillsdale, NJ, 1993.

[6] J.J. Atick, P.A. Griffin, and A.N. Redlich. Statistical approach to shape from shading: Reconstruction of three-dimensional face surfaces from single two-dimensional images. *Neural Computation*, 8(6):1321–1340, 1996.

[7] A. Azarbayejani and A. Pentland. Recursive estimation of motion, structure and focal length. *IEEE Transactions on Pattern Analysis and Machine Intelligence*, 17(6):545–561, 1995.

[8] A. Azarbayejani, T. Starner, B. Horowitz, and A. Pentland. Visually controlled graphics. *IEEE Transactions on Pattern Analysis and Machine Intelligence*, 15(6):602–605, 1993.

[9] T. Bachmann. Identification of spatially quantised tachistoscopic images of faces: how many pixels does it take to carry identity? *European Journal of Cognitive Psychology*, 3:87–103, 1991.

[10] R. Bajcsy and P. Allen. Sensing strategies. In *USA - France Robotics Workshop*, 1984.

[11] D.H. Ballard. Parameter nets. *Artificial Intelligence*, 22:235–267, 1984.

[12] D.H. Ballard. Animate vision. *Artificial Intelligence*, 48:57–86, 1991.

[13] J. Bassili. Facial motion in the perception of faces and of emotional expres-

sion. *Journal of Experimental Psychology*, 4(3):373–379, 1978.

[14] S. Basu, I. Essa, and A. Pentland. Motion regularization for model-based head tracking. In *International Conference on Pattern Recognition*, Vienna, Austria, 1996.

[15] G.C. Baylis and J. Driver. Visual attention and objects: Evidence for hierarchical coding of location. *Journal of Experimental Psychology; Human Perception and Performance*, 19:451–470, 1993.

[16] G.C. Baylis, E.T. Rolls, and C.M. Leonard. Selectivity between faces in the responses of a population of neurons in the cortex in the superior temporal sulcus of the monkey. *Brain Research*, 342:91–102, 1985.

[17] P.N. Belhumeur, J.P. Hespanha, and D.J. Kriegman. Eigenfaces vs. Fisherfaces: recognition using class specific linear projection. *IEEE Transactions on Pattern Analysis and Machine Intelligence*, 19(7):711–720, July 1997.

[18] R. Bellman. *Adaptive Control Processes: A Guided Tour*. Princeton University Press, 1961.

[19] D.J. Beymer. Face recognition under varying pose. AI Memo 1461, MIT, Cambridge, Massachusetts, December 1993.

[20] D.J. Beymer. Face recognition under varying pose. In *IEEE Conference on Computer Vision and Pattern Recognition*, pages 756–761, 1994.

[21] D.J. Beymer. Feature correspondence by interleaving shape and texture computations. In *IEEE Conference on Computer Vision and Pattern Recognition*, pages 921–928, 1996.

[22] D.J. Beymer and T. Poggio. Face recognition from one example view. In *IEEE International Conference on Computer Vision*, pages 500–507, Cambridge, Massachusetts, 1995. (MIT AI Memo 1536).

[23] D.J. Beymer and T. Poggio. Image representations for visual learning. *Science*, 272:1905–1909, 28 June 1996.

[24] G.K. Bhattacharyya and R.A. Johnson. *Statistical Concepts and Methods*. Wiley, New York, London, 1977.

[25] M. Bichsel and A. Pentland. Human face recognition and the face image set's topology. *CVGIP: Image Understanding*, 59(2):254–261, March 1994.

[26] C.M. Bishop. Novelty detection and neural network validation. *IEE Proceedings on Vision, Image and Signal Processing*, 141(4):217–222, 1994.

[27] C.M. Bishop. *Neural Networks for Pattern Recognition*. Oxford University Press, Oxford, England, 1995.

[28] M.J. Black and A.D. Jepson. Eigentracking: robust matching and tracking of articulated objects using a view-based representation. In *European Conference on Computer Vision*, volume I, pages 329–342, Freiburg, Germany, 1996.

[29] M.J. Black and A.D. Jepson. A probabilistic framework for matching temporal trajectories: Condensation-based recognition of gestures and expressions. In *European Conference on Computer Vision*, volume 1, pages 909–924, Freiburg, Germany, 1998.

[30] R.M. Bolle, N.K. Ratha, and S. Pankanti. Research issues in biometrics. In

Asian Conference on Computer Vision, volume 1, pages 2–9, Hong Kong, China, 1998.

[31] S.M. Bozic. *Digital and Kalman Filtering*. Arnold, 1979.

[32] J. Bradshaw and G. Wallace. Models for the processing and identification of faces. *Perception and Psychophysics*, 9:443–447, 1971.

[33] J.M. Brady and H. Asada. Smoothed local symmetries and their implementation. AI Memo 757, MIT, Cambridge, Massachusetts, USA, March 1984.

[34] K. Brammer and G. Siffling. *Kalman-Bucy Filters*. Artech House Inc., 1989.

[35] E. Brown, K. Deffenbacher, and W. Sturgill. Memory for faces and the circumstances of encounter. *Journal of Applied Psychology*, 62:311–318, 1977.

[36] R.G. Brown. *Introduction to Random Signal Analysis and Kalman Filtering*. John Wiley and Sons, 1983.

[37] V. Bruce. Changing faces: Visual and non visual coding processes in face recognition. *British J. Psychology*, 73:105–116, 1982.

[38] V. Bruce. *Recognising Faces*. Lawrence Erlbaum Associates Ltd., London, 1988.

[39] V. Bruce, editor. *Face Recognition*. Erlbaum, London, 1991. Book version of special issue of European Journal of Cognitive Psychology.

[40] V. Bruce. Stability from variation: The case of face recognition. *The quartely journal of experimental psychology*, 47A(1):5–28, 1994.

[41] V. Bruce and M. Burton, editors. *Processing Images of Faces*. Norwood, New Jersey, 1992.

[42] V. Bruce, A. Cowey, A.W. Ellis, and D. Perrett, editors. *Processing the Facial Image*. Oxford. Oxford University Press, 1992. Book version of discussion meeting issue of Philosophical Transactions of the Royal Society.

[43] V. Bruce and G. Humphreys, editors. *Object and Face Recognition*. Psychology Press, 1994. A Special Issue of the journal of Visual Cognition.

[44] V. Bruce and T. Valentine. When a nod's as good as a wink. the role of dynamic information in facial recognition. In M. M. Gruneberg, P.E. Morris, and R. N. Sykes, editors, *Practical Aspects of Memory: Current Research and Issues*, volume 1, pages 169–174. Lawrence Erlbaum Associates, Chichester, UK, 1988.

[45] V. Bruce, T. Valentine, and A.D. Baddeley. The basis of the 3/4 view advantage in face recognition. *Applied Cognitive Psychology*, 1:109–120, 1987.

[46] V. Bruce and A. Young. *In the eye of the beholder: The science of face perception*. Oxford University Press, Oxford, 1998. Written to accompany the exhibition on "The science of the face" at the Scottish National Portrait Gallery.

[47] R. Brunelli and D. Falavigna. Person identification using multiple cues. *IEEE Transactions on Pattern Analysis and Machine Intelligence*,

17(10):955–966, October 1995.

[48] R. Brunelli and T. Poggio. Face recognition: Features versus templates. *IEEE Transactions on Pattern Analysis and Machine Intelligence*, 15(10):1042–1052, October 1993.

[49] H. Bülthoff, S. Edelman, and M. Tarr. How are three-dimensional objects represented in the brain? AI Memo 1479, MIT, Cambridge, Massachusetts, April 1994.

[50] I. Bülthoff, H. Bülthoff, and P. Sinha. View-based representations for dynamic 3D object recognition. Technical Report 47, Max-Planck-Institut für biologische Kybernetik, February 1997.

[51] J.R. Bunch and C.P. Nielsen. Updating the singular value decomposition. *Numerische Mathematik*, 31:111–129, 1978.

[52] G. Burel and D. Carel. Detection and localization of faces on digital images. In *Pattern Recognition Letters*, volume 15, pages 963–967, 1994.

[53] M.C. Burl, T.K. Leung, and P. Perona. Face localization via shape statistics. In *International Workshop on Face & Gesture Recognition*, pages 154–159, Zurich, June 1995.

[54] I.W.R. Bushnell, F. Sai, and J.T. Mullin. Neonatal recognition of the mother's face. *British Journal of Developmental Psychology*, 7:3–15, 1989.

[55] B.F. Buxton and H. Buxton. Monocular depth perception from optic flow by space time signal processing. *Proceedings of the Royal Society of London*, B-218:27–47, 1983.

[56] H. Buxton and S. Gong. Visual surveillance in a dynamic and uncertain world. *Artificial Intelligence*, 78(1-2):431–459, October 1995.

[57] S. Carey, R. Diamond, and B. Woods. The development of face recognition - a maturational component. *Developmental Psychology*, 16:257–269, 1980.

[58] A. Caron, R. Caron, R. Caldwell, and S. Weiss. Infant perception of the structural properties of the face. *Developmental Psychology*, 9:385–399, 1973.

[59] J.E. Chance, A.L. Turner, and A.G. Goldstein. Development of differential recognition for own race and other-race faces. *Journal of Psychology*, 112:29–37, 1982.

[60] S. Chandrasekaran, B.S. Manjunath, Y.F. Wanf, J. Winkler, and H. Zhang. An eigenspace update algorithm for image analysis. *Graphical Models and Image Processing*, 59(5):321–332, September 1997.

[61] F. Christie and V. Bruce. The role of movement in the recognition of unfamiliar faces. *Memory and Cognition*, 26(4):780–790, 1998.

[62] M.S. Chung and D.M. Thomson. Development of face recognition. *British Journal of Psychology*, 86:55–85, 1995.

[63] P.M. Churchland. *The Engine of Reason, The Seat of the Soul: A Philosophical Journey into the Brain*. MIT Press, 1996.

[64] J.J. Clark and A.L. Yuille. *Data Fusion for Sensory Information Processing Systems*. Robotics: Vision, Manipulation and Sensors. Kluwer Academic Publishers, Boston, 1990.

[65] P. Comon. Independent component analysis - a new concept? *Signal Processing*, 36:11–20, 1994.

[66] T.F. Cootes, G.J. Edwards, and C.J. Taylor. Active appearance models. In *European Conference on Computer Vision*, volume II, pages 484–498, Freiburg, Germany, June 1998.

[67] T.F. Cootes, A. Hill, C.J. Taylor, and J. Haslam. The use of active shape models for locating structures in medical images. *Image and Vision Computing*, 12:355–366, 1994.

[68] T.F. Cootes, C.J. Taylor, D. Cooper, and J. Graham. Active shape models - their training and application. *Computer Vision and Image Understanding*, 61(1):38–59, January 1995.

[69] M. Corbetta, F.M. Miezin, S. Dobmeyer, G.L. Shulman, and S.E. Petersen. Attentional modulation of neural processing of shape, colour, and velocity in humans. *Science*, 248:1556–1559, 1990.

[70] C. Cortes and V. Vapnik. Support vector network. *Machine Learning*, 20:1–25, 1995.

[71] N. Costen, I. Craw, G. Robertson, and S. Akamatsu. Automatic face recognition: what representation ? In *European Conference on Computer Vision*, pages 504–513, Cambridge, England, April 1996.

[72] E. Courchesne, L. Ganz, and A.M. Norcia. Event-related potentials to human faces in infants. *Child Development*, 52:804–811, 1981.

[73] J. Coutaz, F. Berard, and J.L. Crowley. Coordination of perceptual processes for computer mediated communication. In *IEEE International Conference on Face & Gesture Recognition*, pages 106–111, Vermont, USA, 1996.

[74] I. Craw. A manifold model of face and object recognition. In T.R. Valentine, editor, *Cognitive and Computational Aspects of Face Recognition*, pages 183–203. Routledge, London, 1995.

[75] I. Craw. Machine coding of human faces. Technical report, Department of Mathematical Sciences, University of Aberdeen, 1996.

[76] I. Craw and P. Cameron. Face recognition by computer. In *British Machine Vision Conference*, pages 489–507, Leeds, UK, 1993.

[77] J.L. Crowley and F. Berard. Multi-modal tracking of faces for video communications. In *IEEE Conference on Computer Vision and Pattern Recognition*, pages 17–19, Puerto Rico, June 1997.

[78] D. Cunado, M.S. Nixon, and J.N. Carter. Using gait as a biometric via phase-weighted magnitude spectra. In J. Bigun, G. Chollet, and G. Borgefors, editors, *International Conference on Audio and Video-Based Person Authentication*, Lecture Notes in Computer Science 1206, pages 95–102, Crans-Montana, Switzerland, March 1997. Springer.

[79] Y. Dai and Y. Nakano. Extraction of facial images from complex background using color information and SGLD matrices. In *International Workshop on Face & Gesture Recognition*, pages 238–242, Zurich, 1995.

[80] T. Darrell, G. Gordon, J. Woodfill, H. Baker, and M. Harville. Robust, real-

time people tracking in open environments using integrated stereo, color, and face detection. In S. Maybank and T. Tan, editors, *IEEE Workshop on Visual Surveillance*, pages 26–32, Mumbai, India, January 1998.

[81] J.G. Daugman. Uncertainty relation for resolution in space, spatial frequency, and orientation optimized by two-dimensional visual cortical filters. *Journal of Optical Society of America*, 2:1160–1169, 1985.

[82] J.G. Daugman. High confidence visual recognition of persons by a test of statistical independence. *IEEE Transactions on Pattern Analysis and Machine Intelligence*, 15(11):1148–1161, November 1993.

[83] G.M. Davies. Face recognition: Issues and theories. In M.M. Gruneberg, P.E. Morris, and R.N. Sykes, editors, *Practical Aspects of Memory*. Academic Press, 1978.

[84] G.M. Davies, H. Ellis, and J.W. Shepherd. Face recognition accuracy as a function of mode of representation. *Journal of Applied Psychology*, 63(2):180–187, 1978.

[85] M. de Haan and C.A. Nelson. Recognition of the mother's face by six-month-old infants: A neurobehavioural study. *Child Development*, 68(2):187–210, 1997.

[86] F. de la Torre, S. Gong, and S.J. McKenna. View-based adaptive affine tracking. In *European Conference on Computer Vision*, pages 828–842, Freiburg, Germany, June 1998.

[87] S. de Schonen and E. Mathivet. A scenario about the development of hemispheric specialisation in face recognition during infancy. *European Bulletin of Cognitive Psychology*, 9:3–44, 1989.

[88] R.D. DeGroat and R. Roberts. Efficient, numerically stabilised rank-one eigenstructure updating. *IEEE Transactions on Acoustics, Speech, and Signal Processing*, 38(2):301–316, February 1990.

[89] A. Dempster, N. Laird, and D. Rubin. Maximum likelihood from incomplete data via the EM algorithm. *Journal of the Royal Statistical Society*, B-39(1):1–38, 1977.

[90] R. Desimone and J. Duncan. Neural mechanisms of selective visual attention. *Annual Review of Neuroscience*, 18:193–222, 1995.

[91] H. Deubel, W.X. Schneider, and I. Paprotta. Selective dorsal and ventral processing: Evidence for a common attentional mechanism in reaching and perception. *Visual Cognition*, 5:81–108, March-August 1998.

[92] P.A. Devijver and J. Kittler. *Pattern recognition: a statistical approach*. Prentice Hall, London, 1982.

[93] U. Dieckmann, P. Plankensteiner, R. Schamburger, B. Pröba, and S. Meller. SESAM: A biometric person identification system using sensor fusion. In J. Bigün, G. Chollet, and G. Borgefors, editors, *International Conference on Audio and Video-Based Person Authentication*, Lecture Notes in Computer Science 1206, pages 301–310, Crans-Montana, Switzerland, March 1997. Springer.

[94] F. Dretske. Meaningful perception. In S.M. Kosslyn and D.N. Osherson,

editors, *Visual Cognition*, volume 2 of *An Invitation to Cognitive Science*, pages 331–352. MIT Press, Cambridge, Massachusetts, 1995.

[95] B. Duc, G. Maître, S. Fischer, and J. Bigün. Person authentication by fusing face and speech information. In J. Bigün, G. Chollet, and G. Borgefors, editors, *International Conference on Audio and Video-Based Person Authentication*, Lecture Notes in Computer Science 1206, pages 311–318, Crans-Montana, Switzerland, March 1997. Springer.

[96] R.O. Duda and P.E. Hart. *Pattern Classification and Scene Analysis*. John Wiley, New York, 1973.

[97] J. Duncan. Selective attention and the organisation of visual information. *Journal of Experimental Psychology: General*, 113:501–517, 1984.

[98] J.H. Duncan and T-C. Chou. On the detection of motion and the computation of optical flow. *IEEE Transactions on Pattern Analysis and Machine Intelligence*, 14(3):346–352, 1992.

[99] S. Duvdevani-Bar, S. Edelman, J. Howell, and H. Buxton. A similarity-based method for the generalisation of face recognition over pose and expression. In *IEEE International Conference on Face & Gesture Recognition*, pages 118–123, Nara, Japan, April 1998.

[100] S. Edelman. Representation is representation of similarity. *Behavioral and Brain Sciences*, pages 449–498, 1998.

[101] S. Edelman. *Representation and Recognition in Vision*. MIT Press, 1999.

[102] S. Edelman and S. Duvdevani-Bar. A model of visual recognition and categorization. *Philosophical Transactions of the Royal Society (B)*, 352:1191–1202, 1997.

[103] S. Edelman and S. Duvdevani-Bar. Similarity-based viewspace interpolation and the categorization of 3D objects. In *Proceedings of Workshop on Similarity and Categorization*, pages 75–81, Edinburgh, November 1997.

[104] G.J. Edwards, A. Lanitis, C.J. Taylor, and T.F. Cootes. Modelling the variability in face images. In *IEEE International Conference on Face & Gesture Recognition*, pages 328–333, Killington, Vermont, October 1996.

[105] G.J. Edwards, C.J. Taylor, and T.F. Cootes. Learning to identify and track faces in image sequences. In *British Machine Vision Conference*, pages 130–139, Colchester, Essex, England, April 1997.

[106] M. Eimer. Mechanism of visuospatial attention: Evidence from event-related brain potentials. *Visual Cognition*, 5:257–286, March-August 1998.

[107] H.D. Ellis. Recognising faces. *British Journal of Psychology*, 66:409–426, 1975.

[108] H.D. Ellis, J. Shepherd, and G. Davies. An investigation of the use of the photo-fit technique for recalling faces. *British Journal of Psychology*, 66:29–37, 1975.

[109] H.D. Ellis and J.W. Shepherd. Face memory-theory and practice. In M. Gruneberg and Morris P.E., editors, *Aspects of Memory Volume 1: The Practical Aspects*. Routledge, 1992.

[110] J. Elman. Finding structure in time. *Cognitive Science*, 14(2):179–211,

1990.

[111] K. Etemad and R. Chellappa. Discriminant analysis for recognition of human face images. In *International Conference on Audio and Video-Based Person Authentication*, pages 127–142, Crans-Montana, 1997.

[112] R. Fantz, J. Fagan, and S. Miranda. Early perceptual development as shown by visual discrimination, selectivity and memory with varying stimulus and population parameters. In L. Cohen and P. Salapatek, editors, *Infant Perception: from Sensation to Cognition: Basic Visual Processes*, volume 1. Academic Press, 1975.

[113] T.M. Field, D. Cohen, R. Garcia, and R. Greenberg. Mother-stranger face discrimination by the newborn. *Infant Behaviour and Development*, 7:19–25, 1984.

[114] R.A. Fisher. The statistical utilisation of multiple measurements. *Annals of Eugenics*, 8:376–386, 1938.

[115] R.H. Flin. Age effects in children's memory for unfamiliar faces. *Developmental Psychology*, 16:373–374, 1980.

[116] F. Fogelman-Soulie, E. Viennet, and B. Lamy. Multi-modular neural network architectures: applications in optical character and human face recognition. *International Journal of Pattern Recognition and Artificial Intelligence*, 8:147–165, 1993.

[117] P. Foldiak. Learning invariance from transformation sequences. *Neural Computation*, 3(2):194–200, 1991.

[118] D.A. Forsyth. *Colour Constancy and its Applications in Machine Vision*. PhD thesis, University of Oxford, 1988.

[119] M. Friedman, S. Reed, and E. Carterette. Feature saliency and recognition memory for schematic faces. *Perception and Psychophysics*, 10:47–50, 1971.

[120] K. Fukunaga. *Introduction to Statistical Pattern Recognition*. Academic Press, New York, 2nd edition, 1990.

[121] A.H. Gee and R. Cipolla. Determining the gaze of faces in images. *Image and Vision Computing*, 12(10):639–647, 1994.

[122] A.H. Gee and R. Cipolla. Fast visual tracking by temporal consensus. *Image and Vision Computing*, 14(2):105–114, 1996.

[123] S. Geman, E. Bienenstock, and R. Doursat. Neural networks and the bias/variance dilemma. *Neural Computation*, 4(1):1–58, 1992.

[124] E. Gibson. *Principles of Perceptual Learning*. Appleton-Century-Crofts, New York, 1969.

[125] J.M. Gilbert and W. Yang. A real-time face recognition system using custom VLSI hardware. In *Proceedings of the IEEE Workshop on Computer Architectures for Machine Perception*, pages 58–66, 1993.

[126] A.G. Goldstein and Chance J.E. Memory for face and schema theory. *Journal of Psychology*, 105:47–59, 1980.

[127] B. Golomb and J. Sejnowski. Computer-based facial expression models and image databases. *NSF Understanding the face*, page ??, 1992.

[128] S. Gong. *Parallel Computation of Visual Motion*. PhD thesis, Department

of Engineering Science, Oxford University, Oxford, England, 1989.

[129] S. Gong. Visual observation as reactive learning. In *International Conference on Adaptive and Learning Systems*, pages 175–187, Orlando, USA, April 1992.

[130] S. Gong and J.M. Brady. Parallel computation of optic flow. In *European Conference on Computer Vision*, pages 124–134, Antibes, France, April 1990.

[131] S. Gong and H. Buxton. On the expectations of moving objects. In *European Conference on Artificial Intelligence*, pages 781–785, Vienna, Austria, 1992.

[132] S. Gong and H. Buxton. Bayesian nets for mapping contextual knowledge to computational constraints in motion segmentation and tracking. In *British Machine Vision Conference*, pages 229–239, Guildford, England, September 1993.

[133] S. Gong, S.J. McKenna, and J.J. Collins. An investigation into face pose distributions. In *IEEE International Conference on Face & Gesture Recognition*, pages 265–270, Vermount, USA, November 1996.

[134] S. Gong, E-J. Ong, and S.J. McKenna. Learning to associate faces across views in vector space of similarities to prototypes. In *British Machine Vision Conference*, volume 1, pages 54–64, Southampton, UK, September 1998.

[135] S. Gong, A. Psarrou, I. Katsoulis, and P. Palavouzis. Tracking and recognition of face sequences. In Y. Paker and S. Wilbur, editors, *Image Processing for Broadcast and Video Production*, pages 96–112. Springer-Verlag, 1994.

[136] S. Gong, M. Walter, and A. Psarrou. Recognition of temporal structures: Learning prior and propagating observation augmented densities via hidden Markov states. In *IEEE International Conference on Computer Vision*, pages 157–162, Corfu, Greece, September 1999.

[137] S.G. Goodridge and M.G. Kay. Multimedia sensor fusion for intelligent camera control. In *IEEE International Conference on Multisensor Fusion and Integration for Intelligent Systems*, pages 655–662, 1996.

[138] I.E. Gordon. *Theories of Visual Perception*, chapter 3, pages 46–75. John Wiley & Sons, New York, 1989.

[139] C. Goren, M. Sartty, and P. Wu. Visual following and pattern discrimination of face-like stimuli by newborn infants. *Pediatrics*, 56(4):544–549, 1975.

[140] V. Govindaraju. Locating human faces in photographs. *International Journal of Computer Vision*, 19(2):129–146, 1996.

[141] H.P. Graf, T. Chen, E. Petajan, and E. Cosatto. Locating faces and facial parts. In *International Workshop on Face & Gesture Recognition*, pages 41–46, Zurich, 1995.

[142] R.L. Gregory. *The Intelligent Eye*. Weidenfeld & Nicolson, London, 1970.

[143] S. Grossberg. How does the cerebral cortex work? Learning, attention and grouping by the laminar circuits of visual cortex. Technical report, De-

partment of Cognitive and Neural Systems, University of Boston, Boston, USA, April 1998. CAS/CNS-97-023.

[144] S. Grossberg and G.O. Stone. Neural dynamics of word recognition and recall: attentional priming, learning and resonance. *Psychological Review*, 93:46–74, 1986.

[145] M. Gu and S. C. Eisenstat. A stable and fast algorithm for updating the singular value decomposition. Technical Report YALEU/DCS/RR-966, Yale University, New Haven, CT., 1994.

[146] P. Hall, D. Marshall, and R. Martin. Incremental eigenanalysis for classification. In *Proceedings of British Machine Vision Conference*, volume 1, pages 286–295, 1998.

[147] L. Harmon. The recognition of faces. *Scientific American*, 229:71–83, 1973.

[148] S. Haykin. *Neural Networks: A Comprehensive Foundation*. Prentice-Hall, 1999.

[149] T.J. Heap. *Learning Deformable Shape Models for Object Tracking*. PhD thesis, School of Computer Studies, University of Leeds, Leeds, UK, September 1997.

[150] M.A. Hearst (ed.). Support vector machines. *IEEE Intelligent Systems*, 13(4):18–28, 1998. Trends and controversies feature.

[151] E.C. Hildreth. *The Measurement of Visual Motion*. MIT Press, Cambridge, Massachusetts, USA, 1984.

[152] H. Hill and V. Bruce. Effects of lighting on the perception of facial surfaces. *Journal of Experimental Psychology: Human Perception and Performance*, 22:986–1004, 1996.

[153] H. Hill, P.G. Schyns, and S. Akamatsu. Information and viewpoint dependence in face recognition. *Cognition*, 62:201–222, 1997.

[154] G.E. Hinton, P. Dayan, and M. Revow. Modelling the manifolds of images of handwritten digits. *IEEE Transactions on Neural Networks*, 8(1):65–74, January 1997.

[155] G.E. Hinton, M. Revow, and P. Dayan. Recognizing handwritten digits using mixtures of linear models. In D. Touretzky, G. Tesauro, and J. Alspector, editors, *Advances in Neural Information Processing Systems*, volume 7, pages 1015–1022, San Mateo, CA., 1995. Morgan Kaufman.

[156] L. Hong, A. Jain, S. Pankanti, and R. Bolle. Identity authentication using fingerprints. In J. Bigun, G. Chollet, and G. Borgefors, editors, *International Conference on Audio and Video-Based Person Authentication*, Lecture Notes in Computer Science 1206, pages 103–110, Crans-Montana, Switzerland, March 1997. Springer.

[157] B.K.P. Horn and B.G. Schunck. Determining optical flow. *Artificial Intelligence*, 17:185–203, 1981.

[158] H. Hotelling. Analysis of a complex of statistical variables into principal components. *Journal of Educational Psychology*, 24:417–441, 498–520, 1933.

[159] J. Howell and H. Buxton. Face recognition using radial basis function

neural networks. In *British Machine Vision Conference*, pages 455–464, Edinburgh, Scotland, September 1996.

[160] J.E. Hummel and B.J. Stankiewicz. Two roles for attention in shape perception: A structural description model of visual scrutiny. *Visual Cognition*, 5:49–80, March-August 1998.

[161] M. Hunke and A. Waibel. Face locating and tracking for human-computer interaction. In *28th Asilomar Conference on Signals, Systems and Computers*, California, 1994.

[162] IAPR. *International Conference on Audio and Video-Based Person Authentication*, Lecture Notes in Computer Science, Crans-Montana, Switzerland, March 1997. Elsevier Science.

[163] IAPR. *International Conference on Audio and Video-Based Person Authentication*, Lecture Notes in Computer Science, Washington DC, USA, March 1999. Elsevier Science.

[164] IEEE. *International Conference on Face & Gesture Recognition*, Zurich, Switzerland, March 1995. IEEE Computer Society.

[165] IEEE. *International Conference on Face & Gesture Recognition*, Killington, Vermont, USA, October 1996. IEEE Computer Society.

[166] IEEE. *International Conference on Face & Gesture Recognition*, Nara, Japan, April 1998. IEEE Computer Society.

[167] IEEE. *International Workshop on Recognition, Analysis and Tracking of Faces and Gestures in Real-Time Systems*, Corfu, Greece, September 1999. IEEE Computer Society. In conjunction with International Conference on Computer Vision.

[168] IEEE Technical Committee on Pattern Analysis and Machine Intelligence. *IEEE International Workshop on Modelling People*, Corfu, Greece, September 1999. IEEE Computer Society.

[169] D.E. Irwin and R.D. Gordon. Eye movements, attention and trans-saccadic memory. *Visual Cognition*, 5:127–156, March-August 1998.

[170] M. Isard and A. Blake. Contour tracking by stochastic propagation of conditional density. In *European Conference on Computer Vision*, pages 343–356, Cambridge,UK, 1996.

[171] M. Isard and A. Blake. A mixed-state condensation tracker with automatic model switching. In *IEEE International Conference on Computer Vision*, pages 107–112, Mumbai, India, January 1998.

[172] A. K. Jain, R. Bolle, and S. Pankanti, editors. *Biometrics: Personal Identification in Networked Society*. Kluwer Academic Publishers, 1998.

[173] G. Johansson. Visual perception of biological motion and a model for its analysis. *Perception and Psychophysics*, 14:201–211, 1973.

[174] M.H. Johnson. Cortical maturation and the development of visual attention in early infancy. *Journal of Cognitive Neuroscience*, 2:81–95, 1990.

[175] N. Johnson. *Learning Object Behaviour Models*. PhD thesis, University of Leeds, Leeds, UK, September 1998.

[176] R.A. Johnston and H.D. Ellis. The development of face recognition. In

T. Valentine, editor, *Cognitive and Computational Aspects of Face Recognition: Explorations in Face Space*, pages 1–23. London:Routledge, 1995.

[177] I.T. Jolliffe. *Principal Component Analysis*. Springer-Verlag, 1986.

[178] M.I. Jordan. Attractor dynamics and parallelism in a connectionist sequential machine. In *Proceedings of the Eighth Annual Conference of the Cognitive Science Society*, pages 531–546, Hillsdale NJ, 1986. Erlbaum.

[179] P. Jourlin, J. Luettin, D. Genoud, and H. Wassner. Acoustic-labial speaker verification. In J. Bigün, G. Chollet, and G. Borgefors, editors, *International Conference on Audio and Video-Based Person Authentication*, Lecture Notes in Computer Science 1206, pages 319–326, Crans-Montana, Switzerland, March 1997. Springer.

[180] D. Kahneman, A. Treisman, and B.J. Gibbs. The reviewing of object files: Object-specific integration of information. *Cognitve Psychology*, 24:175–219, 1992.

[181] R. Kalman. A new approach to linear filtering and prediction problems. *ASME Journal of Basic Engineering*, pages 35–45, 1960.

[182] T. Kanade. Picture processing by computer complex and recognition of human faces. Technical report, Kyoto University, Dept. Inform. Sci., 1973.

[183] N. Kanwisher and J. Driver. Objects, attributes and visual attention: Which, what and where. *Current Directions in Psychological Science*, 1:26–31, 1992.

[184] M. Kirby and L. Sirovich. Application of the Karhunen-Loeve procedure for the characterisation of human faces. *IEEE Transactions on Pattern Analysis and Machine Intelligence*, 12(1):103–108, January 1990.

[185] J. Kittler, Y.P. Li, J. Matas, and Ramos Sánchez M.U. Combining evidence in multimodal personal identity recognition systems. In J. Bigün, G. Chollet, and G. Borgefors, editors, *International Conference on Audio and Video-Based Person Authentication*, Lecture Notes in Computer Science 1206, pages 327–334, Crans-Montana, Switzerland, March 1997. Springer.

[186] R. Kjeldsen and J. Kender. Finding skin in color images. In *IEEE International Conference on Face & Gesture Recognition*, pages 312–317, Killington, VT., 1996.

[187] B. Knight and A. Johnston. The role of movement in face recognition. *Visual Cognition*, 4(3):265–273, 1997.

[188] W. Konen. Comparing facial line-drawings with gray-level images: a case study on PHANTOMAS. In C. von der Malsburg and W. van Seelen, editors, *Proceedings of the International Conference on Artificial Neural Networks*, page 727. North-Holland, 1996.

[189] W. Konen. Neural information processing in real-world face-recognition applications. *IEEE Expert*, April 1996.

[190] W. Konen and E. Schulze-Kruger. ZN-Face: A system for access control using automated face recognition. In *International Workshop on Face & Gesture Recognition*, pages 18–23, Zurich, 1995.

[191] E. Kowler. Cognitive expectations, not habits, control anticipatory smooth oculomotor pursuit. *Vision Research*, 29(2):1049–1057, 1989.

[192] E. Kowler. Eye movements. In *Visual Cognition: An Invitation to Cognitive Science*, volume 2, pages 215–265. MIT, 1995.

[193] F.L. Krouse. Effects of pose, pose change and delay on face recognition. *Journal of Applied Psychology*, 66(5):651–654, 1981.

[194] N. Kruger, M. Potzsch, T. Maurer, and M. Rinne. Estimation of face position and pose with labeled graphs. In *British Machine Vision Conference*, pages 735–743, Edinburgh, 1996.

[195] M. Lades, J.C. Vorbrüggen, J. Buchmann, J. Lange, C. von der Malsburg, R.P. Würtz, and W. Konen. Distortion invariant object recognition in the dynamic link architecture. *IEEE Transactions on Computers*, 42:300–311, 1993.

[196] H.M. Lakany and G.M. Hayes. An algorithm for recognising walkers. In J. Bigun, G. Chollet, and G. Borgefors, editors, *International Conference on Audio and Video-Based Person Authentication*, Lecture Notes in Computer Science 1206, pages 111–118, Crans-Montana, Switzerland, March 1997. Springer.

[197] K. Lander, F. Christie, and V. Bruce. The role of dynamic information in the recognition of famous faces. *Memory and Cognition*, November 1999.

[198] A. Lanitis, C.J. Taylor, and T.F. Cootes. A unified approach to coding and interpreting face images. In *IEEE International Conference on Computer Vision*, pages 368–373, Cambridge, Massachusetts, 1995.

[199] A. Lanitis, C.J. Taylor, and T.F. Cootes. Automatic interpretation and coding of face images using flexible models. *IEEE Transactions on Pattern Analysis and Machine Intelligence*, 19(7):743–756, July 1997.

[200] A. Lanitis, C.J. Taylor, T.F. Cootes, and T. Ahmed. Automatic interpretation of human faces and hand gestures using flexible models. In *International Workshop on Face & Gesture Recognition*, pages 98–103, Zurich, 1995.

[201] K.R. Laughery, P.K. Fessler, D.R. Lenorovitz, and D.A. Yoblick. Time delay and similarity effects in facial recognition. *Journal of Applied Psychology*, 59:490–496, 1974.

[202] C. Leung, editor. *Image and Vision Computing*, 1999. 17(7), Special issue on Content-based Image Indexing and Retrieval.

[203] Y. Li, S. Gong, and H. Liddell. Support vector regression and classification based multi-view face detection and recognition. In *IEEE International Conference on Face & Gesture Recognition*, Grenoble, France, March 2000.

[204] C. Liu and H. Wechsler. Enhanced Fisher linear discriminant models for face recognition. In *14th International Conference on Pattern Recognition (ICPR)*, Queensland, Australia, August 1998.

[205] C. Liu and H. Wechsler. Evolution of optimal projection axes (OPA) for face recognition. In *IEEE International Conference on Face & Gesture Recognition*, pages 282–287, Nara, Japan, 1998.

[206] C. Liu and H. Wechsler. Face recognition using shape and texture. In *IEEE Conference on Computer Vision and Pattern Recognition*, Fort Collins, Colorado, USA, June 1999.

[207] A.G. Livingstone and D. Hubel. Segregation of form, colour, movement, and depth: anatomy, physiology and perception. *Science*, 240:740–749, 1988.

[208] S.P. Lloyd. Least squares quantization in PCM. *IEEE Transactions on Information Theory*, 28(2):129–137, 1982.

[209] N.K. Logothetis, J. Pauls, and T. Poggio. Spatial reference frames for object recognition: Tuning for rotations in depth. AI Memo 1533, MIT, Cambridge, Massachusetts, March 1995.

[210] D.G. Lowe. *Perceptual Organisation and Visual Recognition*. Robotics: Vision, Manipulation and Sensors. Kluwer Academic Publishers, Boston, 1985.

[211] D.G. Lowe. Three-dimensional object recognition from single two-dimensional images. *Artificial Intelligence*, 31:355–395, 1987.

[212] T.S. Luce. Blacks, whites and yellows: They all look alike to me. *Psychology Today*, 8:105–108, 1974.

[213] J. Luettin, N.A. Thacker, and S.W. Beet. Speaker identification by lipreading. In *Proceedings of the 4th International Conference on Spoken Language Processing (ICSLP'96)*, volume 1, pages 62–65, 1996.

[214] R. Malpass. Training in face recognition. In G. Davies, H. Ellis, and J. Shepherd, editors, *Perceiving and Remembering Faces*. Academic Press, 1981.

[215] R. Malpass, H. Lavigueur, and D. Weldon. Verbal and visual training in face recognition. *Perception and Psychophysics*, 14:285–292, 1973.

[216] D. Marr. *Vision*. Freeman, 1982.

[217] D. Marr and H.K. Nishihara. Representation and recognition of the spatial organisation of three dimensional structure. *Proceedings of the Royal Society of London B*, 200:269–294, 1978.

[218] J. Martin and J.L. Crowley. Experimental comparison of correlation techniques. In *Int. Conf. on Intelligent Autonomous Systems*, Karlsruhe, Germany, 1995.

[219] A. Martinez and R. Benavente. The AR face database. Technical Report CVC Technical Report 24, Purdue University, Computer Vision Centre, June 1998.

[220] J. Matas, R. Marik, and J. Kittler. On representation and matching of multi-coloured objects. In *IEEE International Conference on Computer Vision*, pages 726–732, Boston, Massachusetts, 1995.

[221] T. Maurer and C. von der Malsburg. Tracking and learning graphs and pose on image sequences of faces. In *IEEE International Conference on Face & Gesture Recognition*, pages 176–181, Killington, Vermont, 1996.

[222] R.J. McEliece, R.B. Ash, and C. Ash. *Introduction to Discrete Mathematics*. McGraw-Hill, 1989.

[223] S.J. McKenna and S. Gong. Tracking faces. In *IEEE International Conference on Face & Gesture Recognition*, pages 271–277, Killington, Vermont, USA, October 1996.

[224] S.J. McKenna and S. Gong. Non-intrusive person authentication for access control by visual tracking and face recognition. In *International Conference on Audio and Video-Based Person Authentication*, pages 177–184, Crans-Montana, Switzerland, March 1997. Springer.

[225] S.J. McKenna and S. Gong. Gesture recognition for visually mediated interaction using probabilistic event trajectories. In *British Machine Vision Conference*, volume 2, pages 498–506, Southampton, UK, September 1998.

[226] S.J. McKenna and S. Gong. Real-time face pose estimation. *Journal of Real-Time Imaging, Special Issue on Real-Time Visual Monitoring and Inspection*, 4:333–347, 1998.

[227] S.J. McKenna and S. Gong. Recognising moving faces. In H. Wechsler, P.J. Phillips, V. Bruce, F. Fogelman Soulie, and Huang T.S., editors, *Face Recognition: From Theory to Applications*, volume 163 of *NATO ASI Series F*. Springer, 1998.

[228] S.J. McKenna, S. Gong, and J.J. Collins. Face tracking and pose representation. In *British Machine Vision Conference*, pages 755–764, Edinburgh, September 1996.

[229] S.J. McKenna, S. Gong, and Y. Raja. Face recognition in dynamic scenes. In A. Clark, editor, *British Machine Vision Conference*, volume 1, pages 140–151, Essex, 1997.

[230] S.J. McKenna, S. Gong, and Y. Raja. Modelling facial colour and identity with gaussian mixtures. *Pattern Recognition*, 31(12):1883–1892, December 1998.

[231] S.J. McKenna, S. Gong, R.P. Würtz, J. Tanner, and D. Banin. Tracking facial feature points with Gabor wavelets and shape models. In *International Conference on Audio and Video-Based Person Authentication*, pages 35–42, Crans-Montana, Switzerland, 1997.

[232] S.J. McKenna, S. Jabri, Z. Duric, and H. Wechsler. Tracking interacting people. In *IEEE International Conference on Face & Gesture Recognition*, Grenoble, France, 2000.

[233] S.J. McKenna, I.W. Ricketts, A.Y. Cairns, and K.A. Hussein. Cell searching with a neural net. In G. Orchard, editor, *Neural computing - research and applications II*, pages 205–216. IOP, 1993.

[234] A. McLeod. Keeping watch on surveillance. *Image Processing*, 6(1), 1994.

[235] B. Moghaddam and A. Pentland. Maximum likelihood detection of faces and hands. In *IEEE International Conference on Face & Gesture Recognition*, pages 122–128, 1995.

[236] B. Moghaddam and A. Pentland. Probabilistic visual learning for object representation. *IEEE Transactions on Pattern Analysis and Machine Intelligence*, 19(7):696–710, July 1997.

[237] B. Moghaddam, W. Wahid, and A. Pentland. Beyond eigenfaces: proba-

bilistic matching for face recognition. In *IEEE International Conference on Face & Gesture Recognition*, pages 30–35, Nara, Japan, 1998.

[238] J. Morton and M.H. Johnson. CONSPEC and CONLERN: a two-process theory of infant face recognition. *Psychological Review*, 98:164–181, 1991.

[239] Y. Moses, S. Edelman, and S. Ullman. Generalisation to novel images in upright and inverted faces. *Perception*, 25:443–461, 1996.

[240] Y. Moses and S. Ullman. Generalisation to novel views: Universal, class-based, and model-based processing. *International Journal of Computer Vision*, 29(3):233–253, September 1998.

[241] M. Mozer. Neural net architecture for temporal sequence processing. In A. Weigend and N. Gershenfeld, editors, *Predicting the Future and Understanding the Past*. Addison-Wesley Publishing, 1993.

[242] H. Murase and S.K. Nayar. Visual learning and recognition of 3-D objects from appearance. *International Journal of Computer Vision*, 14:5–24, 1995.

[243] H. Murase and S.K. Nayar. Detection of 3D objects in cluttered scenes using hierarchical eigenspace. *Pattern Recognition Letters*, 18:375–384, 1997.

[244] H.H. Nagel. From image sequences towards conceptual descriptions. *Image and Vision Computing*, 6:59–74, 1988.

[245] C.A. Nelson. Neural correlates of recognition memory in the first postnatal year of life. In G. Dawson and K. Fischer, editors, *Human Behaviour and the Developing Brian*, pages 269–313. New York:Guildford, 1994.

[246] B. Neumann. Natural language description of time varying scenes. In *Semantic Structures*, pages 167–206. Lawrence Erlbaum Associates, 1989.

[247] J. Ng and S. Gong. Learning support vector machines for a multi-view face model. In *British Machine Vision Conference*, volume 2, pages 503–512, Nottingham, UK, September 1999.

[248] J. Ng and S. Gong. Multi-view face detection and pose estimation using a composite support vector machine across the view sphere. In *IEEE International Workshop on Recognition, Analysis, and Tracking of Faces and Gestures in Real-Time Systems*, pages 14–21, Corfu, Greece, September 1999.

[249] P.M. Ngan. Motion detection in temporal clutter. In *Asian Conference on Computer Vision*, volume II of *Lecture Notes in Computer Science 1352*, pages 615–622, Hong Kong, 1998. Springer.

[250] A.J. O' Toole, H.H. Bülthoff, N.F. Troje, and T. Vetter. Face recognition across large viewpoint changes. Technical Report 9, Max-Planck-Institut für biologische Kybernetik, December 1994.

[251] E-J. Ong, S.J. McKenna, and S. Gong. Tracking head pose for inferring intention. In *European Workshop on Perception of Human Action*, Freiburg, Germany, June 1998.

[252] E. Osuna, R. Freund, and F. Girosi. Training support vector machines: an application to face detection. In *IEEE Conference on Computer Vision and Pattern Recognition*, Puerto Rico, 1997.

[253] D.B. Parker. Learning logic. Technical report, MIT Center for Research in

Computational Economics and Management Science, 1985.

[254] O. Pascalis, S. de Schonen, J. Morton, C. Deruelle, and M. Fabre-Grenet. Mother's face recognition by neonates: A replication and an extension. *Infant Behaviour and Development*, 18:79–95, 1995.

[255] K. Patterson and A. Baddeley. When face recognition fails. *Journal of Experimental Psychology: Human Learning and Memory*, 3(4):406–417, 1977.

[256] M. Pavel, H. Cunningham, and V. Stone. Extrapolation of linear motion. *Vision Research*, 32(11):2177–2186, 1992.

[257] J. Pearl. *Probabilistic Reasoning in Intelligent Systems, Networks of Plausible Inference*. Morgan Kaufmann, 1988.

[258] K. Pearson. On lines and planes of closest fit to systems of points in space. *Philosophy Magazine*, 2:559–572, 1901.

[259] P. Penev and J.J. Atick. Local feature analysis: A general statistical theory for object representation. *Network: Computation in Neural Systems*, 7(3):477–500, 1996.

[260] A. Pentland, B. Moghaddam, and T. Starner. View-based and modular eigenspaces for face recognition. In *IEEE Conference on Computer Vision and Pattern Recognition*, pages 84–91, Seattle, July 1994.

[261] D. Perkins. A definition of caricature and recognition. *Studies in the Anthropology of Visual Communication*, 2:1–24, 1975.

[262] D.I. Perrett, J.K. Hietanen, M.W. Oram, and P.J. Benson. Organization and functions of cells responsive to faces in the temporal cortex. *Philosophical Transactions of the Royal Society of London B*, 335:23–30, 1992.

[263] D.I. Perrett, A.J. Mistlin, and A.J. Chitty. Visual neurones responsive to faces. *Trends in Neurosciences*, 10(9):358–364, 1987.

[264] D.I. Perrett, P.A.J. Smith, D.D. Potter, A.J. Mistlin, A.S. Head, A.D. Milner, and M.A. Jeeves. Visual cells in the temporal cortex sensitive to face view and gaze direction. *Proceedings of the Royal Society of London B*, 223:293–317, 1985.

[265] M. A. Peterson. Object recognition processes can and do operate before figure-ground organisation. *Current Directions in Psychological Science*, 3:105–111, 1994.

[266] P.J. Phillips, H. Moon, P. Rauss, and S.A. Rizvi. The FERET September 1996 Database and Evaluation Procedure. In J. Bigün, G. Chollet, and G. Borgefors, editors, *International Conference on Audio and Video-Based Person Authentication*, Lecture Notes in Computer Science 1206, pages 395–402, Crans-Montana, Switzerland, March 1997. Springer.

[267] P.J. Phillips and P. Rauss. The Face Recognition Technology. In *Proceedings of Office of National Drug Control Policy*, CTAC International Technology Symposium, pages 395–402, Chicago, 1997.

[268] P.J. Phillips, P. Rauss, and S. Der. FERET (Face Recognition Technology) recognition algorithm development and test report. Technical Report 995, U.S. Army Research Laboratory, 1996.

[269] S. Pigeon and L. Vandendorpe. The M2VTS Multimodal Face Database. In

J. Bigün, G. Chollet, and G. Borgefors, editors, *International Conference on Audio and Video-Based Person Authentication*, Lecture Notes in Computer Science 1206, pages 403–409, Crans-Montana, Switzerland, March 1997. Springer.

[270] G. Pike, R. Kemp, N. Towell, and K. Phillips. Recognising moving faces: The relative contribution of motion and perspective view information. *Visual Cognition*, 4(4):409–438, 1997.

[271] J.C. Platt. Fast training of SVMs using sequential minimal optimization. In B. Scholkopf, C. Burges, and A. Smola, editors, *Advances in Kernel Methods - Support Vector Learning*. MIT Press, 1998.

[272] T. Poggio and S. Edelman. A network that learns to recognise three-dimensional objects. *Nature*, 343:263–266, January 1990.

[273] T. Poggio and F. Girosi. Networks for approximation and learning. *Proceedings of The IEEE*, 78(9):1481–1497, September 1990.

[274] T. Poggio and V. Torre. Ill-posed problems and regularization analysis in early vision. Technical report, MIT AI Lab, Cambridge, Massachusetts, USA, 1984.

[275] T. Poggio and T. Vetter. Recognition and structure from one 2D model view: Observations on prototypes, object classes and symmetries. AI Memo 1347, MIT, Massachusetts, 1992.

[276] M.I. Posner. Orienting of attention. *Quarterly Journal of Experimental Psychology*, 32:3–25, 1980.

[277] W.H. Press, S.A. Teukolsky, W.T. Vetterling, and B.P. Flannery. *Numerical Recipes in C*. Cambridge University Press, 2nd edition, 1992.

[278] C.E. Priebe and D.J. Marchette. Adaptive mixtures: Recursive nonparametric pattern recognition. *Pattern Recognition*, 24(12):1197–1209, 1991.

[279] M. Proesmans and L. van Gool. One-shot 3D-shape and texture acquisition of facial data. In *International Conference on Audio and Video-Based Person Authentication*, pages 411–418, Crans Montana, Switzerland, March 1997.

[280] A. Psarrou, S. Gong, and H. Buxton. Spatio-temporal trajectories and face signatures on partially recurrent neural networks. In *IEEE International Joint Conference on Neural Networks*, pages 2226–2232, Perth, Australia, November 1995.

[281] A. Psarrou, V Konstantinou, P. Morse, and P. O'Reilly. Content-based search in medieval manuscripts. In *IEEE Conference on Speech and Image Technologies for Computing and Telecommunications*, Brisbane, Australia, December 1997.

[282] L. Rabiner and B. Juang. *Fundamentals of Speech Recognition*. Signal Processing Series. Prentice Hall, New Jersey, USA, 1993.

[283] L.R. Rabiner. A tutorial on hidden Markov models and selected applications in speech recognition. *Proceedings of IEEE*, 77(2):257–286, 1989.

[284] Y. Raja, S.J. McKenna, and S. Gong. Colour model selection and adaptation in dynamic scenes. In *European Conference on Computer Vision*,

pages 460–474, Freiburg, Germany, June 1998.

[285] Y. Raja, S.J. McKenna, and S. Gong. Segmentation and tracking using colour mixture models. In R. Chin and T. Pong, editors, *Asian Conference on Computer Vision*, Lecture Notes in Computer Science 1351, pages 607–614, Hong Kong, China, January 1998. Springer.

[286] R.P.N. Rao and D.H. Ballard. Natural basis functions and topographic memory for face recognition. In *International Joint Conference on Artificial Intelligence*, pages 10–19, Montreal, 1995.

[287] R.A. Redner and H.F. Walker. Mixture densities, maximum likelihood and the EM algorithm. *SIAM Review*, 26(2):195–239, 1984.

[288] R.D. Reed and R.J. Marks. *Neural Smithing : Supervised Learning in Feedforward Artificial Neural Networks*. MIT Press, 1999.

[289] R.D. Rimey and C.M. Brown. Selective attention as sequential behavior: modeling eye movements with an augmented hidden Markov model. In *The Proceedings of DARPA Image Understanding Workshop*, pages 840–850, Pittsburgh, USA, 1990.

[290] B.D. Ripley. *Pattern Recognition and Neural Networks*. Cambridge University Press, 1995.

[291] G. Robertson and I. Craw. Testing face recognition systems. *Image and Vision Computing*, 12(9):609–614, November 1994.

[292] S. Romdhani, S. Gong, and A. Psarrou. A multi-view nonlinear active shape model using kernel PCA. In *British Machine Vision Conference*, volume 2, pages 483–492, Nottingham, England, September 1999.

[293] S. Romdhani, S. Gong, and A. Psarrou. A generic face appearance model of shape and texture under very large pose variations from profile to profile views. Technical report, University of Westminster, Harrow, UK, November 1999.

[294] S. Romdhani, A. Psarrou, and S. Gong. Learning a deformable multi-view 2D face shape model. In *IEEE International Workshop on Recognition, Analysis, and Tracking of Faces and Gestures in Real-Time Systems*, pages 31–38, Corfu, Greece, September 1999. IEEE Computer Society.

[295] S. Roweis. EM algorithms for PCA and sensible PCA. In *Neural Information Processing Systems*, 1997.

[296] S. Roweis and Z. Ghahramani. A unifying review of linear Gaussian models. *Neural Computation*, 11(2):305–345, 1999.

[297] H.A. Rowley, S. Baluja, and T. Kanade. Neural network-based face detection. *IEEE Transactions on Pattern Analysis and Machine Intelligence*, 20(1):23–38, January 1998.

[298] Y. Rubner and C. Tomasi. Texture-based image retrieval without segmentation. In *IEEE International Conference on Computer Vision*, volume 2, pages 1018–1024, Corfu, Greece, September 1999.

[299] D.E. Rumelhart, G.E. Hinton, and R.J. Williams. Learning internal representations by error propagation. In D.E. Rumelhart and J.L. McClelland, editors, *Parallel Distributed Processing: Explorations in the Microstructure*

of Cognition, volume 1. MIT Press, 1986.

[300] A. Samal and P.A. Iyengar. Human face detection using silhouettes. *International Journal of Pattern Recognition and Artificial Intelligence*, 9(6):845–867, 1995.

[301] F. Samaria and A. Harter. Parameterisation of a stochastic model for human face identification. In *Proceedings of the 2nd IEEE Workshop on Applications of Computer Vision*, Sarasota FL, December 1994.

[302] D. Saxe and R. Foulds. Toward robust skin identification in video images. In *IEEE International Conference on Face & Gesture Recognition*, pages 379–384, Killington, Vermont, 1996.

[303] F.F. Scapinello and Yarmey A.D. The role of familiarity and orientation in immediate and delayed recognition of pictorial stimuli. *Psychonomin Science*, 21:329–331, 1970.

[304] B. Schiele and A. Waibel. Gaze tracking based on face-color. In *International Workshop on Face & Gesture Recognition*, pages 344–349, Zurich, 1995.

[305] Schineider and Maasen, editors. *Visual Cognition*, volume 5, 1998. Special Issue (1/2) on Mechanisms of Visual Attention: A Cognitive Neuroscience Perspective.

[306] B. Schölkopf, C. Burges, and A. Smöla. *Advances in Kernel Methods - Support Vector Learning*. MIT Press, 1998.

[307] B. Schölkopf, C. Burges, and V. Vapnik. Incorporating invariances in support vector learning machines. In *International Conference on Artificial Neural Networks*, 1996.

[308] P. G. Schyns and H.H. Bülthoff. Conditions for viewpoint dependent face recognition. AI Memo 1432, MIT, August 1993.

[309] G.L. Scott. *Local and global interpretation of moving images*. Pitman, London, England, 1988.

[310] A. Shashua. *Geometry and Photometry in 3D Visual Recognition*. PhD thesis, MIT, AI Lab., 1992.

[311] A. Shashua. Algebraic functions for recognition. AI Memo 1452 (CBCL Paper 90), MIT, January 1994.

[312] J. Sherrah and S. Gong. Exploiting context in gesture recognition. In P. Bouquet, L. Serafini, P. Brezillon, M. Benerecetti, and F. Castellani, editors, *Modelling and Using Context*, number 1688 in Lecture Notes in Artificial Intelligence, pages 515–519. Springer-Verlag, 1999.

[313] J. Sherrah and S. Gong. Fusion of 2D face alignment and 3D pose estimation for robust and real-time face tracking. In *IEEE International Workshop on Recognition, Analysis, and Tracking of Faces and Gestures in Real-Time Systems*, pages 24–30, Corfu, Greece, September 1999. IEEE.

[314] J. Sherrah and S. Gong. Fusion of perceptual cues using covariance estimation. In *British Machine Vision Conference*, volume 2, pages 564–573, Nottingham, England, September 1999.

[315] J. Sherrah, S. Gong, J. Howell, and H. Buxton. Interpretation of group

behaviour in visually mediated interaction. Technical report, Queen Mary and Westfield College, London, UK, November 1999.

[316] H. Shibuya and C. Bundesen. Visual selection from multielement displays: Measuring and modelling effects of exposure duration. *Journal of Experimental Psychology: Human Perception and Performance*, 14:591–600, 1988.

[317] P. Sinha. Object recognition via image invariants. *Investigative Opthalmology and Visual Science*, 35(4):1626, 1994.

[318] W. Skarbek and A. Koschan. Colour image segmentation - a survey. Technical report, Tech. Univ. of Berlin, 1994.

[319] A. Slater, V. Morison, M. Somers, A. Mattock, E. Brown, and D. Taylor. Newborn and older infants' perception of partly occluded objects. *Infant Behaviour and Development*, 3:33–49, 1990.

[320] M. Slater and M. Usoh. Modelling in immersive virtual environments: a case for the science of VR. In *International Conference on Applications of Virtual Reality*, Leeds, UK, June 1994.

[321] A. Sloman. On designing a visual system: towards a Gibsonian computational model of vision. Technical report, University of Sussex, Falmer, Sussex, CSRP 146 1989.

[322] S. M. Smith and J. M. Brady. A scene segmenter: visual tracking of moving vehicles. *Engineering applications of Artificial Intelligence*, 7(2):191–204, 1994.

[323] S.M. Smith and J.M. Brady. Asset-2: Real-time motion segmentation and shape tracking. *IEEE Transactions on Pattern Analysis and Machine Intelligence*, 17(8):814–820, 1995.

[324] S.M. Smith and J.M. Brady. Asset-2: Real-time motion segmentation and shape tracking. *IEEE Transactions on Pattern Analysis and Machine Intelligence*, 17(8):814–820, 1995.

[325] A.J. Smola and B. Scholkopf. A tutorial on support vector regression. Technical Report NC2-TR-1998-030, GMD, Berlin, October 1998. NeuroCOLT2 Technical Report Series.

[326] E.S. Spelke, G. Gutheil, and G. Van de Walle. The development of object perception. In S.M. Kosslyn and D.N. Osherson, editors, *Visual Cognition*, volume 2 of *An Invitation to Cognitive Science*, pages 297–330. MIT Press, Cambridge, Massachusetts, 1995.

[327] J. Steffens, E. Elagin, and H. Neven. Personspotter - fast and robust system for human detection, tracking and recognition. In *IEEE International Conference on Face & Gesture Recognition*, pages 516–521, Nara, Japan, April 1998.

[328] J. V. Stone. Object recognition using spatiotemporal signatures. *Vision Research*, 38(7):947–951, March 1998.

[329] J.V. Stone. Object recognition: View-specificity and motion-specificity. *Vision Research*, 39(24):4032–4044, October 1999.

[330] K. Sung and T. Poggio. Example-based learning for view-based human face detection. *IEEE Transactions on Pattern Analysis and Machine In-*

telligence, 20(1):39–51, January 1998.

[331] M.J. Swain and D.H. Ballard. Colour indexing. *International Journal of Computer Vision*, 7(1):11–32, 1991.

[332] D.L. Swets and J. Weng. Discriminant analysis and eigenspace partition tree for face and object recognition from views. In *IEEE International Conference on Face & Gesture Recognition*, pages 192–197, Nara, Japan, 1996.

[333] M.J. Tarr and S. Pinker. Mental rotation and orientation-dependence in shape recognition. *Cognitive Psychology*, 21:233–282, 1989.

[334] S.P. Tipper, B. Weaver, L.M. Jerreat, and A.L. Burak. Object-based and environment-based inhibition of return of visual attention. *Journal of Experimental Psychology; Human Perception and Performance*, 20:478–499, 1994.

[335] M.E. Tipping and C.M. Bishop. Mixtures of probabilistic principal component analysers. Technical Report NCRG/97/003, Neural Computing Research Group, Aston University, June 1997.

[336] H.G.C. Traven. A neural network approach to statistical pattern classification by "semiparametric" estimation of probability density functions. *IEEE Transactions on Neural Networks*, 2(3):366–378, 1991.

[337] F. Troje and H.H. Bülthoff. Face recognition under varying pose: the role of texture and shape. *Vision Research*, 36(12):1761–1771, 1996.

[338] N. Troje and H.H. Bülthoff. How is bilateral symmetry of human faces used for recognition of novel views ? Technical Report 38, Max-Planck-Institut für biologische Kybernetik, August 1996.

[339] R.Y. Tsai. A versatile camera calibration technique for high-accuracy 3D machine vision metrology using off-the-shelf TV cameras and lenses. *IEEE Journal of Robotics and Automation*, RA-3(4):323–344, August 1987.

[340] J.K. Tsotsos. On the relative complexity of active vs. passive visual search. *International Journal of Computer Vision*, 7(2):127–142, 1992.

[341] M. Turk and A. Pentland. Eigenfaces for recognition. *Journal of Cognitive Neuroscience*, 3(1):71–86, 1991.

[342] S. Ullman. *The Interpretation of Visual Motion*. MIT Press, 1979.

[343] S. Ullman. Against direct perception. *Behavioral and Brain Sciences*, 3:373–415, 1980.

[344] S. Ullman. Visual routines. *Cognition*, 18:97–159, 1984.

[345] S. Ullman. Aligning pictorial descriptions: An approach to object recognition. *Cognition*, 32:193–254, 1989.

[346] S. Ullman. *High-level Vision: Object Recognition and Visual Cognition*. MIT Press, Cambridge, Mass., 1996.

[347] S. Ullman and R. Basri. Recognition by linear combinations of models. *IEEE Transactions on Pattern Analysis and Machine Intelligence*, 13(10):992–1006, October 1991.

[348] C.W. Urquhart, J.P. Siebert, J.P. McDonald, and R.J. Fryer. Active animate stereo vision. In *British Machine Vision Conference*, pages 75–84,

1993.

[349] R. Vaillant, C. Monrocq, and Y. Le Cun. Original approach for the locali-sation of objects in images. *IEE Proceedings on Vision, Image and Signal Processing*, 141(4):245–250, August 1994.

[350] T. Valentine. A unified account of the effects of distinctiveness, inver-sion and race recognition. *Quarterly Journal of Experimental Psychology*, 43A(2):161–204, 1991.

[351] V. Vapnik. *The nature of statistical learning theory.* Springer-Verlag, New York, 1995.

[352] P. Verity. Security camera system for the detection of audio and visual disturbances. Technical report, Department of Computer Science, Queen Mary and Westfield College, University of London, England, May 1998.

[353] T. Vetter and V. Blanz. Estimating coloured 3D face models from single images: an example-based approach. In *European Conference on Computer Vision*, volume II, pages 499–513, Freiburg, Germany, June 1998.

[354] T. Vetter, M. J. Jones, and T. Poggio. A bootstrapping algorithm for learning linear models of object classes. AI Memo 1600, MIT, Cambridge, Massachusetts, March 1997.

[355] T. Vetter and T. Poggio. Symmetric 3D objects are an easy case for 2D object recognition. *Spatial Vision*, 8(4):443–453, 1994.

[356] T. Vetter and T. Poggio. Linear object classes and image synthesis from a single example image. *IEEE Transactions on Pattern Analysis and Machine Intelligence*, 19(7):733–742, July 1997.

[357] T. Vetter, T. Poggio, and H.H. Bülthoff. 3D object recognition: symme-try and virtual views. AI Memo 1409, MIT, Cambridge, Massachusetts, December 1992.

[358] T. Vetter, T. Poggio, and H.H. Bülthoff. The importance of symmetry and virtual views in three-dimensional object recognition. *Current Biology*, 4:18–23, 1994.

[359] L. Vincent. Morphological grayscale reconstruction in image analysis: Ap-plications and efficient algorithms. *IEEE Transactions on Image Process-ing*, 2(2):176–201, 1993.

[360] H. von Helmholtz. *Popular Lectures on Scientific Subjects*, chapter The Recent Progress of the Theory of Vision, pages 93–185. Longmans, Green and Company, 1881.

[361] P. Walker and L. Cuthbert. Remembering visual feature conjunctions: visual memory for shape-colour associations is object-based. *Visual Cogni-tion*, 5(4):409–455, 1998.

[362] G. Wallis. Presentation order affects human object recognition learning. Technical Report 36, Max-Planck-Institut fur biologische Kybernetik, Au-gust 1996.

[363] M. Walter, S. Gong, and A. Psarrou. Learning stochastic temporal models of human behaviour. In *IEEE International Workshop on Modelling People*, pages 87–94, Corfu, Greece, September 1999.

[364] J.Z. Wang, G. Wiederhold, O. Firschein, and S.X. Wei. Content-based image indexing and searching using Daubechies' wavelets. *International Journal on Digital Libraries*, 1(4):311–328, 1997.

[365] H. Wechsler, P.J. Phillips, V. Bruce, F.F. Soulie, and T. Huang, editors. *Face recognition: From theory to applications*. Springer Verlag, 1997. NATO ASI series.

[366] P.J. Werbos. *Beyond regression: new tools for prediction and analysis in the behavioural sciences*. PhD thesis, Harvard University, 1974.

[367] L. Wiskott. *Labeled Graphs and Dynamic Link Matching for Face Recognition and Scene Analysis*. PhD thesis, Ruhr-Universität Bochum, Germany, July 1995.

[368] L. Wiskott, J.-M. Fellous, N. Kruger, and C. von der Malsburg. Face recognition and gender determination. In *International Workshop on Face & Gesture Recognition*, pages 92–97, Zurich, 1995.

[369] C.R. Wren, A. Azarbayejani, T. Darrell, and A. Pentland. Pfinder: Real-time tracking of the human body. *IEEE Transactions on Pattern Analysis and Machine Intelligence*, 19(7):780–785, 1997.

[370] H. Wu, Q. Chen, and M. Yachida. Face detection from colour images using a fuzzy pattern matching method. *IEEE Transactions on Pattern Analysis and Machine Intelligence*, 21(6):557–563, June 1999.

[371] R.P. Würtz. *Multilayer Dynamic Link Networks for Establishing Image Point Correspondences and Visual Object Recognition*. Verlag Harri Deutsch, 1994.

[372] G. Yang and T. Huang. Human face detection in a complex background. *Pattern Recognition*, 27:53–63, 1994.

[373] J. Yang, W. Lu, and A. Waibel. Skin-color modelling and adaptation. In *Asian Conference on Computer Vision*, pages 687–694, Hong Kong, 1998.

[374] A.L. Yarbus. *Eye Movements and Vision*. Plenum, New York, 1967.

[375] R.K. Yin. Looking at upside-down faces. *Journal of Experimental Psychology*, 81:141–145, 1969.

[376] A.W. Young and V. Bruce. Perceptual categories and the computation of "grandmother". *European Journal of Cognitive Psychology*, 3:5–49, 1991.

[377] A.W. Young, E.H.F. de Haan, and F. Newcombe. Unawareness of impaired face recognition. *Brain and Cognition*, 14:1–18, 1990.

[378] A.W. Young and H.D. Ellis, editors. *Handbook of Research on Face Processing*. North Holland, Amsterdam, 1986.

[379] M.P. Young and S. Yamane. Sparse population coding of faces in the inferotemporal cortex. *Science*, 256:1327–1331, 29 May 1992.

[380] K.C. Yow and R. Cipolla. Feature-based human face detection. *Image and Vision Computing*, 15(9):713–735, 1997.

Index

active shape model, 192
    linear, 192
    nonlinear, 195
adaptation, 10, 51
adaptive behaviour, 78
adaptive resonance theory, 250
adulthood, 27, 29, 54, 184
affine transformation, 18, 22, 23, 100, 113, 183
alignment, *see* affine transformation
aperture problem, 60
appearance-based representation, 84, 118, 150, 188
aspect ratio, 129
atemporal, 26, 213
attention, 8, 27, 54, 59, 65, 71, 135
attentional control, 249
attentional windows, 8
authentication, *see* face verification
avatar, 148

back-propagation, 49, 95
background model, 74
basis function, 39, 50
    non-linear, 48
Bayes' theorem, 36
Bayesian belief networks, 238, 306
benchmarking, 273
between-class variation, 173
bias-variance dilemma, 35, 40–41
biometric systems, 254
bootstrap, 10, 53, 60, 145

camera calibration, 271
canonical view, 206

caricature, 28
cells, *see* neuron
childhood, 27, 29, 54
classification, 34, 85, *see* face classification
    linear, 44
    maximum a posteriori, 37, 90
    nonlinear, 48
classifier, 91
clustering, 43
coefficient vector, 169
colour constancy, 65, 136
colour cues, 65
colour models
    adaptive, 136
    histogram, density, 68
combination of 2D views, 20, 119, 190
commercial systems, 11
composite representation, 113
conditional density propagation, 128, 132, 233
conditional probability, 32
configural representation, *see* holistic approach
conjugate gradient algorithm, 49
constant illumination assumption, 61
content-based indexing, 261
contrast normalisation, 94
correlation coefficient, 115, 120
correspondence
    dense, 20, 23, 105
    feature-based, template-based, 23, 105
correspondence problem, 7, 22, 115, 181, 191